Mobile Screens

The Visual Regime of Navigation

Nanna Verhoeff

Amsterdam University Press

This book is published in print and online through the online OAPEN library (www.oapen.org).

OAPEN (Open Access Publishing in European Networks) is a collaborative initiative to develop and implement a sustainable Open Access publication model for academic books in the Humanities and Social Sciences. The OAPEN Library aims to improve the visibility and usability of high quality academic research by aggregating peer reviewed Open Access publications from across Europe.

Cover image: Detail from *Expose* (Jussi Niva, 1998) at Vuosaari Metro Station, Helsinki. Photo: Jussi Tiainen

Cover design: Suzan Beijer, Amersfoort
Lay-out: JAPES, Amsterdam

ISBN   978 90 8964 379 7
e-ISBN   978 90 4851 526 4
NUR   670

Mobile Screens

MediaMatters is a series published by Amsterdam University Press on current debates about media technology and practices. International scholars critically analyze and theorize the materiality and performativity, as well as spatial practices of screen media in contributions that engage with today's digital media culture.

For more information about the series, please visit: www.aup.nl

For August and Lena

Contents

Acknowledgements

First and foremost I want to thank my students. I am grateful for their feedback and inspiration and feel privileged to be in a position to teach and discuss with them the topics of my research. I have developed this work in dialogue with them.

My position at the Department of Media and Culture Studies and the Research Institute for History and Culture at Utrecht University has provided me with a stimulating and collegial environment and I am very grateful for the institutional support for my research. I thank the participants of the Utrecht Media and Performance research seminar in particular, for feedback and regular food for thought.

William Uricchio has been my friend, colleague and mentor. My interest in contemporary screens and the trope of mobility finds its roots in my previous work on early cinema. His perspective on the intersections of new and old media has inspired me greatly. I am also very thankful for being able to work with, and be coached by Frank Kessler, whose work on media dispositifs has provided the theoretical framework for my historical engagement with new and old screens. My colleague Sybille Lammes I thank for inspiring conversations and fun during our travels. I look forward to our continuing collaboration. Giovanna Fossati has been a good friend for years and the best writing partner. I cherish our dreaming and scheming about future directions and intersections of our paths.

Colleagues, friends, and family (most of them fulfilling multiple roles) that deserve special mention are Andrea Battiston, Maaike Bleeker, Marianne van den Boomen, Sarah Dellmann, Karin van Es, Liesbeth Groot Nibbelink, Pepita Hesselberth, Eef Masson, Sigrid Merx, Eva Niën, Katrin Pietsch, Benjamin Schaipp, Mirko Schaefer, Margriet Schavemaker, Iris van der Tuin, Ika Voskuil, Imar de Vries, Lina Zigelyte and Klaas de Zwaan. And a special thanks to Wenche Gerhardson for pointing out that the word *window* has etymological ties with the old Norse *vindauga*, or wind-eye.

My gratitude goes to Jeroen Sondervan, editor at Amsterdam University Press, for working with me on this book, and his gentle managing of the media studies book series. Chantal Nicolaes (AUP) was also very helpful. Thanks to Hein Wils (Stedelijk Museum) and Anna Abrahams (EYE Institute Netherlands) for providing me with some great images on several occasions. Joy Maul-Phillips was invaluable for that last round of corrections, and I am very grateful for her time and for the elevator pitch.

I want to use this occasion to also thank my parents Mieke Bal and Han Verhoeff for their parental, professional and intellectual feedback. I greatly appreciate Han's insightful (and humorous) reflections and his thinking with me. Mieke has helped me immensely with the writing process. They both always support and encourage me and I realize how important that is for me.

Shailoh Phillips helped me finish the first version of this book. She has been invaluable for finding the right words for its main points. I thank her for switching around chapters two and four – and for many other things in my life. I greatly admire her mind, spirit and GPS.

I am so very grateful for Liane and Thomas who have arrived in my life just recently, but have fundamentally changed its course.

Finally, I dedicate this book about mobility to my children, August Voskuil and Lena Verhoeff. No travel metaphor suffices for our lives together and the rapture of watching them grow up.

List of Illustrations

Introduction

Screens are ubiquitous in urban visual culture – colossal screen façades, mobile phones, television sets, game consoles. The architecture and spaces in which we operate are infused with screen technologies. This study explores the connections between two predominant characteristics of contemporary culture at play in the omnipresence of screen technologies and practices. These are visuality on the one hand, and mobility on the other. Together, this conceptual and spatial configuration forms what I propose to call a visual regime of navigation, a guiding principle in how, especially but not exclusively at a certain time in history, we interact with screen interfaces. In navigation, vision is an active engagement, keeping an eye out for where to move or what to do next. This active, creative mode of vision can be found, for example, in the interaction with a touchscreen user interface, enabling navigation within the screen device. This seems utterly new, an innovative practice of our time. However, this is related to a much older paradigm of relational mobility, which forms a broader cultural logic with historical roots long predating the technology of mobile screen devices. The predominant role of visuality in today's culture is tightly bound up with the fundamental role of mobility in modern culture and society – geographical and physical by means of travel as well as visual and virtual through media and communication technologies. The visual turn (Mitchell 1994) and the spatial turn (Soja 1996), including recent emphasis on mobility (Urry 2007) in contemporary theory and culture, can converge in what I propose as a spatio-visual or navigational turn. In this book, I argue that navigation is a primary trope in (urban) mobility and visuality. The intersections between mobility and visuality – more specifically, the mobility of visual experience and the screen-based access to such experiences – constitute, then, the subject of this study.

One of the most striking characteristics of screen-based interfaces is the possibility for people in transit to co-create the map of the spatial arrangement in which they are operating. The coincidence of movement and the creation of spatial representations is what I call a performative cartography. In the visual regime of navigation, that which is depicted, such as maps and panoramic views, emerges simultaneously with someone's interaction with a screen-based interface. This simultaneity of making and image makes movement itself a performative, creative act. Movement not only transports the physical body, but affects the virtual realm of spatial representation. This implies a temporal collapse between making images and perceiving them. In other words, the navigational paradigm that I explore throughout this book, in various contemporary and earlier case studies, entails a shift of focus from texts or objects to relations, practices and processes.

Whereas many current conceptualizations of mobility explore haptic visuality as an embodied, sensorial immersion, in this book, I stress the performativity implied in an active engagement with mobile and urban screen arrangements. The multi-sensory nature of navigation is not only just a physical, but sometimes even a visceral experience, which also underscores the creative ability of embodied motion as a visio-spatial act. Because screens always function within a particular spatial *dispositif*, or configuration, their relation to visual experience varies: screens can shield the spectator from the vulnerability of visual engagement, or liberate from the confines of a particular situation.

Such theoretical statements resonate with the key assertions of several recent blockbuster films, such as *Inception* (Christopher Nolan, 2010), in which the main characters developed the technology to infiltrate people's dreams and thereby manipulate their subconscious by planting ideas. As the lead character Cobb (Leonardo DiCaprio) explains to his new recruit Ariadne (Ellen Page), "in dreams we perceive and create our world, simultaneously". The spatial architecture of dreams is such that one navigates while constructing the space along the way. Hence, experiencing (dream)space enables simultaneous creation and exploration. Like other Hollywood films that play with fantasies of futuristic technologies allowing seamless, weightless and mostly invisible interfaces, such as *Strange Days* (Kathryn Bigelow, 1995), *eXistenZ* (David Cronenberg, 1999), *The Matrix* (Andy and Larry Wachowski, 1999), *Minority Report* (Stephen Spielberg, 2002), or *Eternal Sunshine of the Spotless Mind* (Michel Gondry, 2004), this film is abundant in spectacular visual effects that represent the experience of venturing into virtual realms such as the past, the future, the unconscious, memory, or a completely synthetic virtual realm, such as in *The Matrix*.

Because they suggest tremendous creative and manipulative power, visual representations of experiencing such fantastic interfaces are, within their cinematic representational regime, limited to suggestion only – a limitation inherent to cinema. Obviously, movie audiences can see, but not fully experience what the technologies in question offer to the fictional characters: experiences frequently suggested to be mental states rather than visual experiences. By default, these visual representations are primarily arranged in order to suggest the (weightless) mobility within spectacular spaces and virtual architectures.

As the example of *Inception* shows, the disjunction between representation and its object is not merely visual and narrative, but should perhaps mostly be considered on the level of agency and of what we can call the performativity of the depicted interfaces. Taking interfaces as boundaries where agents (technological and biological) meet, communicate and (inter)act, their performativity entails the intersection of the procedural, the creative and the experiential. Surely, portraying the potential of one medium within another changes its content: a film should not be confused with its content. In the case of science fiction films, the content is imaginary to the core. But, even though they address futuristic, imaginary interfaces, these films are just as much concerned with the technology of cinematic special effects in their present time. In fact, as I will elaborate throughout this book, interaction with screen-based interfaces already entails a performative, creative act, albeit not as visually spectacular as promised in cinematic representations.

What is striking and pertinent here is how these fantasies about futuristic media are grounded in contemporary as well as historical developments. I do not so much mean those of particular technologies, but rather these technologies' affordances, or uses. The relationship between technology (what we have) and medium (what we make) is contingent and to some degree, always fictional. Moreover, what we make stems from what we can imagine, and is in that sense, always already historical. As far as interaction with screens is concerned, the given technology of particular interactive devices entails an ambiguous status of screens: what is shown on the screen has to do with how one interacts with it, that is, we can almost literally see what we are doing.

This study is devoted to a theoretical exploration of intersections between mobility and visuality from a historical-comparative perspective, addressing the mobility of visual experience and the screen-based access to such experiences in a range of case studies. In the following five chapters I will analyze a variety of contemporary screen technologies and the cultural practices involving these screen-based configurations – the ways in which we engage with screens as interfaces with spatial, temporal and haptic experiences. In order to understand visuality and our contemporary relationship to technology, it is helpful to examine this convergence of mobility and screen presence as a historical cultural phenomenon. Screen media participate within a synchronic and intermedial network of media that influence each other, but also within historical dynamics of emergence, change and remediation. (Kittler 1999; Bolter and Grusin 2000; Gitelman 2006) Here, I compare a variety of screen media – their technologies and practices – synchronically as well as diachronically, as sites of virtual mobility, implying a visual regime of navigation. Contemporary screens ranging from panoramas, large urban screens or media façades, micro screens, mobile navigation devices, game consoles, to other cinematic and tele-visual screens are the object of this study. Although at places implicitly, I analyze these technologies and practices from a diachronic comparative perspective in order to understand the ways in which they are involved in a culture of screen mobility, a visual regime of navigation and a paradigm of relational spatiality. In this analysis, I understand a regime as a set of conditions considered valid at a certain time, under which usages of things are taken for granted as normal and legitimate. Regimes are usually mentioned in political terms, but they can also pertain to cultural practice. Martin Jay, for example, uses the term to name certain ways of seeing at specific historical moments; he speaks of a *scopic regime* (1988) Linear perspective, once invented, produced a regime in this sense. Navigation, I contend, produces another.

In adopting a comparative and diachronic approach while focusing on contemporary culture, my aim is to grasp the ways in which mobility and screen technology are inextricably interrelated. This relationship can be traced not only in contemporary culture in general, but specifically as a characteristic of a visual regime with roots in the past long preceding current mobile technology. This requires a view of visual experience not only through a rearview mirror, but also forward-looking. Taking the contemporary imagination of fantastic realms beyond current equipment is indicative of a panoramic desire to view the world from behind the glass of a windowpane. The assault on experience and visuality entailed with the rise of modern cities and modes of transportation, a shift to a modern mode of experience so well addressed by Walter Benjamin, especially in his Baudelaire essays, exposes spectators to an endless number of shocking and thrilling encounters. Benjamin, in reference to Freud, spoke of a psychological shield, protecting our sensibilities from such shocks by filtering out input, resulting in an impoverished mode of experience (*Erlebnis*). Screens do not function solely as windows opening up a field of vision; they can also serve as shields or blinders, limiting our view within the novel mode of panoramic vision. Screens offer an interface with which we can use and co-construct, in order to navigate through, the complex arrangements of modern urban settings. Navigational visuality by no means denies haptic visuality, as I will explain later; here, however, the emphasis is on how our interaction with screens changes the configuration of physical mobility, which can either include the experience of visceral proximity, or the intervention of a screen-based interface in varying arrangements.

Before commencing the diachronic-comparative investigation of various screen practices, interfaces and arrangements, this study is faced with a preliminary question: what are screens in the first place, and what is the significance of the screen for media historians, theorists and analysts? Screens are objects, technologies, apparatuses and machines of vision, all at once. The screen is a technological device, an interface, a flat 2D surface positioned in a 3D arrangement, potentially in a 4D relationship of time and motion, a metaphor for mediation and vision, a frame for representation, a site of innovation and change: what I call a meta-morphing constant in modern culture. Here I allude to the double meaning of the word metamorphosis as pointed out by Vivian Sobchack (2000). When used for the visual effect of morphing of images in animation and computer graphics, there is a literal transformation; this is in addition to the metaphoric meaning of the word for what Sobchack calls a "culture of quick change". (xiii) Similarly concerned with the historicity of change and innovation, and cultural tropes of technology and aesthetics, I want to point out the way in which change always entails constants – instead of negating the change, they are actually exposed in relation to the differences that emerge through change. The complex of the screen's metamorphic nature as material object, as site for mobility and as interface needs to be addressed when tracing the historical presence and the reconfigurations of screens involved with mobility in our visual culture. Rather than proposing a historical genealogy of contemporary screens, however – a project beyond the scope of this study – I will argue for attention, in the analysis of screen devices and uses, to the 'oldness' as well as the 'newness' of each in their dialectical, sometimes polemical, interaction.

Mobility figures as a recurring trope of self-reflection throughout the history of modern visual media. As many have noted, travel was a major preoccupation in, for example, the emergence of the moving image (in early cinema around 1900) and is so again in today's digital imagery (around 2000). (Bruno 2006; Friedberg 2006; Huhtamo 1997) Within this semantic field it is easy to notice that travel is both a narrative and visual trope par excellence. Specifically, new media continually reinvent the age-old relationship between showing and telling by making use of their technological abilities for visualizing movement. Rather than attempting a full history, I use examples from both ends of the twentieth century as well as case studies of current devices and practices, with an emphasis on the contemporary. I seek to demonstrate both similarities and differences between particular visual dispositifs, so as to understand and situate our current fascination with mobility and space in contemporary media technologies and practices. I consider the ways mobility functions as a trope in, and metaphor for, emergent media interfaces, in particular those which are involved in navigation in today's fast-changing media landscape.

Travel owes this prominent position to the fact that it offers a distinctively (post)modern mode of experiencing the reconfigurations of *time* and *space*, at first sight the rightful realms related to telling and showing respectively – a dual distinction I will nuance later on. Travel is a form of transition, between known and unknown territories, between sedentary and provisional lives. Moreover, travel invokes new sensory experiences. In this sense travel can be thought of as a conceptual metaphor for 'new', that is, *transitional* media. This is why in this study, navigation is a central topic, along with its condition – mobility as a state of being – as a metaphor for changing media and what we can do with them. The conceptual metaphor of travel for transitional media allows me to study multiple aspects of mobile practices and experiences, perhaps as a conceptual dispositif, mapping screens, mobility and visuality in different arrangements.

With the diachronic comparison of different screens – large and small, fixed and mobile, public and private – I will also explore how we can approach this variegated field of screens theoretically. But what, then, is subject to comparison in this study of various screens of navigation? The perspective is comparative, but this comparison does not concern an opposition or separation between, but rather the specificities and subsequent synthesis of the participating sensory domains. The interest in the physicality and mobility of perception lies in the alternative it offers to approaches based on binary pairs such as visual-audio, visual-physical, virtual-material, or word-image oppositions. (Altman 1992; Chion 1994; Sobchack 2004) In line with recent rethinking of the specificity of the cinematic and televisual screen in light of today's changing media landscape (Harbord 2007; McCarthy 2001), this study merges the focus in cinema and television studies on temporality (Gledhill & Williams 2000; Mulvey 2006; Steward 2007) with the spatial preoccupation in debates about digital media. (Aarseth 1997; Manovich 2001) Where film theory, television theory and new media theory have focused on the specific nature of certain screens and practices, the current screen culture of intermediality, transmediality, crossmediality and remediation requires a reconfiguring of divergent theoretical approaches. This is necessary in order to explore the convergence of perspectives that are currently often segregated, separated by virtue of different objects of investigation, such as television, cinema and mobile phones.

The screen as site for representation, simulation and perception is in its essence at once a spatial and a temporal domain. In screens of navigation, space and time merge into what I call henceforth spacetime, or timespace, in the sense of temporalizing as well as spatially distributing, and mobility as an experience of moving through space and time, hovering between state and event. Here, I pursue the integration of various media-theoretical approaches, in line with a broader conception of screen studies. Such approaches take recourse to a theoretical perspective, which is neither content- nor object-oriented, but instead focuses on spatial arrangements. This approach can assist me in grasping a broader, more variegated and vastly changing landscape of screens.

Related to this concern with the relationship between temporal and spatial dimensions is the centrality of materiality and physicality of technologies and practices. While the screen has been theorized mainly as a theoretical construction in cinema studies (Metz 1977; Baudry 1978; 1986) and the virtual has long been associated with the imaginary and transient nature of digital culture, this project contributes to current developments in (digital) media theory towards a more material approach (Hayles 2002; Poster 2006; Van den Boomen et al. 2009), thereby expanding the focus on different screens and the physicality and materiality of their practices, rather than adhering to a theoretical, immaterial and ideal construction of the screen.

A helpful point of entrance into this integrated problematic is provided by the concept of dispositif. While developed to provide a theoretical construct of what is often called the cinematic apparatus, this concept also helps us to analyze the material and spatial specificity of the setup within which screens operate. The term, derived from 1970s film theory (Baudry), has emerged from a range of different congenial terms. Like most successful concepts, dispositif filled a void but is at risk of becoming void itself by the wear and tear of over-use. Frank Kessler (2006; 2007) provides not only historical antecedents – such as, for example, in Heidegger and Freud – but also historicizing possibilities the concept affords. He quotes Foucault (1980), who defines the concept of dispositif (there, translated as *apparatus*) as a heterogeneous ensemble of elements connected by relations, which has a dominant strategic function. An often-alleged key example is the Panopticon as a dispositif of surveillance. In a Foucault-inspired moment, Kessler imagines a non-teleological history of cinema as a history of dispositifs. Thus he considers the "cinema of attractions" advanced by Tom Gunning (1990) as a historically specific dispositif that counters point by point the dispositif of classical narrative cinema.

So far, I position this study as an integrative approach, where space and time, but also devices and their uses, converge in the production of a regime of navigation. On a theoretical level, this study engages with discourses on technology, representation, visual culture, historical visual regimes, modes of perception, haptic visuality and debates about space and the visual in cultural analysis. In general, in discussions of media and screen technologies, much attention is paid to issues of visuality. In accordance with the current developments within our screen culture, as well as with theoretical debates engaged with these changes, the focus lies on the materiality and visuality of the digital as well as inclusion of the other senses in fully-fledged embodied experience (Marks 2002; Massumi 2002). However, the multi-sensorial nature of (visual) experience is not in itself the term of comparison. Although I discuss what we could call the haptic operation and perception of the screen as interface as well as a synesthetic dimension, my main interest lies elsewhere. In the screen dispositifs I address, panoramic desire and performative navigation have an ambiguous relationship with the notion of haptic visuality: screens of navigation augment the spectator's mode of haptic visuality, and often are involved in the attempt to protect the spectator from fully merging with the spatial configuration of a position in the world. This is of course not to say that a spectator can actually escape embodiment, however; screens form a crucial part of the visual dispositif that enables someone in transit to view their path as they co-create it.

The thrust of the book, then, is a comparative analysis of contemporary technologies, screen configurations and practices, in which the theoretical scope is inflected with a diachronic slant. In line with media-archeological approaches that have developed since, roughly, the 1990s (Huhtamo; Zielinski; Elsaesser), this focus, which could be construed as historiographic, concerns the critical conceptualization of changing media, remediation, media interfaces, dispositifs and the notion of media synthesis or convergence. (Jenkins 2006) The synchronic as well as diachronic comparison of media technologies and practices implies taking into account the impact of technological and cultural change over time. From my perspective, it is not so much change over time – an adequate definition of what history is – but an assessment of what is new and what is a continuation of the old in contemporary practices that I seek to unpack. In particular, this comparative perspective focuses on media emergence, convergence and transformation; it comprises a reflection on newness and disruptions as well as on continuity; and it considers notions of influence among as well as convergence of media. In sum, while focusing on particular arrangements of screens and viewing practices in our contemporary media landscape, I maintain a diachronic viewpoint and aim to consider media differences and changes, but outside of a linear chronology of development.

The cultural-historical comparative approach in my investigation of a screen culture of mobility and the navigational regime of visuality is comparable to the work by e.g. Anne Friedberg (2006) and Giuliana Bruno (2002), two scholars who have also investigated a modern history of screens (Friedberg) and a history of haptic vision and "cartographic" mobility (Bruno), and whose influence on my project is crucial. While their central perspective is that of visual culture and cultural history, mine is complimentary to theirs in that it is more explicitly engaged with media-theoretical concerns. Whereas both authors trace a cultural history of visuality, I do not foster the ambition to provide a historical genesis; instead, I take recourse to particular historic visual configurations to develop a refined theoretical conceptualization of the particularities of *contemporary* screen technologies and practices and, in retrospect, to better understand earlier media. Even with this diachronic-comparative inclusion, my approach takes as its starting point contemporary practices. Consequently, I consistently view the past through the lens of the present, in search of ways in which the current regime of navigational visuality is not only a property of contemporary screen arrangements but also the provisional outcome of a historical genealogy. Indirectly, my study contributes to the urgent need to reorient the sometimes too rigidly separate fields of cinema and television studies on the one hand, and digital media studies on the other, by integrating cultural-historical and media-theoretical questions. Nevertheless, my primary concern remains theoretical and analytical.

The first part of this book explores two configurations of mobility and visuality: the panoramic and the navigational. In both Chapters 1 and 2, a clear distinction between real, material space and mediated space is problematized through bringing together questions concerning the spatial presence of screens and the spatial constructions that these screens bring about. In an age of media ubiquity, in particular located within hypermodernity's non-places (Augé 1992), a distinction between physical and virtual space does not provide a stable principle of orientation. Mobile orientation is relative, in reference to dynamic coordinates, but does not result in complete disorientation: orientation in a mediatized screen-based environment entails a visual regime of navigation. Navigational visuality is no longer solely based on fixed coordinates. In the visual configuration, the relational mobility of the viewer's position prevails over the longstanding dominance of classical, Cartesian conceptions of time and space. This regime of navigational visuality entails a paradigm shift, which goes against the grain of some of the most basic assumptions about the nature of reality and our navigation in and through reality. Dynamic principles of timespace are, however, not new in the least: they have already been quantified in Einstein's theory of relativity, dramatized in science fiction film, and partially theorized in media studies – albeit not yet in relation to screens of navigation. Media screens constitute in fact a form of spatial regulation; they both provide access to and set limits on the perceptual field. Mobility enables moving perception, but both vehicular and medial mobility rely on the speed, rhythm, and direction of the machines of transport. The viewer is bound to the technology of mobile visibility, subject to the visual regime of navigation. These first two chapters explore some of the ways in which the mobile gaze is constructed and regulated by these technological interventions and how, in turn, space is constructed by the gaze.

In the first chapter ("Panoramic Complex"), I start with an experience that will be familiar to many of my readers. The primary case study is the mobile vision of the highway panorama. Through a comparison with the actual perception of moving landscapes through the windows of a moving vehicle, the screen is considered in terms of a virtual window (Friedberg) providing a framed, visual access to moving images. The comparison between highway panoramas and mobile screens, however, is bi-directional: the concern with the design of highway panoramas for the car window as an interface is only a recent example of a longer history of panoramic desires. Panoramic desire, I argue, is the desire for perceptual, not physical, immersion. It is built on the visual arrangement or dispositif of spectator, visual field, and medium that organizes the gaze. Panoramic desire is part of the regime of navigational visuality, which strives to escape the spatial constraints of embodied haptic visuality.

In the example of the highway panorama I consider the unique viewing position of the driver: the gaze from behind the protective glass of the windshield. I propose that a cinematographic understanding of the panorama is useful for an understanding of panoramic viewing in terms of space, time and experience. Conversely, the specific feature of the windshield as a window to the highway panorama also offers apparent similarities to mediated moving images on film, television or computer screens. In the first place, the view is framed in both cases: the screen offers access to, but also limits the field of vision, just like the windshield; the window is transparent yet it restricts. This makes apparent another similarity with the canvas of a painting or the confines of the photograph's edges.

Secondly, the screen and the windshield are similar to one another because they both function as access points, portals or gateways to the moving image. The window can be opened, literally and figuratively, so that the spectator can gain visual as well as virtual access to the world that lies beyond it. Within media studies, but also in (popular) culture, the window is referred to as a metaphor, and functions as an expedient to better understand the relation between the spectator-subject and the image that is viewed (Friedberg). In the instance of the highway panorama, the sight as seen from behind the (moving) windshield, we are in fact dealing with a similar situation as watching moving images: although seated in a moving vehicle, in fact we sit still behind a window and we look at a moving landscape behind it. A comparison between media and driving spectators can help us understand how viewing is not a one-way operation, but essentially relational and dialogic. With this we return to space, to complicate the demarcation between (media-based) virtual travel and (mobile) physical travel.

In the second chapter ("Self-Reflection") I aim to revamp the notion of representation and display of mobility by considering the collapse of making and viewing that can be witnessed in contemporary screens of navigation. The spatial and physical mobility of portable screens allows for a deconstruction of the usual distinction and separation between the process of making and of spectating. These mobile screens raise questions about the literal borders of screen-based dispositifs. As half-products, unfinished media, screen spaces come into existence in the presence of the user-spectator, who literally finished the work of screening. I consider this co-dependency between screen and user-spectator a form of spatial performativity, in the sense that viewing is an act that enables vision itself. (Carlson 2004; Kaye 2000; McKenzie 2001)

The representation of deixis in the cinematic phantom ride will be compared to deixis as matrix in the navigation of mobile screens. Whereas the previous chapter dealt with the mobility of the screen, the comparison here between narrative and spectacle in two very different regimes – (early) cinema and (contemporary) mobile media – will infuse our investigation with the inseparability, in the latter regime, of seeing and making what is being seen.

In Chapter 3 ("Theoretical Consoles") I zoom in on a specific case. The purpose of this analysis at a microlevel is to integrate instances of spacing mobility with methodological considerations of the relationship between objects and their analysis, as well as of the orienting and resulting interpretation and theory. This touches upon the key issue in cultural analysis of how to construct an object. I seek to address the question how, in a study of contemporary visual culture, one can construe meaningful objects of analysis that yield insights beyond the object alone. If we can no longer limit ourselves to the reading of texts – recognize single, complex cultural-artistic objects such as e.g. specific films or television programs – what kinds of objects bring up insights that reach beyond the meanings of a single text? Moreover, in what way can we include a material and physical understanding of the screen – the screen as object – in our investigation of how screens are used and how they function within visual culture? These questions are of crucial importance for this study.

In this second chapter, the hybrid mobile console offers an example of multiple screen models that can be held in one hand: a mobile screen, a double screen, a touchscreen, and a wired or connected screen. As a multiple, hybrid, and metamorphing object (Brown), the mobile handheld screen invites a renewed inquiry in what the status of the screen is as what has been usefully termed a *theoretical object*. The central case for this chapter is the Nintendo DS game console, an object that offers an understanding of the multi-variegated screen as what I will refer to as a *theoretical console*. Its status as screen rests at once on an abstract notion of site of image presentation and viewing, on a frame for representation, and on a very material object to carry around. Moreover, a game console demonstrates how screens operate when being played, handled, and used. (Cooley 2004) Beyond the narrow focus on its particularities, this object makes clear that the screen only becomes a screen when the software – literally speaking, in the sense of games and digital applications, and figuratively, in the sense of the fugitive screen content – is played *on* it. This insight culled from the object turns it into a theoretical object.

As becomes a theoretical object, it is worth unpacking it, first of all, as what it is. I do so in the chapter that follows, "Theoretical Consoles". The mobile screen as object is, first and foremost, material. As a gadget it is temporal as well as temporary, in the sense of ephemeral. (Baudrillard 1996) Therefore, second, the status of the gadget in the history of media is at issue – its diachronicity. This status is both comparative and diachronic, concerning synchronic differentiations and confluence, as well as transformation over time. Third, concerning its functionality, the status of the gadget is determined by the way any screen-based object embodies possibilities of multiple interfaces. Hence, I will propose, such objects should be considered *theoretical consoles* – to vary on the notion of theoretical objects and make more explicit how these gadgets are theoretically informative. Herein also lies its diachronic status.

In the fourth chapter ("Urban Screens") I investigate the presence of screens 'on site', such as in transitional non-places (Augé) or places of transit, as well as screens in urban, public spaces. The first case is Schiphol Amsterdam Airport, a hypermodern non-place par excellence. At first sight, ubiquity and diversity create a concert or cacophony of screens that subsumes all individual screens. Screens become similar and invisible. On the other hand, a creative use of screen space can mark and deploy the fragmented and varied character of contemporary screen culture. To make the point of the artistic, or if you wish, aesthetic impact of such screens on the cityscape, I discuss the specific spatial relationships that are set up between screens in what is best called exhibition spaces, with reference to and comparison with more traditional exhibition spaces such as museums. The relationship between screens, screened spaces, and the passing, temporary viewer whose temporary loss of direction enables a particular mode of viewing constitute the field of analysis in this part of the chapter.

Following this reflection, in comparison to the airport as a specific site of (im)mobility, a more diverse space of urban screens will be investigated in the second part of the chapter. Urban screens and media façades are a rapidly growing phenomenon in metropoles around the world, and they are part of an extremely varied presence of multimedia in public space. I discuss not only how screens *on site* transform urban space, but also how they are involved in screening practices that are all *about* transformation and mobility of and within urban space.

Screens on site, outdoors or integrated in larger structures and buildings, and in public spaces, can be considered as architectural elements because of their ubiquity, scale, and pervasiveness. They are embedded in or built into constructed spaces, but also open up, make flexible otherwise static, material structures. As screens become integrated in our physical sites and environments, they allow for an almost literal blending of material and virtual spaces. Scott McQuire (2006) calls this phenomenon a *dematerialization of architecture*, in a terminology reminiscent of Marcos Novak's *liquid architecture*. As I will argue, both concepts of material architecture as influenced and transformed by moving images and digital technologies are expressions of an interest in transformations of urban space and the role of media technologies in this process of transformation.

In the last chapter ("Performative Cartography") I again shift to another aspect of mobile screens, now in order to examine touchscreens and the performative nature of navigational visuality. The aspect that most clearly distinguishes the touchscreen from other screen devices such as the cinematic screen, or the television screen for that matter, is the fact that spatial proximity of the screen not only *can* involve the user's body, the screen *must* be touched in order to navigate within the screen interface. Looking at the other end of the interaction, within the mapping applications of such touchscreen devices, I examine the architectural arrangement of the environment within which virtual travel literally *takes place*.

This tactility of the screen extends to a haptic visuality (Bruno) that is enabled by this tactile engagement (Cooley). It is a haptic screen in the sense that the screen is the interface of an interactive architecture and that it positions the user-spectator in a material and spatial relationship to its surface and its imagery. This haptic experience of the tactility of touchscreens primarily meant for viewing inflects the notion – and action – of viewing itself. This particular haptic form of viewing bears consequences for the way the screen enables the viewer-user to virtually travel 'through' the screen. The interface of the screen enables not only a haptic, but also a navigational visuality. And this traversing has a long-standing status as metaphor for screen-based viewing. The idea, or conceptual metaphor, of moving *through* has been dominant in our way of perceiving how visual screen media work. It is as if in retrospect touchscreens were needed to understand this about the past. The novelty of this technology is at least partly wrapped up in a larger paradigm shift regarding navigational visuality, as a new way of understanding what had already been with us for a long time.

The tactile nature of touchscreen technology seems to imply an immediate relationship between viewing, navigating and acting. This transforms the practice of visual engagement with screens (passive spectatorship) by foregrounding the activity involved in navigation, presuming a temporal collapse between creating images and perceiving them. Nevertheless, even if they cannot be disentangled, at the same time paving a way (that is, primarily creating) and following a trace (perhaps primarily perceiving) are different aspects of this double activity. Moreover, a spatial and tactile aspect of surface, materiality and texture enforces the temporal collapse. One way to see this is to imagine that (pre-recorded) cinema becomes live installation as the screen becomes interactive. Paradoxically, it is when haptic activity is most clear, in the engagement with touchscreen devices, that the embodied nature of haptic or visceral experience is complicated by the spatial implications of performative, navigational visuality. The creative turn this can take is clearly visible in what I call live animation. Fantasies we have seen in early cinema of the artist's hands on screen, drawing the animated cartoons 'as we watch', or later science fiction such as *Minority Report*'s magic (data) gloves, resonate with the practice of immediate drawing or manipulating of on-screen images that touchscreen technology makes possible. Immediate as such performative navigation may seem, however, the intervention of the screen that both enables and separates a creative interface is still a technological, mediated mode of visuality. Yet, we can also see this fantasy of haptic creation that meets experience in less physical terms, in films like *The Matrix* or *Inception*, as primarily a mental experience.

The second object considered in the final chapter also warrants something comparable to a close reading, due to the theoretical insights it offers regarding performative navigational visuality: navigation devices mostly used in cars, and augmented reality applications for smartphones. Spatial perception of what is visible on these screens provides what I call liquid landscapes. The fluidity of the perspectival field, the mobility of vantage points that matches the mobile spectator's point of view, not only moves through landscapes – a mobile vision we know from early cinema's phantom rides – but also visually transforms the environments through which the gaze is transported.

The final phenomena that I analyze are GPS-based interactive cartography which makes use of digital photography, geotagging information, and augmented-reality software such as *Layar*, which visualizes mash-up information, layered on a camera view of hybrid smartphones. The chapter then loops back to Chapter 1, where the contemporary highway panorama is connected to its predecessors, and travels back from the present to comparable yet different modes of guiding used in the past, such as maps and road signs.

As I will suggest throughout the five chapters that follow, both in broad brush strokes and in the minute details considered in key objects, we can and must adopt a diachronic-comparative vantage point including earlier media cultures in order to have an inkling of what is happening before our eyes today. The relevance of such a course of study is due to the dialogic perspective on history, and the intermedial perspective on high-tech screen gadgets as well as something as simple but as revealing as a car windshield, which not only offers a view of the world on the other side, but protects the viewer from the discomfort of the experience of travelling at such a speed. With the title of this book, "mobile screens: the visual regime of navigation", I mean to draw attention to the book's dual thrust. On the one hand, it analyzes different 'new' screens and screen practices that put forward mobility; on the other hand, from the perspective of a broader and older regime of navigation, it offers a critical analysis of the ambition to innovate that risks forgetting where many contemporary developments came from, and with which they are in continuity, if not entirely in touch.

1. Panoramic Complex

Let me begin with the contemporary. To be specific, we start out in the Netherlands at the turn of the twenty-first century, with an experience most of my readers will be familiar with. In 1999, during a provocative speech for the Dutch Ministry of Transport, Public Works and Water Management, Francine Houben introduced the concept of the *aesthetics of mobility* as a new principle for spatial planning. Houben, architect and professor of architecture and mobility aesthetics at Delft University of Technology, pleaded for what she called an aesthetic rather than exclusively functional approach to designing roads and the spatial concerns related to mobility:

> [W]e need instruments to realize this aesthetics of mobility. The existing practice of planning fails to do this. The aesthetics of mobility is an aesthetics of movement, of the state you're in when being mobile. It is all about variation. With the alternation of different landscape elements you want to create an aesthetic effect, like the rhythm in a piece of music.[1]

In the project *Holland Avenue* (2003) Houben and her colleagues at Mecanoo Architects made an inventory of the state of highways in the Netherlands for the Dutch Government, using four video cameras in a moving vehicle to generate a visual record of the highway infrastructure from the point of view of the driver. The primary outcome of this inventory was the important suggestion for urban planners that spatial design should develop visually attractive routes rather than strips or corridors. Perhaps more fundamental, however, was the formulation of principles as guidelines for design. According to this perspective, the road is a part of public space, so the design of the highway landscape and roadside space should be organized from the point of view of the experience of the mobile spectator.

Traditionally, in the Netherlands, as in other densely populated countries, space, development, and environmental issues are topics of heated public debate. The enormously high density in population, infrastructure, and mobility networks, the ever-increasing traffic congestion, constructions of so-called *corridor roads*, and diminishing green strips, all provide reason for dispute about the quality of the environment and landscape in the country. A concern for the loss of open spaces and the resulting effects on public health and the environment are also met with the cultural-historical value attached to landscapes: a particular concern for what is referred to as 'panoramic pollution of the horizon' (*horizonver-*

vuiling) and the disappearance of the quintessential Dutch views. From the perspective of urban planning, it is ambiguous, however, what constitutes a panorama – the view, the terrain or the mobilized experience of this constellation – and it therefore remains unclear how to approach the design and preservation of panoramic space. As a media historian and theorist, I have welcomed the opportunity to collaborate with policymakers and urban planners in order to test and develop theoretical insights in relation to the socio-cultural field outside the academy. This allowed me to realize to what extent academic reflection can actually be brought to bear on social and cultural reality.[2]

The first, defining use of the term *screen*, both as noun and as qualifier, is based on something as simple and ubiquitous as the windshield of a car as it moves around the public space. This simple object also demonstrates the obvious importance of navigation, as anyone searching for the right exit, entering a maze of city streets, or trying to find a parking spot will realize. With screens, mobility, and navigation the terms of my study are put in place. The heightened interest in the aesthetics of mobility for the design of public space approaches the panorama in terms of a view of the scenery of an open landscape as seen from the road. Thus conceptualized, the highway panorama is a sequence of views as seen by the driver and the passengers (the back-seat drivers) from behind the windshield of a car, a moving and framed perspective from the highway on the passing scenery. The panorama in this sense is both a spatial arrangement and visual positioning. The positioning in the case of highway panoramas is constituted through motion, paradoxically providing an encompassing, yet distanced view. A similar set of issues is also discussed in media theory, where studies focus on the visual experience of the moving image – in this context not limited to physical mobility, but including the virtual mobility of mediated perception. Starting from mobility as a metaphor for mediality and vice versa, we are led to investigate the crossover terrain between these two domains of media and mobility: media theory and media history meet urban studies, travel and tourism studies, architecture and spatial design.

In this chapter I will explore the intersection of issues in these converging fields of media studies and roadside design, bringing together questions about spatial perception, mobile spectatorship, and panoramic perception. First, I will explore several key concepts at the intersection of vision and mobility. The remaining part of the chapter is devoted to probing the panorama and mobile vision in order to develop a diachronic long view of a visual regime of navigation in contemporary media culture, as well as a social-use context for such a regime.

Building Visions

The construction, design and preservation of highway panoramas puts a set of related issues on the agenda concerning *mobility, perception, performativity* and the *experience* of these within the visual regime of navigation. These key terms require a brief positioning.

The first, most general issue is the changing role of mobility in contemporary society. The technology concerned with mobility and the infrastructure it entails has developed spectacularly in the last century: from the first steam trains, subways, streetcars and automobiles, to the high-speed rail and international airline networks – a development that has accelerated in the last decade. In part due to the exponential growth of communication technologies, from the cellular phone to the Internet, it is possible to travel distances in far less time, as well as to maintain contact all over the globe. The contemporary world is not only reliant on mobility and communication in a social, economic and cultural respect, but it is also spatially arranged, accommodating different modes of transport and mobility.

In his study on mobility as a defining characteristic of modern societies, sociologist John Urry develops a differentiated notion of *mobilities*. From walking to flying, to mobile communication and imaginative travel, as he calls it, he analyzes different historical and contemporary forms of mobility. His study argues for a new sociology based on these mobilities, rather than one based on territorially fixed societies. This historical comparative perspective on different forms of mobility and their impact is pertinent to my analysis. My perspective, however, is focused not on general sociological developments, but rather on a diachronic comparative analysis of the visual regime of navigation, that is, the conditions in which the visual experience of mobility is both possible and taken for granted. This regime – the conditions of mobility as a way of life – is what I aim to offer an analysis of.

Visuality in today's culture is tightly connected to mobility – corporeal by means of physical travel, and virtual through media and communication. Visual perception refers here to the brain's registration of the visible dimension of the world through the visual faculty. This sounds more unbiased than it is. What we see is in fact present, but in looking we select, taint and interpret the visual stimuli. Additionally, seeing should not be considered as separate from other types of perception facilitated through our other senses, such as touch and sound. This ties in with the recent surge of interest in haptic perception. Such a broader conception of seeing makes it necessary to insist on a synesthetic, rather than a merely aesthetic perspective in discussions of spatial perception. In doing so, visual perception is positioned within a larger set of perceptual faculties.[3] In Chapter 5 I will return to this perspective when I analyze what I consider a haptic engagement with space in interactive navigation. In this chapter, instead, I will discuss perception primarily as seeing in relation to motion – including principles of selecting and tainting – exploring the visual regime of navigation at play both in physical movement and virtual (mediated) mobility, without assuming or identifying an absolute distinction between the different forms of perception.

Visuality is not only the perception of the visible, or seeing; it includes the conditions by which we can see. This encompasses the visible world and the technologies that facilitate viewing this world, yet also make it specific or give it shape, as well as the historically changing conceptions related to seeing. Or, as the American art historian Hal Foster says pithily, visuality is "how we see, how we are able, allowed, or made to see, and how we see this seeing or the unseen therein." (1988: ix) In order to understand visuality in our contemporary moment, it is useful to examine this as a historical cultural phenomenon. This does not mean that every scholar should write the history of seeing; rather, the awareness that seeing has a history will inform even the most contemporary analysis of present practices.

Visuality restricts and determines both *what* we see and *how* we see. The reaction of the individual subject – in this case the car driver – is both corporeal and psychological. The concept of *experience* that I use, here, does not make a distinction between these two domains. Moreover, viewing entails agency, as an act that establishes vision: it is a performative act. Performativity, as conceptualized within the philosophy of language in speech-act theory, following J.L. Austin's famous *How to Do Things with Words* (1962), entails the potential of utterances to act. Acting is bringing about change. This notion that saying is doing, and hence also making, can be turned around as well: doing is saying. In this sense, seeing is also doing and vision is an act, one that makes, creates, and establishes.

Later, I will return to the notion of performativity in relation to perception and to the production and construction of space, as it is a key concept at the intersection of mobility, mediation, and the construction and meaning of space, the central concern in this book. Here, the perspective of performativity helps us consider the panorama as constructed through the collaboration of construction, perception and experience. It is in experience that the 'act of looking' (analogous to *speech act*) and the response to it come together. The specificity of navigation as a visual regime, as I will argue in the following, is situated in the intersection of mobility, perception, performativity, and the experience thereof. The movement of the gaze in panoramas, the body in motion in transportation, and the simulation of movement in virtual mobility all rely on principles of visual navigation: the body of the spectator is positioned in the visual arrangement, perched on the lookout for where to go next.

The key terms in this consideration – mobility, perception, performativity and experience – find their nexus in the perception of moving images, that is, in the visual regime of navigation. Or to be more precise, they constitute a *mobile dispositif*: a dynamic arrangement of the viewing subject within a spatial field of perception, including the vectorialization of 'going somewhere', the view or object of the gaze, and the media and/or transportation technology which sets this arrangement in motion. The significance of movement for visuality is that it provides a productive perspective for examining the design of public space from a cinematographic, 'moving-image' perspective. What the cinema and highway panoramas have in common is a particular mode of vision geared towards moving images seen from a fixed seated position, either behind the glass windshield or in the darkness of the movie theater. Such an entry point brings up questions related to design and perception, but also concerning aesthetic and cultural norms. It can even be argued that a cinematographic approach to the highway panorama motivates the contemporary concern for the roadside design in spatial planning. Media are pre-eminently relevant benchmarks for spatial design in terms of mobile viewing of 'moving images'. Therefore, a media-theoretical reflection as part of the way we think about spatial design and the view from the highway can help us understand how media work. In other words, through a comparison between the different types of experiences of and by media, the perspective of cinematography helps when conceptualizing the panoramic experience of driving – and the other way around.

The history of comparing spatial perception in motion with the perception of mediated moving images goes back a longer way than the more recent interest in mobility within media studies and the relevance of media for architecture and spatial design. In 1964, for example, the urban planner Kevin Lynch, famous for his book about perception of the city, *The Image of the City* (1960), co-authored a book with Donald Appleyard and John R. Myer entitled *The View from the Road* (1964), a study based on extensive photographic documentation. This book paved the way for an aesthetic approach to mobility. The authors used motion picture cells and interviews to analyze the visual experience of driving and the view both *on* and *from* the highway. In the preface the authors stress the double-sidedness of their project:

> We became interested in the aesthetics of highways out of a concern with the visual formlessness of our cities and an intuition that the new expressway might be one of our best means of re-establishing coherence and order on the new metropolitan scale. We were also attracted to the highway because it is a good example of a design issue typical of the city: their problem of designing visual sequences for the observer in motion. But if in the end the study contributes something toward making the highway experience a more enjoyable one, we will be well satisfied. (1964: 2; emphasis added)

The authors refer to different media and arts when they write about the constant succession of movement and space, a statement which is used as a motto on the website of the Mobility Studio of the Interactive Institute in Stockholm, Sweden:

> The sense of spatial sequence is like that of large-scale architecture; the continuity and insistent temporal flow are akin to music and cinema. The kines-

thetic sensations are like those of the dance or the amusement park, although rarely so violent.[4]

The Mobility Studio provides this quote in the context of their more recent interest in the perspective of the car driver in their *Backseat Games* project (2001-2006) that addresses very creative questions concerning possibilities for enhancing the experience of road use. This project explores the car as an interface for different purposes: work station, arena for entertainment, site of fiction, or soundscape.[5]

Interestingly, Lynch's statement resonates with Houben's perspective on the aesthetics of mobility, invoking different media and sensory experiences in order to highlight the aesthetic approach. This points to the properly synesthetic nature of the issue: an aesthetic that is built on the synchronization of the senses. As mentioned above, the synesthetic nature of experience in the visual regime of navigation is of crucial importance for understanding not only highway panoramas, but the wider field of mobile screens explored in this book.[6]

These different studies on car mobility share similar interests with media-archaeological studies about the development, theories and practices of screen media, in the sense that both approach mobility as a perceptual and media-shaped experience. Wolfgang Schivelbusch's work (1986) on the impact of train travel on the experience of time and space has been influential for these media-historical studies. Similarly, other cultural historians have focused on the shifts in experience of nineteenth-century modernity and the place of both technologies of transport and of vision. In line with this reasoning a new generation of scholarship on early cinema has made important contributions to this 'modernity thesis' about the reciprocal relationship between media and mobility.[7]

The combination of discourses on media and mobility, on perception and space, and the sometimes highly philosophical discussions about these topics within the fields of architecture and spatial design, raise fundamental questions about the paradoxical relationship between physical mobility on the one hand, and the experience of virtual mobility (mediated) on the other. For the reflection on highway landscaping, the question is how to move beyond mere analogy. I seek to understand how apparent similarities between aspects of media and mobility, between real space and the virtual, can provide insights into both domains that characterize contemporary culture.

Panoramic Desire

What is the significance of the panoramic experience, and why is it something to invest in? In his influential *Non-lieux: introduction à une anthropologie de la surmodernité* (1992) French anthropologist Marc Augé asserts that we live in a culture that puts emphasis on the design and use of non-defined places, places where people pass through instead of in which they dwell. He calls this the culture of *supermodernity*.

According to Augé, the world is increasingly composed of these "non-places" (non-lieux): public places of passage, or knots in networks of mobility, places without history or unique identity that signify mobility, communication and consumption. Due to the increasing mobility in everyday life, residing at these places, but also being on the road, in the car, train or other mode of transport, we increasingly value these non-places as central to our spatial presence. This in part explains the rising interest in the quality of experiences at these places of passage during transportation. That interest responds to a desire to enhance the quality of people's experience of this dwelling in mobility.

The value attributed to the time spent traveling foregrounds the way a landscape is not only a natural, but also a historical area. The design of such a historical, changing place is based on cultural norms. Terms such as heritage, nostalgia, cultural memory, and landscape conservation play a decisive role in this bond between history and cultural normativity. It is therefore not surprising that it was recommended in this project to focus particular attention on developing guidelines for spatial design related to the view from the highway of local landscape identities, defined by means of a cultural-historical landscape analysis. In an attempt to address local specificity as well as uniqueness, a search is conducted for the typical, irreplaceable qualities of certain locations. The objective of this investigation is to make the norms underlying such qualifications explicit in the panoramas within the region. The view allows for a relation to be drawn between the highway as (a series of) indefinable non-place(s), a temporary residence of passage, and the local landscape as a place with an identity, where the quality of the place and the aesthetic experience of the people traversing it can be brought together. In short, the view is transformed to a panorama – fulfilling the desire to transform the non-lieu into a place, into an experience.

In relation to the design of space as a place of experience, I am struck by the mixed discourse in Norman Klein's description of what he calls "scripted spaces," spaces that are

> [...] a walk-through or click-through environment (a mall, a church, a casino, a theme park, a computer game). They are designed to emphasize the viewer's journey – the space between – rather than the gimmicks on the wall. The audience walks into the story. What's more, this walk should respond to each viewer's whims, even though each step along the way is prescribed [...]. It is gentle repression posing as free will. (2004: 11, emphasis in text)

In this brief but evocative description, the design to transform what we can call in reference to Augé's term (non-place) a *non-space* rather than a specific place – an open space of mobility – into a space of experience puts forward the goal of its design: a scripting of experience, which, as Klein rightly remarks, is in part an invisible control of (supposedly) individual experience: a paradoxical scripting of freedom. Moreover, as he continues, with the notion of scripted spaces, he means "primarily a mode of perception, a way of seeing." I find the equation between a scripted space, or to extend this, space as machine of vision, and (resulting) vision itself problematic. It conflates control and experience, as if experience could be fully controlled. Instead, within a visual regime of navigation, the subject has, perhaps paradoxically, a limited control of perception within the parameters of the route. But I do find the close connection between the (pre-) structuring of space and the resulting experience of space helpful in understanding how experiences can be, at least partially, 'tainted' by design. To remain in visual terms, this emphasis on the inherent relationship between design and perception makes it possible to understand culture at work beyond individual experience alone. Because of the complex relationship with perception and the fact that such design is not neutral, it is important to consider the underlying motivations and ambitions of design.

Varied, but co-extending ambitions of science and spectacle maintain the desire to (visually) simulate and augment reality through art and technology. On the one hand, from a scientific ambition we are driven by the unattainable desire to perfect the illusion of reality: to draw out the world, to comprehend, to understand. The operation of human perception is perceived as a direct portal to knowledge. In this sense vision can be seen as epistemologically motivated, in the urge to see and thus know. Yet, on the other hand, we are fascinated by the spectacularity of immersion, an overwhelming aesthetic experience, which is brought about by reality simulation. In this respect, it is not knowledge or understanding but immersive experience that is the primary target of desire. However, my conception of visual *regimes* implies that such distinct desires are integrated. In a visual regime of navigation, visuality entails a combination of epistemological models – ways in which seeing is related to knowing – and aesthetic norms and conventions. These sides to visuality are intricately intertwined, and both purposes of knowledge and aesthetic experience converge. We want to reach our destination effectively, and have a good time looking through the windshield while getting there.

The portrayal of the world from a desire to make an authentic duplicate has a long history, from cave paintings to Disney World, from trompe-l'oeil paintings to digital animation, from the panoramic painting to the Holodeck in the *Star Trek* universe. This trans-historical desire for, or myth of, ultimate reproduction is perhaps akin to what André Bazin (1967) has called the "myth of total cinema" – a desire that long predates the actual invention of the medium of moving images. However, it was when both desires – for understanding and for immersion – converged that cultural transformation occurred. The way in which this desire is fuelled by an ambition, yet also by a fear for an overwhelming, spectacular visual experience is specifically characteristic of the modernity of the late-nineteenth and twentieth century, an era in which technological innovation, scientific discourse and popular spectacle met. In that period, a specifically panoramic desire took shape. Panoramic desire as the urge to have an expanding view, a sense of overview, or survey of the landscape, enabling the viewer to orient herself in relation to landmarks: this is the stuff of the visual regime of navigation.[8]

The contradictory nature of desire – the temporary nature of its fulfillment, the distraction that is sought, and the fears and anxieties that feed it – appears in the way the term 'panorama' has been used. It describes different phenomena, and it is used as a name for a range of different genres within different media – from painting to photography, and from film to digital images and interactive installations. Initially, 'panorama' refers to a view or vista. In addition to this visual experience, the term panorama is also used for media installations and simulation technologies that facilitate realism and emphasize the spectacular nature of the experience of 'looking around'. When we consider media trends over the past 200 years that have been referred to as 'panoramic', it is striking to note the high level of contradiction found in the primary assumptions of what should be considered fundamental to the panorama in terms of its visual effect.

An interest in the (aesthetic) experience of landscape has a long history in the Netherlands. It is, after all, the land of the Van Ruisdaels – both Isaac (1599-1677) and Jacob (c. 1628-1682) and of Philip(s) (de) Koninck (1619-1688), and other painters who have achieved worldwide fame for their depictions of Dutch landscapes. The Dutch painters from the seventeenth century are admired for their fascinating, almost panoramic landscapes. These landscapes are fascinating because the artists did not paint from a detached and objective point of view, but an embodied one. The primary attraction of these paintings is the illusion of depth, which suggests that one is pulled from under the branches of a tree to a lower point in a forest, or that one looks from an imaginary dune top to a flat landscape with a low horizon. Such landscapes can be considered as early attempts to create 3D visions on flat screens. These paintings are marked by a specific use of perspective that constructs a vantage point for the viewer as if she is in fact present in the woods or on top of a dune. Instead of remaining an onlooker, the viewer is invited to be present, as part of the scene depicted: the observer is offered some sort of immersion.[9]

In continuity with this tradition, yet as a radical shift, a change occurs when viewers are no longer placed at an embodied vantage point – when they are no longer fixated, that is, to their place within the arrangement that is configured within the lines of perspective created on the canvas, between the borders of the painting that is marked by its frame. When the viewer is allowed to, or is even required to move around in order to behold, to capture the scene that is presented, the panorama is born.

Fig. 1.1: Jacob van Ruisdael, Dune Landscape with Scrub [Zandweg in de Duinen],
ca. 1650-1655, 42.5 cm x 32 cm (Rijksmuseum, Amsterdam)

Different semi-controllable factors determine the viewing experience, and determine the change brought about by the panorama. I address a few of these factors,
in particular those that are often held in high esteem in the tradition of the panorama. As such the panorama involves more than just a different kind of view,
reformulating that which from a fixed position within the space can be seen at a
glance. More profoundly, panoramas are experiments of the possibility to transform a view into experience. The panoramic desire within a visual regime of navigation, then, is built on the desire to have an unfolding, or unrolling perspective
and the (visual) experience of navigating within this temporally expanding visual
field of moving images.

The neologism 'panorama' is a combination of the Greek words *pan* (everything)
and *horama* (sight, that which is visible). The term was first used in 1791 in an
advertisement for a large cylinder painting where a natural environment was
depicted. Panorama was in fact the second name of an invention that was
patented earlier by the British painter Robert Barker under the name "La nature à
coup d'oeil" (nature at a glance) in 1787. Following this new name of a specific
medium of circular panoramic paintings, the name panorama was subsequently
used for other media and genres, from widescreen or 360° photographic views, to

cinematographic pans (horizontal as well as vertical), in-depth shots, and the IMAX widescreen cinema, to interactive digital simulations on the Internet and virtual reality surroundings. Within the media domain, the term refers to both the realistic and impressive spectacular effect of immersion, in other words, to the visual experience facilitated by these media.[10]

The main reason why the term is used to describe different phenomena is that panorama in fact denotes a form of abstraction, from visual object to visual form. 'Panorama' is primarily used to refer to specific characteristics related to vision: the experience of the limitless visual perception. In this experience in media installations, an omnipotent visual dominance consists of screen encirclement, enabling the spectator to choose the direction in which she looks. In the patent applied for by Barker we find these two characteristics defined. For this reason I cite from the text at some length:

> Now know ye, that by my invention, called La Nature à Coup d'Oeil, is intended, by drawing and painting, and a proper disposition of the whole, to perfect an *entire view* of any country or situation, as it appears to an observer turning *quite round*; to produce which effect, the painter or drawer must fix his station, and delineate correctly and connectedly every object which presents itself to his view as he turns round, concluding his drawing by a connection with where he began. He must observe the lights and shadows, how they fall, and perfect his piece to the best of his abilities. There must be a circular building or framing erected, on which this drawing or painting may be performed; or the same may be done on canvas, or other materials, and fixed or suspended on the same building or framing, to answer the purpose complete. It must be lighted entirely from the top, either by a glazed dome or otherwise, as the artist may think proper. [...] The entrance to the inner inclosure must be from below a proper building or framing being erected for that purpose, so that no door or other interruption may disturb the circle on which the view is to be represented. And there should be, below the painting or drawing, proper ventilators fixed, so as to render a current circulation of air through the whole; and the inner inclosure may be elevated, at the will of an artist, so as to make observers, on whatever situation he may wish they should imagine themselves, *feel as if really* on the very Spot.[11]

The terms in italics reveal the departure points: Barker does not only address *entire view* and *quite round*, but names the *effect*. The sum of the perception is thus not inherent in that which is visible, but is brought forward by the direction of the gaze of the painter, and thus the spectators, who themselves are situated at a fixed point (*fix his station*). At the end of the text great emphasis is placed on the illusion, the reality effect of sensation (*feel as if really*).

Barker is compelled to offer an extensive description as he explains something very sophisticated and to a certain extent 'unnatural'. The relationship between comprehensive panoramic seeing and an individual who determines the duration and direction of the view, for instance, is contradictory. Both are ideals, found also in the descriptions of other media inventions. It can be understood as an ambition, a desire for visual dominance, which has to compensate for the limitations in the field of vision.

When we look at the different phenomena since Barker's invention that have also been given the title panorama, it becomes apparent how different medial features are being used in different versions of the 'panoramic' exploration and the mapping of space. It is a key feature of the panorama painting that the top and bottom boundaries – the borders of the canvas that mark and reveal the framing of the image – are carefully eliminated. At the top this happened by the elimination of the field of vision, below by the so-called *faux-terrain*, a (three-dimensional) foreground that seems to flow over seamlessly into the canvas, to ensure the illusion of unlimited sight.[12]

In this context William Uricchio (1999) points out the difference between the recurring ideal of "all-seeing" against the practice of "always-partial" gaze. This practice goes back to the traditional panoramic paintings and the subsequent panoramas. Setting up a huge circular screen creates a 360° field of vision that can only be viewed entirely by means of the spectator rotating. This contradicts the promise of "nature at a glance" and entails a restriction of perspective. This restriction entails the inherently limiting character of the freedom of movement associated with interactivity. As Uricchio states:

> Despite the name [...] the circular format by definition precluded any all-encompassing glance, requiring instead a series of glances and a mobilized spectator (1999: 126).

This point of the "mobilized spectator" will prove to be crucial for our understanding of the highway panorama. Through this figure of the mobilized spectator, the contradiction inherent in panoramic desire as based on epistemological and aesthetic ambitions – understanding and immersion, or domination and submission – are thus reconciled within a regime of navigation. And through the temporal element involved in this mobilization, desire can be sustained, instead of evaporating.

Fig. 1.2: Panorama Mesdag in *The Hague, the Netherlands. The painting (14 meters high, 120 meters in circumference) from 1881 is still exhibited today at its original site.*[13] *For a digital rendering of this panorama, see fig. 5.1. Photo Panorama Mesdag*

Movement in the Panorama

If popularity is proof, panoramic painting fulfilled a clear cultural desire for machines of vision.[14] In reaction to the immense popularity of the panorama, different variations were developed in the nineteenth century. Part of these developments incorporated movement of and within the panorama, such as the horizontally moving panorama and the diorama created by Louis Daguerre. These types of moving panoramas developed from the criticism of the limits of reproducing the illusion of reality in the immense circular panoramas, as Stephan Oettermann writes (1997:63). The size of the canvas evoked an expectation of movement, but in fact emphasized the images' motionless state. The images of vehicles, animals, and people made it increasingly apparent that these stood still. This was seen as a huge constraint, taxing the panoramic desire. The genre apparently supposes a reality illusion that can function in two ways, two forms of mobility: by movement of the image, or by mobility of the gaze.

The horizontally moving panorama was composed of a long image that was rolled open from left to right (or perhaps the other way around) as the spectator looked. Through this device an illusion of movement was established. However, what actually moved in this imitation was a simulation: the movement that was simulated was that of the vantage point of the spectator themselves, not the 'view' towards which their gaze was directed. The spectators' view seemed to be brought in motion because the object of vision – the depiction of the view – was revealed. This can be compared to the moving perspective of the voyager who, immobile inside her car, makes her way through a seemingly static landscape in a moving vehicle, and the cinematic spectator sitting still while viewing moving images.

The movement of the screen itself, the literal unrolling of the panorama before the eyes of the spectator, can be regarded as a theatrical performance. The duration of the performance, in this instance, coincides with the duration of viewing. This is in sharp contrast to the temporal liberty intrinsic to the spectator of the circular panorama. The unrolling variant of the panorama has its roots in the stage decorations of the theater. At the beginning of the nineteenth century these painted rolls formed an independent source of entertainment, albeit temporarily. For this reason I find it useful to refer to this kind of (horizontal) moving panorama as theatrical panorama.[15]

The diorama by Daguerre, a semi-circular panorama with many visual effects that simulate motion, is based on different principles. This type is also theatrical; it too stems from a tradition of performance culture. However, the term 'diorama' has been established so firmly that I am compelled to treat it as a different genre. The diorama is composed of two screens painted on both sides. Through lighting an illusion of motion in the image is created, such as a sunset or a wreath of smoke from a chimney. Additionally the stage, centrally positioned in relation to a seated audience, would rotate approximately 73°. This rotation facilitated interchanging one screen for the other. A noticeable difference with the theatrical panorama is that the diorama specifically visualized the lapse of time. It was not the sense of spectator movement that was being simulated through shifting the field of vision, but a more general sense of time passing that lies at the foundation of a different experience of movement, the movement of the earth in relation to the sun in the course of a day. This experience arises from the transition from one scene to another, or from a natural temporal dynamic symbolized in the sunrise and sunset.[16]

Another genre within the panoramic culture with a paradoxical relation to time is panoramic photography. In a strict sense the photographic image offers no movement, but rather a fixation with the illusion of reality. Photographic realism, founded in the indexical characteristic of the photo-chemical image – the literal imprint on sensitive film of light at a specific moment – offers an anchoring in time and place that in our culture is considered to guarantee authenticity (Barthes 1981). Despite the fact that the indexical characteristic of the photograph fixes authenticity in time – the moment at which the photo was taken has actually passed – movement is not necessary. In contrast to circular panoramic paintings, panoramic photography emphasizes the horizon of the image, just as the horizontal moving panoramas do.

The size and the circumference of the large-scale painted panorama that invites observation in a horizontal fashion is reduced, and flattened in panoramic photography. Reading the image happens either from left to right, or vice versa. This can be compared to experiments in cartography where the sphere of the earth is flattened out, translated to a two-dimensional image. Digital photography adds to this the possibility for individual authority: the spectator can move around 'in' a digital panorama. The mouse, joystick, or touchpad can navigate not only horizontally, vertically and diagonally, but also in or out of depth. As such, you do not view panoramic photos at a glance; rather, you scan the visual field. However, there is no space for zooming in and out of the image. The space of the spectator engaged with the panoramic painting is simulated but may be enhanced, since the depth of field of the image can be manipulated.[17]

The aspect of movement, inherent to exploring space, from and within the panoramic image itself is characteristic of panoramic cinematography. In contrast to the panoramas mentioned earlier, where movement is reliant on the spectator (panoramic paintings) or the user (digital panorama), the movement of the gaze in panoramic cinematography has been previously recorded, registered, and also fixed by the eye of the camera. It has been scripted. In the beginning of film the term panorama was used to describe different film experiments. As Uricchio (1999) has pointed out, it was not only the most frequently used genre label in film titles prior to 1915, but the term was a way of categorizing a large range of films: from train films to stationary total shots, to images shot from high buildings or hot air balloons. The most striking similarity between these films is their dynamic exploration of the depth of images, in contrast to the horizontal orientation of the two-dimensional panoramic paintings and panoramic photography. Cinematography not only added a temporal element to the static image when the moving image had yet to be discovered, but this movement also offered the ability to explore the dimension of depth in the image. Here, the panoramic film can also be perceived as the successor of the stereo photography. In the nineteenth century, this was the basis of popular entertainment using 3D photography.[18]

A panorama concerned with both movement and depth frequently crystallized into what were known as *phantom rides*. These are films shot from a moving train, subway, boat, car or even hot air balloon, in most cases avoiding visual references to the mode of transportation so as to ensure that the spectator is transported through the screen as a ghost. This film archetype is still very popular and takes on different forms. Consider, for example, the excess of car chase scenes on television and in films such as *Speed* (Jan de Bont, 1994), *The Fast and the Furious* (Rob Cohen, 2001) and its sequels, or *The Matrix Reloaded* (Andy and Larry Wachowski, 2003). The attraction of these images is the result of a combination of spectacle, evoked by the sensation of a visual rollercoaster, and the stimulating urge the spectator shares with the main character.[19]

A panoramic desire is conspicuous in all these inventions and panoramic genres. Whether it concerns simulating circular vision through panoramic paintings, in this extension, the moving view offered in panoramic theaters, fixating movement by film, or the interactivity in digital panorama, this desire consistently fuels such inventions and their popular success. The aspiration that is fundamental to the continuing cultural desire for panorama is fed, satisfied, and further clarified by such visual inventions and technological experiments. Therefore a panorama in all its manifestations is best considered a scripting of a (theatrical) performance: it solicits in the viewer a performance based on a script. Such performances are, indeed, enactments of a script. In music, this would be the score; in theater, the scenario; in song, the lyrics plus the score. In a panorama, the script or the configuration of the dispositif is the route along which the spectator is guided – either the gaze or the entire body. A concept can also be the script when the performance is thought. Or, as in this case, it can be an image that solicits the performance of a visual act. Performativity pertains to that act itself. The performance is performative if and when the scripted act, beyond the execution of the script (performance), brings about a change in the subject, his surroundings, or the object seen, e.g. when an interpretation becomes a new script for others. Here – in the intricate and temporal relationship between performance and performativity, lies the fundamental movement of the panorama. The panorama is created as the viewer engages with the view. The visual regime of navigation reigns over this script, informing the spectator how to look, how to move, and how to understand what is being seen in terms of the spatial construction.[20]

Modes of Viewing

The crucial question is, then, what is the spectator's part as a participant in the panoramic performance? Within art and media studies, there is a lot of discussion about visual perception, the construction of perspective and the role that movement and mobility have in this.[21] First of all, within this theoretical debate, the mode of viewing where the spectator is left out of the scene of looking is separated from a more dialogic, engaged way of looking. This first form we can call monologic; it is also sometimes referred to as colonizing. Linear perspective is based on this. In a strict sense the spectator stands at the boundary of the field of vision, but crucially, outside of it. A partial circle encompasses this field of vision, creating a horizon and a vanishing point. The principle is directly applicable to driving on the highway, but this is the only similarity that can be established, for the perspectival spectator is motionless. She represses – to use a psychoanalytical term – the participation of her own body in the viewing process, and embraces the field of vision without participating in it.[22]

In the extension of this perspectival view stands another form of monologic viewing, namely voyeurism. Here the spectator is also left out of the scene altogether. Instead of optically falling outside the field of vision, the spectator, who is utterly object-oriented, closes himself off, by staying behind a curtain or otherwise staying invisible. Here, however, a crucial distinction must be made, which impacts on the cultural appreciation of this mode of looking. The object of the voyeuristic eye is not a segment of the world, but in fact a person. The arousal this stirs in the spectator is dependent on her invisibility. As such, it remains a monologic way of viewing. Despite the fact that there is a similarity of principle between perspective and voyeuristic viewing, the effort necessitated by the voyeur in order to stay clear of the spectacle seems to suggest that the assumptions central to perspective viewing are incorrect. Not a single spectator actually manages to stay out of the scene of looking. The exhilaration, fundamental to voyeurism, takes place within the body of the spectator – hence this body is implicated.

The panoptic gaze, made prominent by Michel Foucault in *Discipline and Punish* (1979), is another variety of monologic viewing that implies appropriation. Here, with regard to the corporeal, the spectator remains less bodily engaged than in voyeurism. However, this gaze demands – just as with panoramic painting – a mobility of the body (turning around), albeit not for the looker's own exhilaration, as with voyeurism, but to exercise a restrictive power over the objects seen. In summary, these three types of monologic viewing, that is to say perspective, voyeuristic and panoptic gaze, are based on one-way traffic. They therefore they carry with them a tendency to appropriation. Hence, the idea of perspective is inherently colonizing.

On the other end of the spectrum are the modes of viewing based on dialogue, on mutual relations and engagement. Here the spectators are thoroughly aware of the implications viewing has on them and their bodily experience. This can be a physical sensation, or a form of psychological effect, such as aggression, repulsion, or attraction. Because of the acknowledgment of response, this mode of looking can be termed dialogic. Here the one being looked at is able to return the gaze. The spectator is not only the subject but also the object of the gaze. Such viewing is emphatically anchored in time. This is where we find a similarity to the experience of the motorist.[23]

Within a visual regime of navigation, looking is dialogic and self-referential, searching for landmarks and points of interest from the point of view of one's current location, the movement of travel, and often a destination. This experience bears comparison with all the modes of looking outlined above. As with the perspectival spectator, the car driver has an overview. This view is limited, by either the horizon or by roads, bridges, industrial terrain and residential areas. But, just as is the case with the dialogical spectator, the driver is influenced by what she sees. The driver is not protected, as is the voyeur, and has no fixed position, as the spectator of the panoramic painting does. As a consequence of a combination of these gazes, it is possible to circumscribe a unique highway aesthetic. Unlike the panoptic gaze of the prison guard, the driver is unable to turn around at will in order to achieve an overview. The experience of viewing and driving – from moving with and sitting still inside a car – is dialogic in the sense that it may evoke aggression, repulsion and attraction or amusement, as well as arouse such responses in the driver herself. The realization that the position in the car is not one of separation, as with the perspectival spectator, is of vital importance for the driver. After all, the illusion of such exclusion would lead to safety hazards on the road.

The Gaze in Motion

To attain a more precise understanding of the gaze of the driver, it is necessary to bring the notion of the gaze in relation to movement and mobility. This is precisely what Anne Friedberg does in her study of the role of film in what is often termed a postmodern experience (1993). She terms her synthesis, which is relevant here, a *mobilized gaze*. 'Mobilized' can mean two things. First, it means a 'mobile' gaze – one put into motion. However, mobilized also means 'summoned' (for military duty, for instance). In order to foreground once more the contradictions of panoramic desire, I wish to emphasize and activate this second meaning of mobilization. The gaze is put in motion, made mobile, but also steered, put forward, and shaken up – even exposed to danger, like the mobilized soldier. From this perspective it is possible to discuss a mobilized gaze. Friedberg seeks to emphasize the way in which nineteenth-century modern man makes use of different technologies through which the world can be admired in motion. Examples of these are the bicycle, the tram, the train and later the automobile and airplane, but also the elevator and the escalator, and even window-shopping.

For, in addition to those modes of transport, 'wandering' within typical urban architectural environments such as shopping malls, museums and city parks is a novel and modern phenomenon. In the 1920s and 1930s, cultural philosopher Walter Benjamin devoted his work *The Arcades* (*Das Passagenwerk*, published posthumously) to researching the topic of the nineteenth-century predecessor of urban shopping arcades. Composed of separate fragments, in its structure (or lack thereof) this book offers its readers a chance to wander on their own account (Benjamin 1999; for a commentary, Buck-Morss 1989).

Friedberg establishes a relation between the literally 'mobilized' gaze as a preoccupation in contemporary society, with the development of media technologies that enable the virtual gaze. She defines the latter as follows: "The *virtual gaze* is not a direct perception but a *received* perception mediated through representation." (1993: 2; emphasis in text) This formulation allows me to discern the causal relation between mobility and virtuality: transport and mobility nourish a desire to simulate this (and vice versa); they nourish a desire to the secondary experience of looking *by means of* media technologies. This is also relevant when considering the view of the highway panorama. After all, drivers too can choose their own path (albeit within the maze of roads and streets) – they cruise in automobiles, unfettered by fixed tracks or routes, wandering on wheels. And here as well, in fact, the perpetually changing view offers the world as a moving image. Trees and buildings flash by, the horizon is constantly changing; the structures of bridges and waterways appear, transforming, then vanishing.

The panoramic painting, the theatrically moving panoramas and the (stereo) photograph transport the spectator in a virtual fashion. The moving image, of film, television, and video, but also later the more interactive technologies such as virtual reality, can be regarded as developments in which the virtual gaze – already familiar from paintings and photography – is mobilized again. This re-mobilized virtual gaze stems from two traditions within modern visuality: mobilizing the gaze and virtualizing the gaze, that is, putting vision into motion and presenting the world as a moving image. These come together in the highway panoramas, which are real and stable – think of the roads, bridges and residential areas – but also virtual: the movement of the panorama itself is a perceptual effect of the mobile gaze. This effect is of great significance to the experience of the motorist, who experiences the mobilization in a physical, sensory and psychological fashion.[24]

Through the combination of mobility with virtuality – the nineteenth-century visual revolution – a paradox is made explicit. The movement of viewing, supported and enhanced by the moving image, has become dependent on the immobility of the spectator. Only the gaze is moving, virtually through media or literally through modes of transportation – whether the spectator is sitting in the chair of the cinema, behind the computer, in the train, or in the car. But sitting (still) is the starting position from which the moving image can be experienced. Friedberg finds that this paradoxical fact stems from the principle of "compensation":

The [cinematic] spectator is not really moving – his/her head and body remain relatively immobile. The visuality here is compensatory, in line with the paradox that I have emphasized elsewhere: as the mobilized gaze became more virtual, it grew to involve less physical mobility, and became located within the confines of a frame. (2006: 162)

The added value of sitting still while watching comes from the desire to have an overview and to optimally experience the sequence – in other words the sequential (and re-edited) shots, as a series of glances. Hence, the image seen is that of the *single shot*, a recording of a single fluid (camera) movement. According to Schivelbusch, the desire for such a visual experience is especially apparent in the experience of transport by technology, such as by train (1986). An appreciation of Schivelbusch's theory enables a better understanding of how the highway panorama stands, in continuity and disparity, in relation to the phenomenon I have recognized above as constitutive of the visual revolution of the nineteenth century.

Schivelbusch does not limit his attention to the consequence of traveling and tourism in modern society and of cultural expression such as literature and painting. His primary concern is the way in which the experience of modern, technological modes of transport brings forward a fundamental transformation in our experience of time and space. A comparison with the way in which media technologies, such as machines for virtual travel, have rigorously changed the experience of time and space, is inevitable. Consider for instance the impact of the Internet and cellular phones on the acceleration and globalization of the world.

A development that cannot be overestimated is the radical acceleration of travel due to the train. Specifically, the speed facilitated by technology in certain modes of transport has had great implications for the relation between the traveler and the landscape. As a result of such velocity and the associated distance between the traveler and the environment, a particular way of viewing has emerged. Schivelbusch calls this panoramic viewing. The panoramic gaze is fast, *scanning* almost, superficial and focused on the depth of the image. That which is close disappears – the objects in close proximity of the moving window are literally rendered seemingly invisible by the speed of motion – and that which lies far away slows time and is visible for a longer period. The panoramic gaze is static and restricted: the window frames the field of vision, and the railway track makes the train a projectile. The traveler does not feel the ground; rather, s/he can be said to glide through the landscape. In such a line of reasoning, the highway panorama is in fact a prolongation of the panoramic experiences such as mediation and mobilization – to use these terms again – by panoramic painting, circular and immobile, theatrical and mobile, and by photographic, filmic and digital panoramas. And, like traveling in a train, the body of the driver remains immobile, regardless of travel speed. But what she sees does, in fact, have an effect, and so it should. This makes the performance (in the theatrical sense) of the panorama also performative (in the speech-act sense) so that it becomes generative of a 'solicitation effect' in the recipient; the mobile gaze, first mobilized, is also mobilizing.

A Panoramic Complex

At this point it becomes possible to have a closer look at the aspects of the panorama that stem from the panoramic desire and the complex relation between mobility, perception and experience. To that end, I introduce the term *panoramic complex* after which this chapter is named. The classic cinematic viewing arrangement or dispositif is a voyeuristic one, due to the spatial position of the unseen and immobile spectator; within the panoramic complex, the spectator is a mobile agent, requiring movement in order to see. This movement can take place to varying degrees, in various viewing arrangements, either with the turning of the gaze from a fixed point, or the vehicular movement of highway panoramas. The point is, however, that the mobile dispositif implied in the panoramic complex arranges a visual regime of navigation.

To see everything – the 'pan' in panorama – a view is necessary. It requires a spatial but immaterial fact: void space. This void gives depth and length to the lines of vision when looking. Scale is also of importance here, the relative proportions of the objects in the visible landscape through which people move. But this space is also necessary to act as a borderline and accommodate the objects that can be seen. Borders and objects are the material elements within the spatial void of depth. Remarkably, the term panorama is used in particular to mark those sites from where the view 'begins': the look-out points from where the spatial arena is viewed. The panorama perceived as location affords visual access to the arena of the gaze, the field of vision, or scopic terrain.

These different points of departure, from shifting attention from the scopic terrain, or the visual field itself, to the vehicle or medium that transports the gaze, and across this field, to the concrete framing of the spatial and material specific objects within the field, can be seen as fundamental to the panoramic complex. The panorama understood as a complex encompasses the total spatial-visual arrangement of the following: the point of view (the point of departure of the gaze, in other words: the position of the spectator), the field of vision (the full width and height of the scopic terrain that encompasses the gaze) and the lines of vision (the lines of movement of the gaze), as well as 'eye-catchers' – the material elements of that which can be seen within this field.

A panorama can thus be regarded as both a view and a mise-en-scene. A staged scene is more than a view. It is a picture that can be seen in a glance, while its unfolding occurs in time. It may require a specific amount of time to 'happen', to unfold. A scene also appeals to its experience, of its temporality for example, and in terms of aesthetic experience. It is the arrangement of the frame in which objects and people are found, and events can take place. The scene suggests that all that occurs within the frame belongs together; that it forms a unity. From this perspective, architects can arrange these elements. If we assume that the spectator perceives the frame as a unit, then their activity can be seen as staging. Staging implies directing experience, as in scripting. In light of this, staging can be thought of as composing or arranging the elements in view of the aesthetic effect. This aspect of staging also demonstrates that the elements that are put on display have an aspect of attraction: the elements within the arrangement have an aesthetic and attractive function. The view can thus be regarded as the (aesthetic) effect of a staging of elements that is seen with a panoramic gaze, facilitated, enhanced, restricted or influenced by a medium.

The panorama complex points to something that is crucial for my investigation into the visual regime of navigation. I have demonstrated that, aside from the (void) space that it requires, the panoramic gaze is also supported by mobility.

Without movement, without the mobility of the gaze, the space is not seen in its entirety. The panorama is never just a static visual experience, it is an experience based on movement. This movement is plural and diverse: it is in the movement of the eye and the alternating focus on different points in the field of vision – zooming in and out, scanning over the territory. But it is also in the movement of the entire body, assisted as it may be by a means of transportation or a technology of movement. In this movement, the corporeal fixation of the gaze is an essential component of the panoramic complex. This has consequences for the experience: by means of varied roles of movement, the panoramic gaze is inseparable from the temporal dimension of the panorama. This makes it a complex. The panoramic complex is best understood as dynamically viewing, a visual complex that consists of a relation between the spectator or subject, space, and time.

The Windshield as Screen

This leaves the second key term of this study as suggested in the title, and the one that binds these reflections to contemporary media practices: the screen. As I have explored above, a fundamental characteristic of the panoramic mode of experience is the integration of movement and perception. We can also view the panorama as a spatial concept, as something that can be shaped, configured, designed. Matters become increasingly complex, however, when we approach the phenomenon from multiple angles: the panorama is not restricted to a spatial and material conception, it is rather a dynamic combination of spatial aspects (the scopic field, the material elements, the staging of the arrangement), temporal aspects (movement, rhythm, speed) and subjective viewing (the experience of the spectator).

In conclusion, we should consider the unique viewing position of the driver in the example of the highway panorama: the gaze from behind the glass of the windshield. I proposed that a cinematographic understanding of the panorama is useful for understanding panoramic viewing in terms of space, time and experience. But we can also reverse this comparison: the windshield as a window to the highway panorama offers apparent similarities to the film screen. In the first place, the view in both cases is framed: the film screen offers access to, but also limits the field of vision, similar to how the windshield the window is transparent but also restricts the view. Screens and windshields are not the only things that exhibit such framed views; this is obviously also akin to the canvas of a painting or the confines of the photo. Secondly, the screen and the windshield are similar to one another because they both function as access points, portals or gateways to the moving image. In contrast to the canvas or photograph, they are mobile frames. Finally, this parallel also holds true when we compare the way the body of a spectator is aligned and configured in space in relation to the windshield and the cinema screen. In both cases, there is a fixed distance, positioning the gaze towards the window or screen. As I will discuss in Chapter 5, a navigational mode of viewing is already at play here, not only for the driver, but also for the other passengers who are aware that the driver is partly in control of the panorama presented.

The window can literally and figuratively be opened, and the spectator can gain visual as well as mediated, imaginary, virtual access to the world that lies beyond. Within media studies, the window is used as a metaphor and functions as an expedient to better understand the relation between the spectator-subject and the image that is viewed. In the instance of the highway panorama viewed from behind the windshield, we are in fact dealing with the inverse situation as well. A comparison to the moving-image spectator could help us understand how viewing from an automobile works, and what considerations we should make when designing the space that is being viewed. This makes the area along the highway an aesthetic object of the (mobile) gaze of the passerby. This brings us back to the space: mediated travel becomes genuine travel yet again.

The speed at which people move through a landscape determines how people see and experience the scenes passing before their eyes. Combined, these scenes create a sequence in the order of their perception. It is no coincidence that the term 'sequence' can be traced back to the language of cinema. But in contrast to highway traffic, the film spectators themselves remain immobile. Drivers, however, cannot entirely determine their own speed on the road. The conditions of the road, the traffic rules, the presence of other vehicles that pass through the landscape at the same time demonstrate the restrictions of individual choice. Every driver is part of an ensemble, of a set of drivers determined by time and place.

This situation invokes the need for another concept, namely *flow*. Road-users are the combined participants of a flow, from which they view and see the landscape. Flow refers to a combination of a series of factors, which transforms scenes into a smooth consecutive sequence: scenes, speed, scale and experience together structure the flow. The comparison to the film spectator implies that a visual experience of the driver can be interpreted as a sequence, a flow or current of scenes that are sequential, parallel to the filmstrip that passes through a projector.

To extend the idea from vehicular traffic to media traffic: Raymond Williams (1975) introduced flow as a concept for television programming. While succession of elements is, indeed, at the heart of the flow of images in the 'montage' of movement, in our case here, Williams used flow to analyze something very specific to programming, going back to precisely that: television programs as discrete elements and modularity of their succession within programming. Lauren Rabinovitz uses *flow* to describe the visual impression of movement in phantom rides: "The continuous flow of motion delineated the visual and temporal information within the frame as that of objects rushing toward the camera." (1998a: 140)

Viewing individual panoramas is embedded in a long sequence of views, a panoramic stream if you like. This should be taken into consideration in the design and preservation of designated panoramas. Certain areas along the highway can be entitled to a 'panoramic' status, with pragmatic consequences demanding that dilapidated objects should be cared for given the aesthetic concerns of the panorama composition. Nevertheless, the highway panorama is best understood as a long stretched-out panorama. Not only rhythm and variation within a panorama, but also variations of the sequence between a series of diverse panoramas along certain routes, must be included in the strategies for design in the regions that the highway intersects. From this perspective, a proposed route design should, at the very least, be juxtaposed with regional design and spatial planning.

Comparing the windshield with the moving-image screen particularly emphasizes the aesthetic experience that is central in the design. Aesthetic and cultural values therefore play a large role in the design aspects and principles, but may also collide. That which is deemed valuable or useless from a cultural-historical perspective is not always granted sufficient appreciation. In addition, no degree of design can prevent some highway panoramas from being monotonous or messy.

It is impossible to address these issues by drawing up general guidelines from this starting point. Every region should be addressed in the context of its individual cultural historic characteristics and scenery. But in the case of the panorama, the old panoramic paintings as well as panoramic film, it becomes clear that what counts is not the elements within the panorama. It is the combination between the experience of mobility and the dynamics of viewing that matters. Designing panoramas as moving images entails a cinematographic approach to the view from the highway.

The panoramic desire and panoramic complex that I have described here bring forward a paradox: a paradox between freedom and control, immersion and spectacle; in other words, between scripted performance and uncontrollable performativity. As it happens, precisely these tensions are frequently involved when media reflect upon themselves. In line with the case presented in this chapter, it was in the report to the government that such reflection was found. There, the paradoxical pairs-in-tension compelled a revisioning of our design of vision and experience. Mobility as a dominant trope in modern visual culture transposes visual relationships and spatial coordinates of earlier visual regimes. The project on panoramic perception of (auto)mobility in the case of the spatial design of highway panoramas, therefore, underscores the paradoxical status of screens of navigation as both stationary objects and as sites of mobility. As will become clear in what follows, such reflections are also embedded in the media themselves.

2. Self-Reflection

Self-reflection in media offers insights into how a culture sees itself; that is why it matters. As a dominant trope in modern visual culture, at moments of transition, emerging or transforming screen media often self-reflect on the virtual mobility that the new media enable for its users. More specifically, in the following I will argue that today's media's self-reflections insist that navigation is effectively the primary paradigm driving digital screen media. This primacy of navigation entails more fundamental positions regarding the relations between our culture's predominant modes of address: narrative and spectacle. Both modes are centered on sense-making: from making sense as bringing logic, making understandable, and bringing about (or privileging) meaning, to mobilizing the sensory domain of attraction and affect.

To bring these implications out, I compare contemporary digital media with the first years of cinema. This comparison will show how the intimate, inextricable relationship between narrative and spectacular tendencies manifests itself, especially in navigation. I will demonstrate how media present these twin tendencies as converging in a trope of virtual mobility. This melding together of spectacle and narrative is most clearly visible in screen visions of navigation. These visions establish a particularly dynamic space of which the screen is the ground, the conduit, and the organizer at the same time. I call this simultaneous on-screen construction and representation of navigation, this dispositif where seeing and making converge, 'screenspace'. The screenspace at issue in this chapter has a particularly revealing center, which, as I argue below, is deictic. The ride films from early cinema will make clear how this centrality of a converging deictic center makes self-reflexivity a useful tool for the understanding of the present navigational complex – to coin an analogue to the panoramic complex – as both different from and yet continuous with the early moment of the moving image.

The Point of Self-Reflection

Self-reflection is a doubly ambiguous term. This makes it both rich and at risk of becoming vague. As Mieke Bal has pointed out, both elements of the term are subject to further specification. The 'self' may be the work, or it can be the subject looking at it. 'Reflection' can refer to a visual mirroring, and it can be an intellectual activity of thought. (1991: 247-48) Moreover, each pole of these two ambiguities can be crossed with each of the other pair, so that four types of self-reflection may occur: the mirroring of the work, as in *mise-en-abyme* – about which more in the next chapter – or of the viewer, as in literal mirroring effects; reflection on the work, or reflection on the viewer, the act of viewing, and the effect of it – its performativity. This rich ambiguity can be mobilized as a whole, or in any of its specifications. The situation becomes even more complex, as is the case here, when 'work' is not the right term; when a situation, an installation, or a combination of screens are the object of the self-reflection. In what follows, it is useful to keep in mind this complexity of the term.

Fantasies about virtual mobility have fueled our imagination and colored our conceptions of how visual media work. Technologies of transportation have been used, literally, as models for the possibilities of technologies of vision. Yet, where the train stood as a model for cinema, and auto-mobility has been regarded as homologous to television, applications of digital technologies seem to lack such a literal model of vehicular transportation. Instead, in the cultural imaginary, more so than analogue media, the digital has been framed as immaterial and disembodied; in order to be imagined as a machine for virtual mobility, the digital has therefore taken this virtuality to a new level, so to speak.[1]

We see a paradoxical imagination at work, where digital virtual mobility is symbolized as mobility and the disembodiment of the digital involves the body itself as the locus of mobility. Sometimes digital technology is presented as offering a *weightless* mobility, as we can see in some contemporary commercials that depict e.g. mobile phones floating through the air, or underwater. In other instances, however, digital mobility is conceptualized as a mobility that dispenses with such propelling machines, one where the body appears to suffice: a kind of pedestrian rather than vehicular mobility. With this term I do not seek to characterize the transformed experience of walking with mobile screens, as analyzed for example by Ingrid Richardson and Rowan Wilken (2009, esp. 27). Here, the qualifier pedestrian refers to the imaginary characterization of the media experience *as* walking. Unlike trains and cars that are spatially bound to tracks and roads, as well as temporally tied to timetables, stop signs and traffic jams, digital pedestrians can make space their own, on their own, in their own time and place. They compose their own, individual trajectories, which demonstrate liberation from the spatial and temporal constraints of vehicular mobility. In line with this fantasy of freedom and autonomy, surfing, skating, snowboarding or skateboarding figure as metaphors for the fluidity of individual digital mobility. More flexible, faster, swifter, and more anarchistic than walkers, these boarders can truly construct new spaces. In short, in the absence of a key trope comparable to the train or the automobile, a great variety of figures of mobility rival for attention. It is precisely because of this variety that I seek to propose a more solidly anchored, single trope. As it happens, these visions of mobility have in common that they all point self-reflexively to navigation as characterizing new screen media.

The fantasies I am exploring concern less simultaneity or immediacy, based on the conflation of time and space – a trope in emerging media that has been pointed out by others – than navigation, as the activity that makes that conflation central. Navigation is so central because it constitutes a practice that unifies time, space and agency. The appeal of navigation is based on the desired power over one's own mobility. As figures that metaphorically stand for the possibilities of digital media in commercials, the surfer, skateboarder or pedestrian do seem to have that power. Such metaphors, commercial as they are, signify a point of self-reflection in the culture in which they function.[2]

Self-reflection is meaningful for the understanding of a cultural moment due to the metaphors that specify what is at stake in that moment. This is how self-reflection can become a privileged tool for a methodology adequate for a cultural moment which is no longer captive of canonical works of art. What, then, are the self-reflexive metaphors for virtual travel through navigation that we can distill from presentations of digital screen technologies, and what do they specify regarding navigation? The answer to this question harbors a view of cultural history and its methodology as I see it. This is the point of self-reflection. In this instance, its central metaphor is travel.

As I have argued in my book The West in Early Cinema (2006) on emerging cinema and the depiction of the American West, particularly as a frontier, the popularization of travel is not only contemporaneous with the advent of cinema; it is also structurally congruent with cinema. In light of this temporal conjunction, it is significant that, similarly, at the heart of both 'new', modern culture and the 'new' medium are the hot topics of movement, vicarious displacement as well as both spatial and perceptual expansion. Therefore, the recurrence of the theme of travel in the popular deployment of the moving image in both moments of my diachronic bipolar vision – around 1900 and around 2000 – is no coincidence, and the self-reflexivity of the films in the first decade of the medium points out how this theme's frequent occurrence is best understood. Within the fragmentation and variability we can discern a logic of kaleidoscopic connections and attractions that celebrate the moment of radical change: a change evidenced by new mobilities and the new medium that provides ways to show them. I contend that the self-representation of media reflects the ways their screens give us access to space – indeed, determine our relationship to space. In this sense, the media always precede and thus, pre-write (if not to say pre-scribe) the way scholars and users later come to understand them. The object pre-formats how we can study it.

Of course, I am not the first to draw attention to media in transition as being acutely self-reflective. For example, as David Thorburn and Henry Jenkins have pointed out, "the introduction of a new technology always seems to provoke thoughtfulness, reflection, and self-examination in the culture seeking to absorb it." (2003: 4) The terms of these self-reflections are grounded in a strong bond (either positive or negative) between the old and new media. A reassessment of old media is sometimes even more apparent than an examination of new media. This is the reason that, as I explained in the introduction to this book, I took as the starting point for my cases the examination of media behavior at not one but two moments of transition, one hundred years apart: the first years of cinema, and the present-day use of digital screens. Both moments are marked by a self-reflexive foregrounding of the possibilities of the new screen to navigate virtual space. This systematic relationship between new cultural practices and the collective imaginary it contributes to shaping enhances the relevance of a study such as this one within its own field of study, but also beyond, as it helps us understand how cultures self-express.

However, with the advent of postmodernism, perceiving self-reflexivity is becoming a bit of a platitude, and is only helpful for our understanding of media culture if we specify what it is that self-reflection puts on the table. When referencing each other, pointing out their own mediated status, media texts suggest very different agendas, different degrees and directions, even destinations, of self-reflexivity. Moreover, this discursive operation of reflection even suggests a critical agency of media artifacts. To give some examples: they may seem self-satisfied or critical of themselves or of the media they have the ambition to replace, of social and cultural situations, related or not to the emerging media, of the consequences of their popularity. As a result, reflection on this reflexivity may yield insights of a methodological nature, concerning the ways we study and write cultural history, as well as of a philosophical nature, concerning the self-critical perspective of a culture.

In line with this differentiation of self-reflexivity, I offer the following double contention – theoretical and historical. Media reflection means that an artifact in a particular medium probes that medium's features and impact. Moreover, as Mary-Ann Doane suggests in her discussion of medium specificity at the moment of innovation and transition, this entails not only highlighting possibilities, but also its technological and material limitations:

> Proper to the aesthetic, then, would be a continual reinvention of the medium through a resistance to resistance, a transgression of what are given as material limitations, which nevertheless requires those material constraints as its field of operations. (2007: 131)

Such reflections (phrased here as "reinvention") on the possibilities and limitations of the medium are not a mere issue of aesthetics, nor can they be reduced to commercial self-promotion. Theoretically speaking, I contend that reflexivity in a broad sense is an inevitable cultural mode pervasively present in all media artifacts. This is so because cultural existence implies the desire to understand how things work. However, this need for exploring the possibilities, limitations, and medium-specificity is particularly pertinent to moments of innovation and transition. Specifically at those moments, the artifacts are reflexive in that they inform us about the historical position of their newness, including its future, as well as, consequently, our own. This can easily be assessed in an analysis of the meeting of two moments of increasing and accelerated development of new media, a century apart. Whether we consider these moments as ruptures or as modifications does not matter. This double contention has a systematic and a historical side to it. I will elaborate both through an analysis of different modes and levels of self-reflexivity in a range of disparate cases. Each of these cases address in their own way changing relationships between spectator/user and (urban) space. They do this through, on, and by means of the screen. This centrality of the screen brings up the question of the relationship between spectator, screen and image. A particularly useful concept to investigate this relationship is *deixis*. I propose to use the concept of deixis to probe the way mobility and space-making work through the address to and solicitation of the spectator.

The term deixis is borrowed from linguistics to explain how language is context-dependent. In fact, as Émile Benveniste (1971) has argued, deixis and not reference is the essence of language. Deictic words, or shifters, function as mobile focal points, often within an oppositional structure such as 'here', implicitly opposed to 'there'. Deixis indicates the relative meaning of the utterance, tied to situation of utterance, an 'I' in the 'here' and 'now'. They have no fixed, referential meaning. Deixis establishes the point of origin, or deictic center, of the utterance: the 'I' who speaks, as well as its point of arrival, the 'you' who is spoken to. These terms are by definition mutually exchangeable. Moreover, or consequently, deixis frames the statement in temporal ('now') and spatial ('here') terms. Deixis helps set up the world to which the text relates. In contrast to e.g. nouns or adjectives, deictic words or shifters have meaning only in relation to the situation of utterance. Their meaning is produced through indication rather than reference – think of pointing. Personal pronouns of the first and second person – 'I', 'we', or 'you' – are shifters. But 'he', 'she' or 'it' are not. The latter, although also in need of identities to fill them in, do not change when the situation of utterance changes. But when I speak and *you* answer, *you* become I, and I, *you*. *She* remains the same, since both I and *you* know the person to whom we are referring. If we do not know who is speaking, the first-person and second-person pronouns have no meaning. Similarly, we cannot *place* the meaning of such words as 'over there' or 'right here' if we don't know from where the speaker is speaking. Nor can we *time* the meaning of 'yesterday' without a determined time frame.

I allege these examples of shifters to suggest that time, place and person are their primary anchors. While the term was first introduced in linguistics, the perspective on the construction of space, time and subjectivity is particularly useful for analyzing how the spectator is bound to the image. Hence, the 'represented' images of, for example, the ride films that are central to my case below, are not simply presented as from an internal point of view – a diegetic spectator – but also produce the subjectivity of the implied looker, (the 'I' doing the looking) as well as of the looker's 'you', the second person who mutually constitutes and affirms the 'I'. A filmic image is what tells us about, and thus constitutes, a (fictionalizing) gaze that emerges through the inflection of the vista that invests it with subjectivity. This inflection can also be called focalization, as a term from narrative theory that expresses this mediating and subjectivizing function, a visual equivalent of deixis. That is to say, these images in their self-reflexivity address the meaning of the screen.[3]

Meanings of the Screen

At the first point of my diachronic comparison, phantom rides were a typical attraction in early cinema that proved to have a staying screen presence. I position this genre in confrontation with other screens of navigation as the typical dispositif that, I submit, constitutes the contemporary visual regime. The features of the mobile screen exemplify new technologies and practices that influence the relationship between the screen's user or spectator, or perhaps best called the screen's engager on the one hand, and the urban environment on the other. GPS technology and personal, handheld navigation systems are mobile technologies that provide access to urban space through virtual 'tours'. Initially, the train was a medium, for it transported vision. Now the medium has become our vehicle, for it visually transports: it accompanies, guides and represents movement of the screen.[4]

The cinematic phantom ride and the mobile screen have in common that they not only display but also constitute an experience of travel. Simply put: the medium is the message. Both deploy the imagery of travel to underscore the (new) medium's capacity as a virtual travel machine. The dynamic of travel as topic-trope-metaphor results in a mirror image or synecdoche – specifically in the form of a *mise-en-abyme* – when the medium *in* the image comes to stand for the mobility *of* the image. This shift from a thematic to a metaphoric reflection of mobility is visible throughout the history of media. I am referring in particular to those moments when physical mobility was first used to establish and demonstrate the virtual mobility of the medium.

In early cinema, phantom rides are exemplary for this mobility model. But we can see how this developed, or split, into a new trend in which the situation has become partly reversed, so that mediated mobility is used to convey physical mobility. In the case of phantom rides, the screen is the tool for movement through vision. The result of captured mobility refers back to the mobility-in-motion (the moment of shooting) and enables the spectator to travel back in time to the moment of this mobility; the handheld screen conflates the moments of mobility and capture, resulting in a highlighting of simultaneous temporality; touchscreen technology shifts the activity to 'before' mobility. There, agency and physical activity and contact on part of the engager-spectator redefine the screen not so much as tool, but as site for mobility – the construction of timespace. For the sake of consistency, I will reserve the word timespace for moments when I am concerned with the particular type of space that is created in navigation.[5]

Central in the construction of media as a travel machine is, then, the screen. The screen, even if it can represent a temporal mediation, is always also a spatial object, a tool for, but also part of spatial transgression. And this transgression is the desired object for the media user. Both the time of experience and diegetic time become *spatial* as a result of the screen – indeed, it is the locus of that transformation. The screen is where it all happens: at once a technological device, a metaphor for mediation, for vision, a frame for representation, and a site of innovation. The screen has many meanings.

In the course of the history of visual representation, the screen has been understood as *mirror*, as *magnifying glass, window, lens,* but also as *veil,* even as the *walls of a cave,* or, today, as *interface.* This multiplying of metaphors through which the screen is conceptualized is significant in highlighting its specific manifestations. In these metaphorical comparisons, the screen is positioned at once as a tool intended for determining the conditions of perception – and result – of mediation. What is on-screen, is aired, or is entered, is the result or the product of the medium. But once the image hits the screen, this image as product becomes a producer, namely of experience, hence becoming the medium itself. A film becomes a film when it is screened, a television show becomes television when it is aired, and a game is a game when it is entered – as in accessed as well as activated by the 'enter' key. And once in progress, the process of screening can be captured.

These terms may seem to be just different words for the same thing – an argument Lev Manovich puts forward when he states that in the end "[w]e still have not left the era of the screen." (2001: 115) This may be true, since there is undeniably a certain continuity. But within that continuity of media ambition in which the screen is the key, the differences in screen concepts point to fundamentally different constructions of spectatorial engagement or agency – differences that range from encapsulated bodies (Hutamo 1995) and tele-present viewers (Uricchio 2004) to my focus here on digital navigators. With the concept of deixis, we can now see that navigation puts a particular spin on the deictic center of the screen, which converges with the center of the off-screen space that is the viewer. Early cinema's phantom rides demonstrate this.

Spatial Attractions and Visual Deixis

Phantom rides are ride films from a first-person point of view – usually shot from the front of a moving vehicle. The phantom ride's attraction is bound up with the deictic relationship between the camera, the viewer and the landscape. This is most important for an understanding of the films in their moment of cultural history. Through the device of the camera attached to the locomotive machine, the visual representation of landscape constitutes a truly shared environment. As a consequence, landscape does not stand on its own, as a geographical setting 'out there' only, but rather functions as a shifter between ways of life. It stands as the point of access to the other of modern and diverse culture.[6]

In this sense landscape has a specific role in the representation of modernity, mediating in the ideological opposition, strongly present in the culture, of nature versus culture. And as binary oppositions tend to do, they declare either one of their terms positive, the other negative. But this valuation is fraught with ambivalence, as the one becomes the attraction for the other. To put this more strongly, the representation of nature partakes of a specific representation of its negative, culture, and is therefore an oppositional representation of the urban. The terms of the binary couple nature/culture, or wild/urban, need each other. From the vantage point of the second term of the opposition – which is that the one with which the viewer is aligned – the first term opens up to a spatial otherness, an elsewhere. The elsewhere, just like *elsewhen* and the cultural *Other*, only has meaning in an oppositional structure which, by means of the mapping of meaning through a shifter, organizes itself around the 'I' /eye of the (urban) viewer that is its focal point – its deictic center.

Many travel films that include fictional characters films play with this ambivalence of the traveler/spectator as being part of the landscape yet, inherently, also not part of it. Films like *A Romance of the Rail* (Edison, 1903), *The Hold-Up of the Rocky Mountain Express* (American Mutoscope and Biograph, 1906) or *A Railway Tragedy* (British Gaumont, 1904) combine footage from a train ride with romantic, comical or dramatic scenes. *A Railway Tragedy* opens on the streets, at the arrival and departure of the train at the station, and it ends with the train's arrival at another station. In this film, both trajectories, the nonfictional display of landscape and the fiction of the characters on the train with their urban point of departure, are literally intertwined by the insertion of views of passing landscape into the frames that show the interior of the train. As if they were traveling companions of the characters on screen, spectators can see the same view from the window, and they can also take a peek into the train compartment. The combination of shots and their modes of address sustain a fluid boundary between different forms of address, both fictional and nonfictional, providing shifting points of reference from 'he'/'she' to 'you' and, in the case of primary point of view, a phantom 'I'.

The cinematic ride films and the mobile screen have in common that they not only display but also constitute an experience of travel. Both deploy the imagery of travel to underscore the (new) medium's capacity as a virtual travel machine. The dynamic of travel as topic-trope-metaphor results in a mirror image when the medium in the image comes to stand for the mobility *of* the image. Such mirror images are synecdoches, where a part or detail stands for the whole. Specifically they take the form of a *mise-en-abyme* – a figure where a detail not only stands for the whole, but is a summary or mirror-image of it. (Dällenbach 1989) This shift from a thematic to a metaphoric reflection of mobility is visible throughout the history of media. I am referring in particular to those moments when physical mobility was first used to establish and demonstrate the virtual mobility of the medium. In early cinema, phantom rides are exemplary for this model of visual, or virtual mobility. In the case of phantom rides, the screen is the tool for movement through vision. The result of captured mobility refers back to the mobility-in-motion (the moment of shooting) and enables the spectator to travel back in time to the moment of this mobility.

Let me point out how mobility and visuality are tied together in travel imagery of early cinema to produce a space of mobility. This interest in mobility, in the unbreakable bond of space and time in timespace as a trope of early moving images, stems from the insight that (virtual) travel and transport are, precisely and intensely, both visual and narrative in their appeal, so much so that these two aspects can no longer be disentangled. Transport is an experience consisting of a temporal sequence of micro-events; of movement through space and of (resulting) encounters: a series of movements in time that appeal to the spectator's desire for immersion in space. It allows for "new ways of seeing".[7]

This new way of seeing is a temporally structured, at times immersive experience of visual engagement with new phenomena, environments and people. These are all set, importantly, in space. The spatio-temporal imagery of travel thus establishes narrative as twin or partner, not oppositional "other" of visual spectacle. According to André Gaudreault (1990), time or *chronicity* is the primary aspect of narrativity. He distinguishes two levels of narration in moving images: micro- and macro-narratives. This distinction is that between the level of the single shot and the narrativity that is created between shots by means of montage. The single shot – as micro-narrative – is the barest form of narration because it shows the passing of time that is *change* over time within the image. Spectacle, or attraction, can be regarded as things happening; things that have a direct effect on the spectator, drawing primary attention to themselves, or in temporal terms: happenings that punctuate the moment. In this view it makes sense to consider spectacles, attractions, as narrative, yet in a different timeframe than the (longer) narratives that surround them.

At first sight, narrative is the account of the passing of time (and its results) outside the world of the spectator, whereas spectacle draws the engager-spectator into that world; from a grammatical third-person account to a first- and second-person interaction, as if by synchronizing watches: not in some other time, or *elsewhen*, but *right now*. This makes such spectacles, or narratives that are also spectacles, deictic, and sets them in the present tense. Nevertheless, if narratives can *also* be spectacles, this is because as concepts, narrative and spectacle are derived from different logics. Narrativity is constructed by means of interpretation, whereas spectacle is often conceptualized as an 'effect', a forceful one that takes the spectator out of an immersive diegesis, breaking through the narrative barrier.

Although this conception of narrative and spectacle as opposing forces seems to be clear-cut, disentangling their relationship is still on the agenda of media studies, whether as debate in the study of narration in moving images, in film history, or in the study of (digital) special effects. Problematically, this oppositional conception blinds us to the intricate connections between the two. These connections become prominent in mobility. When mobility predominates, the distinction between temporal and spatial constructions is no longer meaningful.[8]

The concept of cinema of attraction as it was originally proposed makes this clear. Tom Gunning (1990) initiated a rehabilitation of visual attractions as belonging to a register different from but equal to narrative, in order to understand a mode of address that did not fit with (classical) narrative models. Identification, suspense and laughter are typical responses to narrative that demonstrate the mechanism of what I would call a *heteropathic immersion*. The 'pathos' of such immersion is 'hetero' when the viewing subject goes, as it were, out of herself and makes the leap to immerse herself in the 'other' field visible on the screen. The opposite would be an 'idiopathic' immersion where the subject appropriates the image and absorbs it into her own world. The distinction as I propose it here is based on a distinction between the off-screen world of the spectator and that of the on-screen events she engages with. There, heteropathic means that the immersion takes place on the terrain of the diegesis, an elsewhere/elsewhen into which the spectator enters.[9]

Gunning draws attention to a different set of responses, such as a primary spectatorial confrontation, aesthetic fascination and an appreciation for the novelty of 'direct' cinematic imagery. This he sets off against the diegetic absorption that results from narration, the unfolding of a story. Gunning considers the phantom ride as a key example of the cinema of attractions. He also proposes that its relative, the chase film, is the original truly narrative genre which provides a synthesis between attractions and the linear logic of narrative editing. Both train and chase films rely on a primary narrative format of spatial mobility, but in a different way. The phantom ride shows this in a first-person perspective from a moving vehicle; the chase film 'follows' characters traversing space. These generic formats show different perspectives on the experience of mobility: one that invites a primary identification, and one that binds the mobility to a third person. Both solicit a heteropathic immersion based on spectatorial transportation via the visual mobility on the screen.[10]

I would underscore this view and extend it for my purpose here, which is to clarify the new look that contemporary media help us cast on early cinema. As an exemplary motive in moving images, phantom rides constitute an *arch*-genre –

let's call it a paradigm – that precedes and predicts, and is continuous with contemporary screen-based ways of constituting ever-changing (media)spaces. As such, movement, especially that of the traveling camera of the phantom ride, establishes a synthesis between narrative and spectacle. Gaudreault discerns micro-narratives in shots that show movement, using the example of the famous single-shot arriving train film Arrivée d'un train à La Ciotat (Lumière, 1895). Following this, I propose a temporary typology of train films to think about contemporary screen-based relations to space. Together, these types demonstrate how movement as cinematic form reflexively embodies the ways that narrative and attractions are essentially tied together – inextricably.

Foregrounding the intricacies of what some have, perhaps, tried too hard to disentangle, I argue that different types of train films function as visual motives, in which both attraction and narrative can be discerned. It is primarily deixis that defines attraction; through deixis, narrative can therefore (also) become attraction. Let me depart from this point with some examples from Zoomscape, a 2010 compilation program of early train films by EYE Film Institute Netherlands, on which I will have more to say in Chapter 4. In the Zoomscape program we see a representative sample of the variety of train images from the early period. The program comprised titles such as Arrivé d'un train à La Ciotat (Lumière, 1895), Conway Castle (British Mutoscope and Biograph, 1898) and Irish Mail (American Mutoscope and Biograph, 1898). Like any program, a (thematic) compilation program is a creative product of selection and collage. Similar to the exhibition practices of early cinema at its time, spectators today were presented with a wide array of images, viewpoints and attractions. Let us see how the spectator is deictically addressed by these images.

A first form is that of the arriving train. Perhaps the most canonical example is Arrivé d'un train à La Ciotat. Shot with a camera positioned on the platform, a train arrives and people step off while others board the train. A more dynamic – more clearly deictic – variant is the approaching-then-passing train film: the train moves towards the spectator, but passes on one side. An example of this is Fast Mail, Northern Pacific Railroad (Edison, 1897), not programmed in Zoomscape. In some cases the camera pans, following the train ride towards the distance. This produces the sensation of seeing something being hurled at you, and the subsequent relief of seeing it as it misses you as the target and disappears into the distance. The physical sensation this can produce is evidence of the deictic nature of such ploys. This is what Gunning points out as the relationship between early cinema attractions of train rides and the visual spectacles of the fairground (1990: 383). What they share is the visual-physical sensations of the roller coaster.

In another type, the phantom ride of Conway Castle shows a first-person perspective, tracking the perceptual field as seen from a moving train, without showing the train itself. While named after the castle that was a popular tourist attraction, the film mainly shows the train track and the passing landscape. In the promotional text from the American Mutoscope & Biograph Company, this is advertised as such:

> Without a doubt this is the finest railroad moving picture ever made, and for variety and beauty of scenery it can hardly be surpassed the world over. This view is taken from the front of a rapidly moving locomotive, over a stretch of track made up of a continuous series of reverse curves; and every turn opens a vista of surpassing beauty. Conway Castle itself, one of the most picturesque and historic spots in Wales, appears from time to time in the picture. (reprinted in Brown and Anthony 1999: 251)

Fig. 2.1: Conway Castle (British Mutoscope and Biograph, 1898). Courtesy of EYE Film Institute Netherlands

Besides the tourist attraction of the film, the rollercoaster effect is very strong. The film consists entirely of a first-person perspective or deictic center and follows the twists and turns of the track. The train also goes through a tunnel and, much like in a true ghost ride, vision is temporally suspended. The vista of the emerging landscape after the darkness of the tunnel in the colored print of the film is very spectacular in its effect, even today. The spectator 'lives' the moving perception, so that the phantom ride has become the measure of dynamic time-space. In deictic terms: the 'I' is in the point of view that the spectator can adopt and from which the landscape is infused with meaning, for whom the image has an effect. The deictic center is positioned by the camera perspective.[11]

Today's cinema offers plenty of examples, as it is a conventional way of shooting ride or flight chases, as we see in contemporary 3D blockbusters *Avatar* (2009) or *Toy Story 3* (2010), but also in older special-effects vehicles such as *2001: A Space Odyssey* (1968) or the first *Star Wars* trilogy (1977; 1980; 1983). Racing games deploy this form consistently. The game player rides as a chasing phantom along the racetrack, while also chasing the other cars on that track.

Fig. 2.2: Screenshot from Shift 2 Unleashed *(2011) for iPad. Courtesy of EA Games*

These four kinds of train films each exemplify a different relationship between the screen and its engager-spectator as she experiences space as dynamic, ranging from static beholder to virtual passenger. These categories of attractions, based on mobility, time and the perception of spatial consequences of this mobility, are irreducibly self-reflexive as they show on screen how we are to relate to the screen, in a troping of the train as vision machine. They are not only to be considered as micro-narratives, but, as a commercial for a JVC video camera demonstrates, can become entire macro-narratives in and of themselves.[12]

This television commercial was an element in the appropriately called *Ride the Wild Side* lifestyle campaign from 2007. It showed a complex, integrated elaboration of these forms. This JVC skateboarder is a close relative of the four types of 'train spotters', but here the mobility of the screen itself redoubles the mobility already demonstrated by the phantom ride.[13]

This short film borrows from the phantom ride model the mobility of vision; the spectator joins the ride while the camera follows the skateboarder filming his own ride with the camera in his hand. This joining is possible thanks to the attraction (Gunning) of the convergence of the deictic center. The movement is embodied in the figure of the screen, whose movement is both utterly realistic and utterly appealing, so that the viewer or engager inadvertently moves along, rocking on the rhythm of the skater's pace. The film then mixes the train-ride formula with a second layer of movement in the image. For, while he is riding, the skater is recording the ride, creating an image of movement within the image of movement. This is a *mise-en-abyme* of motion in motion, so to speak.

Fig. 2.3: *JVC commercial, Ride the Wild Side campaign (2007)*

The skateboarder is our exemplary pedestrian. Moving over car roofs, staircases, ignoring traffic lights, leaping over benches, he embodies the weightlessness, the fluidity, the anarchistic freedom and the speed so eagerly pursued in contemporary culture. In doing so, this commercial borrows the tropes of screen mobility to sell cameras that are desirable for precisely those features. We see movement of the character-boarder who is navigating while looking through the camera lens, and we see him simultaneously recording his movements.

The short film triples the movement through the city: it follows his movement (1), we see movement in the image (2), and we see, implied in this image, the future of the movement he is creating-recording (3). Even if we do not see the full result (the phantom ride he is making), we see the creation of the ride: the process is proof of the result. At the end, we even get to see a glimpse of it. The temporal layers in this film are thus extremely complex, but nevertheless clearly focused on the conflation of physical mobility and medium mobility, both constructed as spatial transgressions. We can think of wired or shared screens, as I called them in the previous chapter – interconnected screens such as we use in multi-player games – in a similar vein, as they make tele-presence or televisual simultaneity more interactive. Because both users have the same screen content, they can interact in/on the same screen, regardless of the distance between them, as long they are in the same timeframe. The small LCD screen on his camera fulfills the double function of capturing, showing and constructing the navigation.

Navigating the Screen

This double function of the screen as both site and result of navigation leads to what I have called screenspace; in a sense, this screenspace is at the heart of many mobile screen devices. I am thinking of devices such as the Nintendo DS game console, on which more in the next chapter, or other hybrid and mobile media that combine different interfacing possibilities (touch, voice or shake, as is the case with smartphones), applications (games, navigation, photography, browsing, text or voice messaging) and different forms of connectivity (GPS, 3G, WiFi). As I point out in the following chapter in relation to the Nintendo DS, the double screens allow for different interactions and a multiplicity of screen uses in different screen spaces on the same device. Multi-tasking on PDAs and smartphones is similar, but then on a single screen. The possibilities for touch add to the dynamic space of the screen. Where the phantom ride proposes the spectator to move *through* the screen, using the screen but making it invisible at the same time, the touchscreen in a way *flattens* the surface. The screen, here, becomes a thin, but essential and visible membrane. Its materiality has become quite literally the surface we need, the surface we touch, trace and imprint. And given the centrality of navigation, we can say that the screen here becomes our *map*.

This warrants the term screenspace. Let us consider simultaneous on-screen and off-screen navigation in this context. The screens of navigation devices, both in cars and on mobile phones, help scores of people move through the city. Some devices include ways of memorizing itineraries; such a device is a map, a camera, a photo album and a racing game all at once.

Navigation devices or applications for smartphones combine touchscreen technology with digital photography for navigation. This principle of navigation by images is founded on principle of traditional photographic representation, but extends – or rather reinstates – the indexical nature of the photographic image by attaching (invisible) geographical coordinates to the visual image, thus enabling navigation in an on-screen spatial simulation.

I use the verb *reinstates* to refer to the alleged ontological loss of indexicality with digital photography, where the photograph no longer functions as visual evidence of the literal imprint of reality (i.e. the rays of light on a sensitive surface). The analogue photograph is a literal imprint of light, which ontologically 'proves' spatio-temporal reality and thus provides the image with a sense of authenticity, yet also with material decay. Digital photography has lost this direct relationship from reality to image. But there is also a gain. To understand the nature of this gain, we can look to a distinction proposed by Mary Ann Doane. In her contributions to a special issue of *Differences* devoted to the index, Doane conceptualizes a very different characteristic of the index.

She problematizes the issue of authenticity by proposing the distinction between two kinds of indexes, or rather, indexicalities: the trace and deictic index. I seek to implement the temporal aspect of that distinction. The trace is the remnants of pastness from which the present cannot disentangle itself. The analogue photograph of an object that was once before the lens would be a prime instance of such a trace. As we have seen above, deixis concerns the situatedness of the image in the present of its emergence: the sense of place in 'here was the object' of the photograph is the 'here' which positions the spectator in relation to the image. The here constitutes presence and positions relationality. Moreover, the trace and deixis are not mutually exclusive. For my concern here, geotagging is a typical practice of the deictic index, no less than analogue photography is the key practice of the trace index. But there is more. As we will see in Chapter 5, it is thanks to its deictic indexicality that geotagging allows the trace of the past – of the navigation it can retrieve – to become in the present the deictic index from which the traveler looks, so that – as a third temporality of the index – the image points to the future where the traveler can go: a destination index.

The screen of navigation devices functions as an interactive remediation of the traditionally flat, limited and fixed map, a new cartographic principle that will be further examined in Chapter 5 in its temporality. Let us here consider the screen as a simulation map. The map emerges on the screen of the navigation device, structuring, or constructing, real, physical and geographical mobility. What is doubled here is mobility before and after the interaction with the screen: the usual arrow or other avatar on the screen-map represents the simultaneous movement of the navigator. It enables the user to map future movements, as it shows the options of where the user-navigator may go. But the navigator suggests and determines the destination. Content is constantly updated as the navigator changes her path, producing the fluid screenspace. Moreover, photographs, like footprints, of previous sights along the road become travel destinations of the future – inroads into the hitherto unknown corners of the city. What is stored and used as source for retrieval are not the sights that are displayed in the photographs, but the sites from where these vistas were recorded. Geographical attractions or 'points of view' become (in navigation jargon) POIs or 'points of interest', and as such are possible destinations for future travel.

The mobility is thus still a fantasy, 'in the air', or into the future. For this mobility, the constantly evolving technology offers ever-more appealing forms. In the phantom rides, it is by looking at movement that the spectator or user moves along. With reference to this older tradition and making a claim for radical newness, the JVC commercial for digital cameras proposes the possibility to make your own phantom ride. And it deploys deixis to make that claim plausible. Commercials for the Nintendo DS go even further. These suggest that the power of the touch makes the doubling of the screen redundant. The navigation-by-pictures through geotagging digital photographs depends on physical mobility of the media user for its on-screen representation of this mobility, while simultaneously routing future movement. This conception of screenspace leads to a new way of experiencing space. Not only is space continuously framed by the lenses and screens of our mobile devices, but our temporal experience of space is also not based on a presence in the here and now. Instead, this experience is emphatically layered as an unfolding presence that can be captured, revisited, expanded and linked at different moments in time. This will be further explored in the next chapter.

There are clear differences between these cases regarding the way the activity of the engager-spectator relates to the vitality of the image as put forward by the screen. The train ride is dependent on the stillness of the body as well as on the transferred mobility of the eyes of the spectator. The screens in this case offer only a suggestion of mobility. The means of transport invoked and used – the train – still rides on pre-established tracks. In the second case of the handheld camera, the mobility is a prerequisite: you have to move to capture movement. In both the phantom ride and the JVC commercial, the screen fixates the relationship between on-screen and off-screen space. The screen has become mobile, but according to the commercial for the JVC handheld camera, media navigation only promises an ideal of simultaneous agency and movement of screen and image. Here, viewing happens during and in the space of shooting.

The touchscreen, on the other hand, allows for direct image manipulation. Here, the moment of shooting is eliminated. At first glance, the user makes the image directly with her finger, but seen from the opposite perspective, she can no longer make anything: she can only conjure up what is already there, on the other side of the screen. The screen does not show the result of navigation, but is the navigation. This is even more apparent in smartphones' hybrid of touchscreen technology and moving maps.

With mobile screens, the ideal of ubiquity seems close at hand. You can look everywhere, and connect anywhere. Navigation suggests that this ubiquity comes with a total, or at least a fundamental agency. But as soon as the navigation occurs not at sea or in cars but on screen, this agency is yet again subjected to those limitations inherent in the screen as tool for mediation. Simultaneity, ubiquity and control have been added to the mix, but the screen remains the surface beyond which we cannot go. The regimes of viewing may be changing, but the question the metaphor raises is: is viewing still what is at stake? Perhaps the touchscreen metaphor in its self-reflexive guise helps us realize that development and chronology, technological or otherwise, also bites itself in the tail. The thrill of the phantom ride that spectators felt in their bodies when watching the dizzying images rush by has, perhaps, not been enhanced but eliminated when the agency over the movement was given over to the engager-spectator. Looking ceased to be looking only. Perhaps, then, with this agency, it could be said that spectators lost touch of looking.

Navigation as Narration

This brings us back to the time-space dichotomy implied in the opposition between narrative and spectacle, or visual attraction. I insisted above that time necessarily includes movement through space; indeed, that movement itself evidences the untenability of the distinction, since time becomes space. The other side of this argument comes to the fore on the basis of the examples discussed. In this doubling of virtual movement we can see how space, in fact, becomes time; stories are spatial in the sense that they are set (or embedded) in, or evoked by space, but more than that, they construct visible space. Here, the two are collapsed. Given its near-dogmatic status in discussions of media, I now zoom in on this opposition between narrative and spectacle.

Space has often been opposed to time, as the support of visuality versus time as the backbone of narrative. The moving image already defeats that opposition, and that may well be its primary attraction. For, whatever the attraction that holds the gaze, the image unfolds in time, in fact dictating the temporal involvement of the spectator who is subjected to the film's pace. Symmetrically, as Henry Jenkins has argued, even the most stable of spatial arrangements, such as architecture, have a temporal dimension as well, so much so that Jenkins speaks of *narrative architecture*. By using this provocative term of narrative architecture, Jenkins accounts for the particular form of narrative that can be discerned in digital games. He discerns four different ways in which spatial narratives can result in immersive experiences of media spaces: "[S]patial stories can evoke pre-existing narrative associations; they can provide a staging ground where narrative events are enacted; they may embed narrative information within their mise-en-scene; or they provide resources for emergent narratives." (2004: 123) His notion of narrative architecture – the narrative design of space in digital environments – makes it possible to recognize a new kind of constructing space: that of player navigation.[14]

The interactive possibilities of digital media are crucial for the narrative potential of mediated spaces. A player's navigation of digital games, for example, enables not just an active reading of space, but rather – and more fundamentally – an active construction of place into space. Janet Murray (2001) therefore considers digital navigation as a form of agency – interactivity in which actions are autonomous, are selected from choices, and determine the course of the game. In line with this somewhat optimistic view we can state that navigation is an active and narrative practice, even if this type of narrativity is different from the classical model of characters or actors that experience events while the spectator ('passively') witnesses these. The narrative of navigation is creating a narrative of space by reading place as space. Instead of being an external focalizer who does or does not espouse the diegetic focalization of the characters, the navigator is a narrator, focalizer and actor in one. Moreover, when the player is the navigator, or more precisely – and this distinction is important – when she navigates the diegetically-bound avatar, the borders between playing and seeing are blurred.[15]

Bernadette Flynn takes up Jenkins' notion of embedded narratives. Flynn emphasizes the difference between such embedded narratives and classical narrative in the following terms: "adventure games [...] are not narrative spaces and operate outside of the narrative causality structure." (2003: n.p.) I assume Jenkins would concur, but the formulation begs the question of causality's role in narrative. For Jenkins has demonstrated, precisely, that narrativity can operate outside a dominant narrative causality, and that the navigational, "ludic and aesthetic pleasures" that Flynn argues to be "unrelated to narrative," can, in fact, be understood as having a narrative core – namely, a development or outcome, but not necessarily a traditional causality.

This argument can perhaps be reversed. In light of the centrality I am claiming for navigation in the construction of screenspace, it is possible to argue here that, more than just having a sense of narrativity about it, navigation is at the heart of narrative. Michel de Certeau's claim that every story is a travel story (1984), which I will discuss in Chapter 3, makes sense in light of this generalization. This is the case if, as I contend, we need the navigator to explore places and turn them into spaces. The navigator, then, fulfills the triple narrative role of narrator, focalizer and actor. This is why it is necessary to come to an understanding of narrative that is different from the traditional sense in which it is opposed to spectacle. The visual regime of navigation bridges this gap. The nature of the tour, ride or navigation involves events in some kind of coherent sequence, and thus is narrative, even if it also functions on the basis of attraction. Thus, navigation binds narrative and spectacle inextricably and crucially in screenspace. This conclusion changes the traditional conception of narrative and undermines its bias to privilege time over space.

Boundary-Crossings

When we look back from these two poles where intense visuality meets narrative – cinema of attraction (phantom rides) and digital screens (navigation) – it is possible to argue that even still images such as photographs and paintings have a temporal, and therefore a potentially narrative dimension. They are narrative to the extent that they require a certain amount of time to be processed. Less dictatorial in time management than film, a photograph requires that someone stops, looks, thinks and responds, moves on – a requirement that assumes the occurrence of a series of small events liable to become a micro-narrative. Similarly, urban spaces of architecture – houses, public buildings, department stores – once they are visible and visually displayed and processed, entice the engagement of the people entering them, moving in them, and exiting, into the small stories of everyday life. These spaces attract because of – not in spite of – the fact that they can be entered and navigated in a narrative.

I have noticed that movement is thematically in the forefront when it comes to flaunting the visuality of screen media. This thematic centrality can be taken as a pointer to a self-reflexivity that has methodological and philosophical consequences. As we have seen, in early cinema the phantom ride and its relatives that exploited mobility make virtual mobility visually imaginable; hence, possible. Digital mobility, in turn, multiplies modes of mobility even further. Multiple tropes of mobility are at work in both media in transition: the cinematic form itself, but also a mobilization of the (inter)active navigator in cyberspace. Mobility is a topic and trope in media, so that self-reflexivity becomes prominent. Self-reflexively, new media spaces come to stand for new mobilities that subvert or at least qualify the old notions of narrative.

This bond between visions of mobility and narrative harbors the self-reflexivity I keep insisting on. This is most prominently demonstrable in relation to cartography. Tom Conley points out the close analogy between cinema and cartography, both of which he sees as forms of "locational imaginings". (2007: 2) Conley borrows this term from David Buisseret (2003). This author argues that cartographic media locate subjects within the places they represent. In this analogy that Conley makes between maps and movies, we can recognize two points that are useful for our comparison between early cinema's phantom rides and interactive screens of navigation. These are the cartographic texture of images of mobility and the inherent self-reflexivity this entails.

When discussing the role of maps in movies, he writes that the image of the map "brings forward these elements of the image in which it is found" – a self-reflexivity by means of mise-en-abyme. He uses two sets of terms. In the first place he uses Bazin's terminology of fact and event to point out how both movies and maps "produce space through the action of perception, especially perception that both perceives and perceives its ways of perceiving." This – his locational imaging

– is an event of space-making. This event occurs in the process of perception and, according to Conley, has a haptic quality. (20) A second, less conspicuous but for me equally important terminological choice is the term deixis, which he evokes in a footnote (216). He borrows this use from the French semiotician Christian Jacob, whose seminal book The Sovereign Map (2006; or, L'empire des cartes, 1992) Conley translated. Jacob, in turn, bases his theory of the deictic nature of maps on Emile Benveniste's linguistic theory, of which I have spoken above. The linguist proposed this term to account for the implication of the speaker in what is being said. Examples are 'I' and 'you' – as distinct from 'he' or 'she' – and 'here' or 'there'. The combination of these two examples lead to the key phrase 'I am here' that defines the cartographic act.[16]

The phantom ride discussed above offers the focalization that this phrase entails. It gives the illusion that the viewer is on the train and sees the world through that vantage point. The map requires that the subject decode the (imaginary) phrase. The map is only usable once the subject knows where 'I am here' exactly is. Interactive maps, as I will further elaborate in the next chapter, visualize this situation in two ways. The interactive map embodies the user's position as focalizer of the map. It also reflects what the user does with the map, what itinerary the user creates and simultaneously travels.

Indeed, in the current inquiry of moments of media transition foregrounded in self-reflection, concepts such as attractions, ludology, navigation, and narrative architecture or spatial narrativity have infused our theoretical vocabulary. These terms have in common that they are deployed to conceptualize the changing relationship between the user, spectator or engager, and screen media as essentially different from classical notions of reading strategies, textuality, and distinctions and hierarchies between spectator, performer and character that inform classical modes of identification in narrative even in the broadest sense.

Screens of navigation show us that in our present visual culture viewing and making collapse. Moreover, the spatial boundaries between screen and physical space become blurred. In Chapter 5, I will further explore the notion of the cartographic, both as property of moving-image media, and as characteristic of our creative engagement with these images: cartography as practice. In screenspace, we are simultaneously narrator, focalizer, spectator, player and, perhaps most fundamentally, navigator. But first, in the following chapter, I will further develop the methodological issues put forward here through self-reflection. I will examine the consequences of our approach to screens of navigation as interfaces for mobility and spatial navigation for our understanding of the mobile screen as theoretical object.

3. Theoretical Consoles

Theoretical objects are things that compel us to propose, interrogate and theorize. They counter the influence of approaches that try to define, position and fix. The handheld, mobile screen offers us a specific kind of theoretical object. Smartphones and tablet computers are a rapidly developing type of screen object. Hybrid screen devices that encompass multiple interfaces, they raise questions about the specificity of the screen gadget as object, and about the entanglement of technologies, applications and practices. Moreover, the very speed of the development of this type of technological object demands an assessment of their historicity: how can we understand their specificity if they are changing so very fast? Taking the current moment – in which smartphones and tablets are at the forefront of innovation and commercial marketing – as a provisional halting place and point of departure, I will go back just a few years. Through an analysis of the Nintendo DS game console, launched in 2004 and updated in 2008 to include a camera (the DSi) and re-released in 2010 with a larger screen (the DSi XL), and in 2011 adding a 3D screen (the 3DS), I argue that handheld gadgets like mobile gaming devices, smartphones, and tablets like the iPad are best understood as *theoretical consoles*: objects that raise theoretical and historical questions, precisely, about their inherently temporary and hybrid status. In order to demonstrate that this function is theoretical rather than object-specific, after the case study in this chapter, I will take this perspective in Chapter 5 to look at the hybrid interface of the iPhone as a theoretical console.

The Status of the Gadget: The Case of Nintendo DS

In 2004, a new handheld and portable computer game console was released: the Nintendo DS. With the DS, Nintendo updated and expanded their successful earlier mobile consoles, the Game Boy and the latest generation to date, the Game Boy Advance with which Nintendo had dominated the market of mobile consoles since 1989. Like any new console, Nintendo's latest version was faster than its predecessors, allowed for more detailed game graphics, and had an updated design. The DS, however, was marketed as a revolutionary console because it allegedly offered radically new possibilities for game play. The new 'specs' or technological features of the DS were, indeed, multifarious: voice-control options, WiFi connectivity, touchscreen technology, and last but not least, a double screen.

I did not choose this object because the range of these characteristics is particularly 'impressive' – a term used so often in the descriptions and evaluations of newly-launched technological devices and gadgets – in comparison with the whole array of other handheld, hybrid electronic devices such as mobile phones, PDAs, media players, and navigation systems, or competing handheld game systems such as the PlayStation Portable (PSP). It is not. In fact, as a piece of technology, at its time of appearance it did not even represent the forefront of technological innovation. I selected it, rather, because it is so ordinary; the very fact of its generalized use makes it characteristic for the (technological) culture of its time.

Fig. 3.1: *The Nintendo DS Lite (black edition) with screenshots of the game* Pokémon: Mystery Dungeon. *Courtesy of Nintendo, Benelux*

Moreover, I chose this object for historical as well as theoretical reasons. It helps me articulate the intertwinement of historical and theoretical thought, allowing us to turn from the one to the other. This turns the DS into a *theoretical object*. This term has been brought into currency by French thinker Hubert Damisch. First casually used by Damisch and his circle at the EHESS in Paris, the concept became more precise when, asked about its precise meaning, the philosopher and art historian replied with an insistence on such objects' agency. He contended that a theoretical object

... obliges you to do theory but also furnishes you with the means of doing it. Thus, if you agree to accept it on theoretical terms, it will produce effects around itself ... [and] forces us to ask ourselves what theory is. It is posed in theoretical terms; it produces theory; and it necessitates a reflection on theory. (Bois et al., 1998, 8; emphasis added)

Such objects do not form an empirical class of things by themselves. They emerge in the convergence of people discussing through and around them. But once they acquire the status of theoretical objects, they become things that appear to attract debate, thought and arguments.

In particular, looking at the 2004 Nintendo DS as a theoretical object helps me break open the still rather rigid distinction between historical and theoretical approaches to media studies, and specifically to propose a methodology for analyzing contemporary gadgets. Since my proposal is modeled on the console-like structure of the way in which historical and theoretical approaches interconnect, I submit the term *theoretical console* for such a specific theoretical object. Theoretical consoles raise questions about their own hybrid status.

Like any technological gadget, the Nintendo DS flaunts its historical position. First, as an instance of commercial gadgetry, the object represents the state of the art of applied technology available to the average consumer at the time of the gadget's appearance on the market. Its commercial value lies in the discourse of an ever-changing horizon of technological development. Moreover, as Baudrillard has put it in his critical analysis of the system of fashionable objects, this discourse is even embedded in the technological make-up of the object itself. (1996, esp. 115-138) In the "permanent state of revolution" of technology, it is the object that "speaks [its] *time*" (9). In the midst of a continuous push for innovation and development, accompanied by ubiquitous marketing, the Nintendo DS speaks of its historical status, its moment within the longer history of the screen.

It speaks to us about the ongoing quest for innovation of the ubiquitous and polymorphous screen. If the historical flux of technological change is a moving image, the gadget is a still of it. More clearly than the snapshot, the metaphor of the still – a single frame out of the series of 16 or more frames per second that compose the illusion of movement – intimates that immediately before, and immediately after its appearance, other, related image frames scroll by. The still is a fugitive and artificially arrested moment in a longer, constantly changing moving environment. However, the moment of the gadget is as relevant as any moment in the longer history of media development and media change. It is significant precisely because of its temporal state.

The DS console offers a distinctive interface and enables quite specific possibilities for engaging, for interacting with its screens and with their on-screen content. This makes the DS suitable to explore the complex issues that emerge from a theoretical-object approach to the Nintendo DS as a time-bound piece of material screen technology – a time-boundedness that compels a historical consideration. This includes applications that explore the new possibilities and limitations offered by the interface for the use of the object in screen practice.

The second, theoretical reason for my choice of the DS is that it is a screen-based *console* – a significant term, literally as well as metaphorically. As a console, it is a platform or interface for the games and other software that can be played on it.[1] Like any screen-based apparatus, its technology and the ensuing possibilities for its users prescribe and require content and interaction. This is the case with any screen-based interface, be it the classical movie screen, TV screen, desktop computer screen, or any other hybrid or derivative screen. It requires, that is, an on-screen image or application, on the one hand, and the actual viewing or handling of the screen on the other. This dual need makes it necessary to consider the DS as more than an apparatus; it must be seen as a *practice*. Screening, thus, involves screen technology, screen content or application, and screen use. And when we take the gadget not simply as a material object but as a time-bound object-in-practice, it becomes productive to consider a handheld console such as the DS in terms of theoretical console. As a true console, it raises questions of the articulation between theoretical and historical concerns.

The concept-metaphor of the theoretical console raises theoretical questions about the object's status and gives access to various strands of media research. The console thus conceived is infused with approaches to media archaeology, entailing theoretical and even cultural-philosophical considerations. Such a set-up is best described with the untranslatable concept of *dispositif*, a viewing configuration. The DS can be taken as an instance of issues that emerge from the integrated examination of screen, application and use – all three both historical and theoretical. Mobile consoles raise related questions about the mobility *of* media (media mobility) and the mobility *by means of* media (mediated or virtual mobility, as discussed in the previous chapter). This focus on mobility also invokes a historical approach, attentive to transformations over time – hence, the notion that this gadget can be seen as a still, a moment within the narrative flow of media development. Therefore, in the end, the two focal points that the theoretical console revolves around – the DS as historical and as theoretical console – are really only one.

The temporal status of a commercial product of the media industry is what makes it relevant for such a console approach that examines crossroads of history, theory and, in relation to both, practice. When new media are launched, the focus of the advertising prose is understandably on innovation. But paradoxically, presenters of products offered as new then foreground features that hark back to older products. This connection between older and newly-launched products acknowledges the inevitable historicity of even the most ephemeral gadgets. The very concept of newness, of innovation, is fundamentally historical.

It is this historical nature of any new product that offers the starting point for my reflection. From the perspective of media archaeology, then, I consider how this application of screen technologies and their material practices relates to older screening arrangements and practices, or dispositifs. The DS is an example of a *mobile* dispositif: a screening arrangement that encompasses both the perceptual positioning of the screen's beholder, and the physical set-up for interactive interfacing by the screen's use. The 'theoretical-console' motivation of this focus lies in the idea that a mobile console prompts comparison with other (older) screen technologies and dispositifs – specifically the televisual and the cinematic – and at the same time raises questions about how to regard, study and analyze the new ones.

For Joachim Paech (1997) the perceptual positions brought forth by modern modes of transportation such as the train, the airplane and the automobile, by optical media such as the panorama or the cinematographer, and by new forms of public space such as the department store, can all be considered as different dispositifs of perception, with the modern metropolis as a 'hyper-dispositif'. This approach takes the concept of dispositif into the field of the specific visual culture of modernity.[2]

What I consider to be different and new is the fact that the mobility of this mobile dispositif is multifaceted; it is a mobility of screen, user and image. In consequence, as a mobile medium it raises questions about the screen as related to movement, touch and the process of spatial transformation. I also consider it 'old', that is, in line with older visions of the cinematic and the televisual screen. This intersection of new and old can tell us something about *change over time* – which is the most succinct definition of the historical. Thus, it is here, at the moment the historicity emerges when innovation and continuity converge, that the historical entwines with the theoretical.

To demonstrate the usefulness of attributing to a somewhat banal object such as the Nintendo DS the status of a theoretical console, I now zoom in on three of its features that make up the particular mobile dispositif of the DS: the touch control of the screen, the mobility of the screen, and the doubling of the screen. This chapter is an exploration of the range of issues and questions that emanate from this mobile configuration. The result is the notion that even such an ephemeral object as a gadget can further our understanding of media culture in its inextricable knot of historical and theoretical, as well as practical complexities. The next section develops this argument concretely.

Portrait of the Gadget as a Theoretical Console

This gadget is, then, both new and not new at all. Even though the screen features of the DS are central in the console's marketing campaign – if only because the name DS (Dual Screens) underscores these features – the use of a multi-screen format is not new for Nintendo's mobile gaming devices. Dual screens in a 'clamshell' case were already used in the company's *Game & Watch* series (1980-1991). There are, however, some important differences between these earlier portable video games and the DS console. The first obvious difference is the fact that the *Game & Watch* series offered single games – of which *Donkey Kong* is perhaps the best known – rather than operating as a platform for multiple games on interchangeable game cartridges, as does the DS.[3]

A second difference is that the screens of older games were partly pre-printed with both a foreground and a background setting – much like in theatrical set design. These preprints situated the versatile game characters moving on the screen behind and in front of the print within a specific spatial environment. Moreover, the double screens offered one possibility only. The player was able to move the game characters from one screen to the other, a move that resulted in a linear spatial continuity between the two screens. The DS, in contrast, allows for a wide variety of game applications of the possibilities a double interface offers. The two screenspaces can be related to each other in very different ways in each game.

A third difference concerns users' control of the lower screen by touch. The lower screen is operated by a different kind of screen handling than the more traditional button controls serving the upper screen. Thus, this one gadget object comprises two different screen interfaces. This is what makes it a true console: a technologically hybrid platform for multiple dispositifs. Moreover, as a game console, the DS is a platform of an array of games that each provides different applications of the dual screens and the touchscreen capabilities.

This dual-screen feature gives the company's advertisers an argument to enhance novelty. On the Nintendo DS consumer service FAQ website, the producers stress that the letters DS, in addition to being an abbreviation for *Dual Screens*, have another meaning: "[t]o our developers, it stands for "Developers' System", since we believe it gives game creators *brand new* tools which will lead to more innovative games for the world's players."[4] In spite of the hyperbolic rhetoric deployed to accentuate innovation and global scale, the producers do have a point. The two-screen features that distinguish this console from other portable, hybrid or convergent game systems, such as Sony's PSP or Nokia's N-Gage, invite specific types of games – newly designed, or versions or modifications of existing games. Conversely, these games explore the particular possibilities of the DS screens.

Moreover – a fourth difference from the older *Game & Watch* games – as Nintendo announced, with the double screens, different screen functions converge. Read the combination of the following statements, for example:

> With Nintendo DS, dual screens and touch-screen technology allow you to interact with games like never before. Wireless communication allows you to

experience real-time multiplayer game play, while built-in PictoChat software gives you the power to draw, write and send messages wirelessly. Nintendo DS revolutionizes the way games are played.

Two LCD screens offer one of the most groundbreaking gameplay advances ever developed. Imagine the possibilities. In a racing game, you might see your own vehicle's perspective on one screen and an overall track view on the other. Soon, games could be created allowing you to play games on one screen while sending text messages on the other.

Each 3-inch screen can reproduce a true 3D view, with impressive 3D render-ings that can surpass images displayed on the Nintendo 64.The lower screen offers something never before provided by any dedicated game device: touch-screen capabilities. You no longer have to rely on just buttons to move your character or shift perspectives. Navigate menus or access inventory items sim-ply by touching the screen with a stylus or fingertip. The possibilities are lim-ited only by developers' imaginations.[5]

These instances of a commercial rhetoric that stresses innovation ("like never before") nevertheless foreground the different aspects of what I intend to put my finger on, not just as newness (the historical aspect) but as a vision of what the screen is, what we can do with screens, and what makes a particular screen-based device stand out as singular (the theoretical aspect). Along with their claim to newness, the writers emphasize time, space and practice at once. Their concept of time is not just historical but theoretically elaborated. They address the real-time aspect of communication through wireless connectivity and touchscreen interaction. They position the gadget's spatial properties, the spatial multiplica-tion it allows, when they speak of multiple perspectives enabled and visualized by the double screens. The writers also foreground practice, with the suggestion of a more intuitive interaction with the screen by direct touch.

In addition to that theoretical-historical analysis of newness, the passages inti-mate a triple theoretical point the DS makes concerning the status of the gadget as object – the thing I am portraying in this section. First, the gadget as object is material. Second, a screen-based gadget is temporal as well as temporary, ephem-eral. This engages the status of the gadget in the history of media. This status is both comparative and historical, concerning synchronic differentiations and con-fluence, as well as transformation over time. Herein lies its historical status. Third, the gadget's functionality is determined by the way any screen-based object embodies possibilities of multiple interfaces. This is another reason why such multifaceted objects should be considered theoretical consoles rather than (sin-gular) theoretical objects. The issues the gadget raises offer a constellation of concepts for use in media history and theory together – not conflated or merged but articulated together, flipping from the one to the other and back according to the 'thought-console' of our two disciplinary approaches. In other words, these concepts draw lines that cross at the intersection between those two approaches and thus suggest ways we can shift from the one to the other at the hub that is the console itself.

The first issue this gadget raises concerns method: how to study it from a media-archaeological perspective? Within media history, a gadget is a commercial and vernacular technological object that is designed as interface and platform for multimedia applications. Its innovative character primarily determines its market value. Paradoxically, however, its innovation is recognizable through its similarity to other, previously marketed gadgets. The fact that we speak of *generations* of mobile phones, mobile game consoles, or media players indicates this assumption of a family resemblance and a lineage among gadgets.[6]

Elsewhere, I have used Wittgenstein's concept of family resemblance – a resemblance that can be based on different features between any two members of a 'family' and does not comprise essences shared by all members – for an analysis of early cinema's open genre-structure (2006). Early (roughly pre-1914) cinema, like most if not all 'new' media technologies that are just taking shape in cultural practice, shows a wide variety of genres that are not as rigidly demarcated as in the classical period, or what Noël Burch (1973) has called the *Institutional Mode of Representation* (IMR). The argument for early cinema holds, I think, for all moments of transition and innovation, as periods of experimentation and shifting modes of use. Family resemblance allows us to consider similarities of formations within genealogies, without thinking in terms of core essences and without keeping out of sight that which is not covered by the category.

In the case of newly-launched technological gadgets, we see an explicit foregrounding of the older family relations, while emphasizing the new aspects of the latest generation. Specifically, a gadget is a pocket-sized, handheld object designed for individual, everyday use. Its status lies somewhere between practical tool, fun object, means of expression, and shiny piece of technology. As Lev Manovich stresses in his essay on the playful interactions with mobile phones, it is also an aesthetic object in which such different functions and meanings converge as "friendly, playful, pleasurable, aesthetically pleasing, expressive, and fashionable; signifying cultural identity, and designed for emotional satisfaction" (2006: 1).

The gadget's historical character lies in that newness. For, as a product of rapidly changing and passing technology, the gadget is a fugitive object. Therefore, we study the gadgets/objects in their newness, without merely considering them as new. Its media-historical questioning can now no longer be disentangled from its theoretical one: the gadget as theoretical console asks how we can deal with passing technologies, passing newness, within a media-archaeological comparison? Moreover, it suggests we consider the range of meanings these apparatuses have, e.g. as tool, aesthetic object, commodity, and as both self-effacing and self-affirming piece of technology.

As a technological object, a gadget is an apparatus, a device and an appliance, all in one. First, a gadget is an apparatus, a piece of machinery. Second, as a device it is a technological object designed to produce a particular effect. Third, as an appliance it is geared towards application. This means we use it as a tool in order to perform tasks. The outcome of the device's operation is what is called *mediality*. I understand mediality as the integration of these three aspects. Hence, mediality is the process of an apparatus producing effects that emerge in application. The somewhat artificial distinction I am making of mediality as result of the operation of a device from that resulting from the use of the gadget by a viewer/ user, as well as from discursive operations that play a part in the process of mediation, is only meant to clarify the multiple understandings of the materiality of the gadget as instrument. I call mediality the result of the convergence of these three aspects. This convergence of three aspects in mediality distinguishes the DS from, say, the vacuum cleaner, which results in dust-free cleanliness, or a pen resulting in shopping lists, lecture notes or poetry. In the case of this (hardware) appliance, several (software) applications can run on the apparatus. The products of this performance of both appliance and application are various and versatile and have different types of use-value. Moreover, as pointed out by David J. Bolter and Diane Gromala, the value and meaning of computers and, as I would suggest especially, electronic gadgets is different from appliances such as vacuum cleaners, in the sense that we do not want them to be functional and invisible only:

> Computers don't feel like toasters; they feel much more like books, photograph albums, or television sets. For us today – and it's a realization that our culture has made gradually over the past thirty years – the computer feels like a medium. It is providing us with a set of new media forms and genres, just as printing, the cinema, radio, and television have done before. These digital media forms stage experiences for us. As producers and as users of digital technology, we don't want our computers to disappear, any more than we want books, films, or paintings to disappear. (2003: 5)

The specificity of gadgets is their value as material objects, not unlike other much-cherished media objects and artifacts.

As a technological moment, the gadget provides a historical anchoring of technology. In this status of the gadget between apparatus, device and appliance, a convergence becomes visible. Convergence is a useful notion to account for the other side of history, namely the ephemeral synthesis of a moment, a synchronic slice of time where different issues, possibilities and desires converge. Here, media technologies and (therefore) media usages converge. The issue is not that different technologies join in one appliance, however, but that a singular constellation of technologies emerges in one console. This mixture offers a platform – console – for a whole array of possibilities for the gadget's applications. It is not a singular medium; it is, rather, a composite convergence of screen paradigms within a single dispositif. Therefore, the features of the screen that both *converge* and *transform* in this apparatus bind synchrony to diachrony and thus embody its status as theoretical console. This central position of the screen warrants a closer look at the many-sided screen of the DS: the touchscreen, the mobile screen, and the double screen.

Touch Screen: Dirty Windows

The first element in this convergence of screen paradigms is touch; the aspect that distinguishes the touchscreen from the cinematic or televisual screen is the fact that the screen can be, indeed, must be touched. This tactile form of access to viewing bears consequences for the way the screen enables the viewer-user to virtually travel by means of the screen. This feature is, again, both new and old. Traversing has a longstanding status as a metaphor for screen-based viewing. The idea of moving *through* has been dominant in our perception of how visual screen media work. It is as if touchscreens were needed to understand this about the past. If novelty there is, then this novelty is at least partly of a cognitive kind, as a new way of understanding what had already been with us for a long time.

As has been insightfully traced by Anne Friedberg, seeing has an established cultural meaning that is metaphorically expressed in the window (2006). Not coincidentally, the DS happens to be promoted by Nintendo as a dirty window. The lack of transparency of its 'windows' thus underscores the double function as both a screen or window *on* or *through* which to see things, and an object or tool to do things *with*.

A boy approaches the dirty rear windows of a van and writes "GO" with his fingers, upon which the van drives away. This short evocative clip speaks of the main feature of the touchscreen technology: like on a dirty window, on the touchscreen we can write commands.

The dirty window resembles Freud's famous mystic writing pad. This children's toy on which drawings or writings could be made with a stylus that could then be erased always retained the traces of the erased marks. Freud alleged this toy to be a metaphor of the unconscious (1940 [1925]). According to Derrida, Freud 'staged' this founding metaphor long before he actually wrote the essay (1976). Mary Ann Doane rightly remarked that Freud could as well have chosen cinema or photography, rather than this quaint and cheap toy, as his model for the storage of time (1996: 315). It rather suits my purposes here that Freud chose a toy comparable with the status of the mobile screen today and the case I selected for this reflection, the Nintendo DS.

Fig. 3.2: Nintendo DS commercial Dust (Leo Burnett advertising agency, 2005)

And so does, I contend, the ad. The analogy between a dirty window and a touchscreen, here a visual comparison, suggests two directions in which to think the two elements. From window to touchscreen, it says both simplicity and availability. Certain informality suggests that everyone can do this, and hence that everyone should own this. Conversely, from touchscreen to window, the clip suggests magic conferred upon the everyday, as if the world becomes more wonderful when we own such a gadget. Things will happen when we touch the opaque glass shield. Far from being transparent, the screen becomes a thing.

The commonplace comparison between the screen and the window demonstrates what is at stake. When a window is dirty, is it the window we actually see, or is it the impossibility of seeing *through* the window, its opacity, that marks its presence as a thing? This is how Bill Brown explains what he calls thing-ness. He refers to a novel by A.S. Byatt:

> [...] the interruption of the habit of looking through windows as transparencies enables [Byatt's] protagonist to look at a window in itself in its opacity. (2004: 4)

When the screen functions as a transparent window, it is invisible as object. It is when it is opaque that its materiality, its thing-ness, surfaces. This paradox of non-functionality that correlates visibility to thing-ness is particularly intriguing in the case of the screen. Unlike the window, the operation of this screen necessitates opaqueness for virtual transparency: it needs the surface to reflect the images on screen.

In a similar context of opacity and transparency, Heidi Rae Cooley defines what she calls tactile vision, a vision "activated by the hand" and "a material and dynamic seeing involving eyes as well as hands and a MSD [mobile screenic device]." (2004: 137) With this term she does not refer to touchscreen technology but to the more general manual handling – mind the word "hand" here – of mobile screens; the 'touched screen' as we may call this broader category. Tactile vision, according to Cooley, is based on the principle of the fit: "the particular relationship between a hand and a MSD, which opens onto a relation of interface through which vision becomes and remains tactile." (137)

Cooley rightly argues for a tactile notion of *interfacing*. I would derive an even stronger point from this tactility. To put it simply: touchscreen technology invites one to touch in order to see. Thus it transforms the practice of screening as tactile *activity* into a haptic *experience* of this practice. This formulation sums up what distinguishes tactility from the haptic, on which more in Chapter 5. The activity as such foregrounds the temporal collapse of making and viewing images. It merges the experience of these activities when the screen becomes interactive and viewing, at least partly, a haptic experience of productivity. Using the screen of the DS is a physical and performative activity. Viewing is no longer a matter of looking alone, nor of perceptually receiving images. It entails movements with the hand that holds the stylus. This simultaneity of touching, making and viewing connects the viewing experience of the cinematic, to the television viewing as live, to the installation-art experience of performativity – in the sense of effect-producing semiotic action – and to the physical experience of drawing. There are no images prior to the moment the user conjures them up by touch. This temporal aspect is clear in the ad, where looking and doing occur at the same moment – are, in fact, one act. This is a literal enactment of performative looking. Temporally, this breaks with the cinematic dispositif; the touchscreen implies live image-*making*. The activity of making shifts the focus from cinematic as well as televisual receptivity, to production. This feature of the screen-as-window metaphor demonstrates the gadget's enhanced newness in relation to its equally enhanced oldness.

The discourse surrounding the DS displays symptoms of the recurrence of old media within the new.[7] According to its advertisers, the Opera Browser for the Nintendo DS replaces the mouse-directed feature of scrolling with the cinematic feature of panning:

Forget the scrollbar – Nintendo DS Browser users prefer panning. When in either browsing mode, simply touch the screen and drag your stylus to move the screen up or down.[8]

Another allusion to (pre-)cinematic techniques is made in the art of *Pictomation*. Here, the drawing feature of the PictoChat application that is installed on the DS is used for creating animations, appropriating the pre-cinematographic animation technique of the flipbook or flickbook.[9]

This puts a particular spin on Bolter and Grusin's further development of Marshall McLuhan's notion "the medium is the message" (1964) in their concept of remediation (1999). Their term refers primarily to a revamping of the old in the new. This uni-directionality fails to do justice to these creative interventions. While we could consider pictomation and machinima as a remediation of flipbooks and animation, the techniques and technologies deployed to make them are part of the mediality proper to this gadget. Therefore, the historical referencing is not only retrospective, toward previous techniques and modes of representation, but also forward-looking, in terms of innovation and modification.

The tactility of the DS touchscreen is humble and inconspicuous. This is especially so when it is compared to the much more elaborate movements we must make when holding a controller for the Xbox or PlayStation, but especially the controller for the Wii which allows you to swing the controller like a tennis racket or a golf club. Those larger sweeping movements are physically very different from the touchscreen 'nitpicking'. Rather than engaging the full body, the latter is closer, more intimate. In both cases, looking at the screen is something that can, itself, be looked at, as well as felt in the body. But in our case of the touchscreen, the physical connection of hand and screen matters most. Like a master draftsman, the user produces the images with subtle movements of touch.

The shift from screen/window and touched-screen/thing is thus preceded by that other, temporal shift: from eye to hand as the primary organ activated not qua seeing, but in order to see. Meanwhile, the hand also makes what is seen. It is the hand of the observer that changes the status of the screen from transparent to opaque. This is in line with Cooley's argument about what she calls "screenic, seeing":

In this instance, vision is not a practice of seeing through, i.e. a window, but looking at, i.e. the screen. And this shift from window-ed seeing to screenic seeing reconfigures one's relationship to that which is seen. Whereas a window distances viewers from what they are looking at, the screen draws them toward the images that are displayed on the screen (not beyond it). In which case, window-ed seeing institutes a detached engagement, while screenic seeing encourages an experience of encounter. Vision, no longer a property of the window and its frame, becomes an extension of the screen. Likewise, that which is being viewed (and perhaps recorded) no longer exists separate from that which is framing it. The object, formerly located on the other side of the frame, converges or fuses with the screen, its physicality becoming the physicality of the screen. In this way, vision involves opacity, not transparency.

Screenic seeing acquires a sort of tangibility, a physicality of its own. In looking at the screen, the MSD user engages the screen and, subsequently, enters into a relationship with the screen. This relationship is material and unfolding; it does not involve containment but contingency. (2007: 143)

This screenic seeing as a result of touching screens thus concerns not only *what* we see and *how* we see, but also the experience of seeing itself. As an experience, touchscreen seeing involves the experience of sight by means of touch in duration.[10]

The moment the images appear on the screen, or when their shapes and sizes change, the image becomes animated. A live form of animation, this procedural textuality evokes, again, machinima. Machinima are recordings of gameplay and as such they are essentially films made of playing games, turning a ludic activity into a performance. Compared to machinima, the touchscreen animations are live, not recorded, and more difficult to bracket as texts. The process of touching the screen collapses with the process of watching. Machinima separates this once again: there, the moment of making precedes the moment of watching – much like film.

This point concerning the consequences of the way players are positioned in relation to screens can also serve to highlight the historical perspective. Touchscreen technology can be regarded as one of many explorations of interface possibilities. These range from *eye candy* – a popular term for special effects and scopic pleasures – and *eye ware* – the term for virtual reality head-sets – to *eye toys* – named after Sony's Eye Toy extension of the PlayStation which is based on webcam technology and allows you to become part of the image on screen. In this lineage, we now move to touchscreens. In this genealogy, however, something drastic happens: the metaphor of the screen is substituted for that of the eye, a substitution that is in itself a shift of focus – to use yet another optical metaphor. Each of these poetic and playful terms inflects the eye, and in doing so, they each point to fundamentally different constructions of spectatorship – from the more distant scopic pleasures, via the phenomenon of frame-less visual immersion, to ideals of in-screen (tele-)presence, and now, via the touch, to tactile continuities. For my perspective here, the point is that this range does not present a linear and singular development, as an ongoing series of eye-related words would suggest. We can consider these interface technologies as different forms of *interfacing*. With this term, a verb form, I refer to the practices rather than technologies of the screen-based interface. These practices depart from fundamentally different ideals about the relationship between screen, content and spectatorship. While vision remains the common denominator, all these visual ideals inflect the relationship between vision and the other senses; hence, they concern a sense of perception larger than vision alone. The fact that with touchscreen, the tactile aspect is actually named in the terminology, retrospectively draws attention to that synesthetic aspect of the other technologies.

From the vantage point of the touchscreen and its shifted emphasis on tactility, the eye had it coming; it needed to be dislodged as the queen of sense organs for perception in the traditional hierarchy of the senses. Scopic pleasure (eye candy) is presented as a literal satisfaction of taste. The special effects are so stunning that they seem to melt in the mouth, or make the viewer's mouth water. Eye ware's equipment involves hearing as much as seeing, and influences the entire sensate body. Immersion entails total proximity but also a loss of boundaries, perhaps a loss of self. Eye toys allow the viewer to play with transformations of dimensions, when, Alice-like, the viewer becomes part of the smaller image while distant others can be approached closely. In spite of the playful term, this is a very serious issue. This visual proximity is a much craved-for form of contact in communities of migrants, when thousands of kilometers can be visually and aurally bridged.

But if touchscreen shifts the metaphor from eye to touch, from vision to tactility, something else also happens. The idea of the touchscreen signifies a definitive leave taken from the illusion of retinal looking – of looking with the body aloof, uninvolved, and protected from influence. This is why space becomes such a central category. When retinal looking is no longer even an illusion, and the eye is replaced within the body with its other sense organs, the experience of viewing must be considered as, literally, taking place.

In February 2006, Jeff Han demonstrated an "intuitive, interface-free, touch-driven computer screen" which can be manipulated with multiple fingers: "bimanual, multi-point, and multi-user interactions on a graphical display surface" as he calls his multi-touch interaction research on his website.[11] The multi-touch principles expand touchscreen technology and open up the possibilities for a whole range of new applications, among which map navigation, image manipulation, and the creative and intuitive animation of abstract shapes which stood out in the presentation Han gave at the TED (Technology Entertainment Design) Conference in Monterey, California.

When Apple CEO Steve Jobs presented the iPhone a year later at the Macworld Conference & Expo 2007, it became clear where the first appearance of this new touchscreen technology was to appear in commercial, personal gadgetry. As Apple announced then, the primary feature of the iPhone is this multi-touch principle:

iPhone features the most revolutionary user interface since the mouse. It's an entirely new interface based on a large multi-touch display and innovative new software that lets you control everything using only your fingers. So you can glide through albums with Cover Flow, flip through photos and email them with a touch, or zoom in and out on a section of a web page – all by simply using iPhone's multi-touch display.[12]

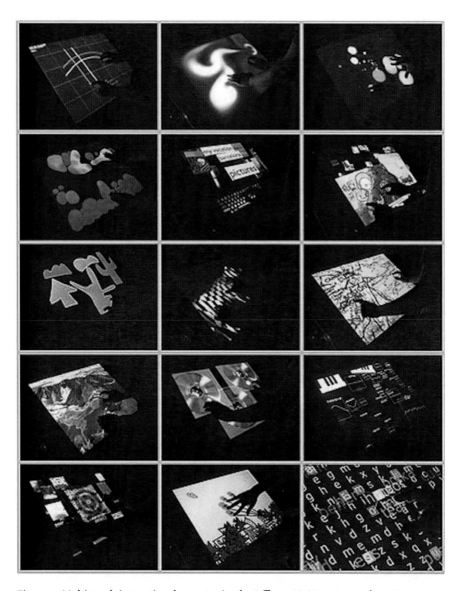

Fig. 3.3: Multi-touch interaction demonstration by Jefferson Y. Han. Image: http://www.flickr.com/photos/millynet/98031764/

According to both men, we are once again witnessing a revolution. In both visions, the presence of a finger is noteworthy. This is the tool to image the small size, hence, the handheld quality of the gadget. But there are important differences between the two gadgets.

True, this application in the iPhone indeed seems new in the way it changes the button interface of phones and allows you to slide and re-arrange images in the vein of the fantastic and futuristic screen technology represented fictionally in *Minority Report* (Spielberg, 2002). This technology allows for the live arrangement and editing of a sequence of images. Yet, the small size of the apparatus – an average mobile phone – and its screen does not really accommodate multi-touching. According to the developers, the multiple touch as demonstrated by Han made a promise for multiple fingers, hands and user interfaces.[13]

For my exploration of what the hybrid apparatus of the Nintendo DS can tell us, it seems relevant that the touchscreen aspect is imbricated with a new sense of flexibility and continuity between eye/hand, screen, and image, and between space and time. This is both new and old when compared to cinematic and televisual dispositifs, their recorded-ness and liveness, and the ensuing spatial relationship between onscreen and off-screen spaces.

As part of a body that can move around, the hand that touches the screen can also take the gadget to different places. I now turn to the mobility resulting from this as a second fundamentally new, yet also continuous aspect of the gadget. The manual engagement with the screen, not only in the case of touchscreens but in the wider category of touched screens, also makes the screen mobile. As I argue below, multiple takes on mobility – of device, screen, and user – can be brought to bear on the particular touchscreen interface.

Mobile Screen: Carrying, Sharing, Transporting

One form of mobility results in the possibility that touchscreens offer for sharing the screens. Sharing, however, is a problematic characterization of the touchscreen. True, as a handheld device the DS can be taken anywhere and handed over to others. The portability of the device makes it a mobile medium but, because of its pocket size, also an individual one. Yet, as per the marketing of the DS, sharing is part of the fun – part of its social ecology. Even though the console is designed for individual use (the small screens allow for one simultaneous user only), thanks to that same small-size mobility it is easy to pass around. Unlike the paradoxical public-yet-private viewing experience of the movies, you cannot share the moment of watching and playing, but you can still share the object. Sharing concerns the way the mobile screen as a handheld object can be passed around, a mobility not of space only, but also of use and even property. Although mobile gadgets are often also called 'personal electronic devices', the DS campaign explicitly targets connectivity, communal play and media use.

In addition to the possibility of passing around the whole gadget, the gadget as apparatus has WiFi Internet connectivity built-in. As device, it produces connectivity. As appliance (as toy), it makes playing together possible; it enables game playing among multiple players using this connectivity. Hence, this feature of connectivity enables another way of sharing. Wireless connection makes it possible for the user/player to share screen space, simultaneously in multiple-player games or by sending messages and drawings, for example with Nintendo's DS application PictoChat. Screen space is not literally the space of the hand that holds the screen. Instead, the experience of space can be considered in terms of a spatial continuity of eyes, hand, screen, and screened space. In response to earlier screen technologies, the mobility of the gadget is therefore best understood as the spatial extension not beyond the screen (into the screened space) but before the screen (between eye and screen). More intimate than a distant screen, more individual than a large screen, more intuitive than a separate screen, the handheld aspect of the mobile screen emphasizes the continuity between spaces, allowing for what can be called space-binding. As will be explained in the next chapter, this is a particular characteristic of televisual connections between spaces that fundamentally alters the experience of time within a place (McCarthy 2001: 74).

This brings me to another aspect of spatial continuity, namely the impact of time on space. Continuity is spatial but inevitably also temporal. Simultaneity and the sharing of screen space is a way of temporalizing space. Continuity and, in its wake, sharing are, however, not only clarifying but also mystifying terms. They suggest a social advantage, an overcoming of individualism and loneliness. When speaking of the "bi-located psyche" of the player, Parikka and Suominen (2006) argue that this discourse of connectivity does not disrupt the traditional separation between public and private domains. In this respect, the term *sharing* is deceptive, and clearly belongs to the discourse of advertisement parasitical upon social needs and problems of our time.

In fact, this discourse expands on another trope, that of virtual mobility. Sharing and connectivity concern transport. Space itself is transported: the expansion of space through the media device, whether or not its windows are 'clean', allows the player to do something else, somewhere else. Thus, the mobility of the device comes to stand for the mobility of the medium.

It follows that mobility operates on different levels: that of the mobility of the device, the mobility of the player/user, and the mobility between places and users. The device itself can go wherever the owner wants to take it. The owner can play while moving herself, for example in public transport. And they can play with a fellow-player who can be anywhere else, in turn either static or in movement. What is most significant for the mobile game console is the way the mobility *of* the screen and its user meets the mobility *on* the screen; the mobility of the screen relates to the virtual mobility that the screen 'images'. Drawing attention to that double-edged mobility turns the console as gadget once more into a theoretical console.

As I have explained in Chapter 1, in the case of the traditional media of the moving image, there is, however, a paradox at the heart of this mobility: the spectator remains immobile. Anne Friedberg has pointed out this paradox of the cinematic viewing arrangement (2006). The virtual mobility of the medium is made possible, precisely, in the space between the immobile (cinema) viewer, the static screen or frame, and the mobility of the images on screen. This is yet another way in which our console is both new and old; it derives its newness from its compliance with desires provoked by older screen media.

In the case of the DS, the spectator is a player, a user, and is physically engaged when using the console. The touchscreen is screen and controller in one, requires physical action, and such action entails movement. But movement is not mobility; moving one's hand is not the same as moving around. This brings me, once more, to the oldness aspect of this gadget. The immobility of the spectator is required for the classical screen, of which the film screen is the paradigmatic example. The player is sitting or standing; the relationship between screen and player is still, immobile, even if she is in a state of mobility, for example, taking a bus ride. The newness resides in the fact that mobile screens not only allow mobility of both body and screen, but position the mobility of the body within a number of relationships.

The DS embodies a newness it has in common with many other contemporary gadgets. The fact that this newness is quite common further enhances the Nintendo's status as (a relatively arbitrarily chosen) theoretical console. As Ingrid Richardson argues, many contemporary gadgets set up a distinctive relationship between body, screen/technology, and environment/space:

The idea that embodiment is possible relies largely on the supposition that our engagement with screen media requires a stationary body, such that one's awareness of the corporeal recedes. Yet, as I have suggested mobile media complicate this relation, and facilitate a physical mobility of the body, whether pedestrian or vehicular, partially returning one's attention to physical location and the navigation within and around material environments. (2005: np)

This hybrid mobility with mobile screens is most emphatically demonstrated in the case of navigation devices. There, our literal being in the world, our physical occupation of space and the inhering coordinates, make on-screen navigation possible. Therefore, we are becoming familiar with the principle that not only can the body become mobile, but it has to move in order for the screen to function.

This mobility is similar to the movement of the avatar as representation of the player on the screen of racing games. There, the cars even represent the vehicle, which virtually transports the player through the virtual space of the racetrack. There is, however, a difference. The navigation of the screen itself – in the hands of the user or in the car/vehicle that transports both user/viewer and device/screen – pulls the avatar through the represented space on the screen of the navigation device. In contrast, the movement of buttons, finger or stylus pushes the avatar across the screen space in the case of racing games.

All these aspects of mobility overdetermine the simple fact that the gadget itself, as a thing, can be transported wherever the user wishes to go. It is pocket-sized, handheld, and lightweight. This mobility of the thing *qua* thing is only the outer shell of something of which the mobility is multiple and constantly shifting. In giving us a freedom within space-time that no longer holds us, but that we, as owner of this gadget, can hold, it is new in relation to the old. Rather than a screen-window through which we can look outside, the gadget is like a remote control for the subject itself. It transports us while being on the move.

Double Screen: Split, Insert, Map

In combination with the mobility and tactility of the screen, the DS raises the stakes of screen technology by a doubling of the screen. It does so not only literally, by offering two related screens that split up screen space, but also conceptually, thus thickening its potential as theoretical console. As a material site for interfacing, the screen can be multiplied by combining different interfaces. The clamshell case not only makes closing the screens possible, but also divides them, splitting up single screenspace into two separate screens.

Obviously, screens within screens, or perhaps more appropriately, frames within frames have a longer history than Nintendo's invention. Split screens, inserts, *mise-en-abyme*: we have seen it all in cinema – and before that in painting.[14] Yet the primary difference here is the aspect of navigation. In her section on multiple frames and screens, Friedberg explains how the digital, multiple screen allows for multitasking. This implies simultaneity of different activities in parallel spaces. (Friedberg, 2006: 233) Following the historical metamorphoses of the screen, a temporal and spatial doubling of multiple screens is perhaps the most significant newness of the digital screen. Therefore, I focus here on the fractured, yet connected, spatial arrangement of screen-based activity; the exploration of or navigation within one screen space, for example, which results in a representation of that process in another space.[15]

Through its multiple screens the DS makes connections between multiple (virtual) spaces, but also to multiple interfaces possible; and it makes that possibility visible. The games developed for the DS explore these possibilities for double vision. One of the clearest cases is that of racing games. Since the early days of racing games, we have been familiar the screen insert with a little map of the racetrack in the upper or lower corner of the frame. These maps show little arrows, or avatars that resemble the cars that are driven in the game. On the larger screen we see a first-person perspective from a car on the racetrack.

These representations exemplify what Michel de Certeau calls map and tour paradigms. Through this theoretical view the gadget becomes a true interlocutor; the technological console is, at the same time, a theoretical one.

Fig. 3.4: *Simultaneous screens of the racing game* Mario Kart *and adventure game* The Legend of Zelda: Phantom Hour Glass. *Courtesy of Nintendo Benelux*

As I mentioned above, in their article "Nintendo® and New World Travel Writing: A Dialogue", Henry Jenkins and Mary Fuller compare exploration games to old travel narratives with the help of de Certeau's writing on *spatial stories* in *The Practice of Everyday Life*. De Certeau claims that "every story is a travel story – a spatial practice." (1988: 115) Reversing this idea, I propose that every space contains potential travel narratives – and so do the tactile, mobile, and dual screens of the Nintendo DS.

In his logic, de Certeau makes a distinction between *place* and *space*: "space is a practiced place." (116) Hence, every place can be turned into space by the practice of narrative. This practice is infused with ambitions. Fuller and Jenkins see in these ambitions a certain colonizing violence:

> Places exist only in the abstract, as potential sites for narrative action, as locations that have not yet been colonized. [...] Places constitute a "stability" which must be disrupted in order for stories to unfold. Places are there but do not yet matter, much as the New World existed, was geographically present, and culturally functioning well before it became the center of European ambitions or the site of New World narratives.

The comparison between narrative and the conquest of the New World demonstrate the sociohistorical, indeed political relevance of this view. Both are ways of turning place into space, or insignificant into significant space. As the authors continue:

> Places become meaningful only as they come into contact with narrative agents [...]. Spaces, on the other hand, are places that have been acted upon, explored, colonized. Spaces become the location of narrative events. (1995: np; emphasis added)

If the latter is the model of the former, then narrative is a form of conquest.

For de Certeau, maps are formalized, abstracted accounts of spatial relations, whereas tours are spatial movements, described from the point of view of the traveler-narrator. Fuller and Jenkins compare the rhetoric of the tour and the way this rhetoric produces attention to the effects of the tour, including its ethics expressed in terms of obligation – the other side of gaining control over narrative spaces. They signal the narrative aspect of touring which involves "a constant transformation of unfamiliar places into familiar spaces." Spatial control needs to be reaffirmed as the tour-narrative continues. As a consequence, moving through space is a narrative appropriation of place, which involves an inherent struggle for control. In double screens this can be represented simultaneously as narrative and as spatial abstraction.

If tours are visual narratives, in the case of screen-based spatial representation, maps are visual abstractions of space. These two forms of space-making announce the simultaneity that double screens make possible. De Certeau was talking about traditional, analogue cartography when he used these terms as metaphors for spatial relations – the old to which the new relates. With interactive digital maps, shifting perspectives and navigation on screen become possible. This is where the doubling of the screen becomes relevant – both practically, for the gadget, and theoretically, for its deployment as theoretical console. The virtual movements of the avatar on digital maps allow an experience of navigation that results from the transfer of physical movement of tactility to another spatial realm that can be visually entered with haptic engagement, as I will explain in more detail in Chapter 5. When the navigator moves, the avatar on the screen moves along with it. The continuity between spaces makes navigation between the converged mapping paradigms possible. This the DS demonstrates, proposing for our reflection the implications of mapping according to de Certeau, the way these implications respond to the old cartographies, and to what extent the newness, with all its rhetoric of sharing, truly innovates the ecology of screen technology.

Gadgetivity

Gadgets, then, are defined by activity and they afford this activity – let's call it gadgetivity. As I have argued above, the Nintendo DS prompts a reflection on the gadget as a hub where many different preoccupations of contemporary visual culture and its study intersect – the historical approach to media, in two directions; the theoretical understanding of how gadgets work, how they are practiced; and, superimposed on both, the ethical implications that de Certeau added to this crossing. As a theoretical console, the DS offers insight in the mobile screen, both as a technological gadget and in relation to the cultural practices it allows – an intersection, precisely, of history and theory. With its historical status it suggests the interrogation of the gadget as "speaking its time" (Baudrillard 1996) through its combination of recognizable, old and exciting new features. Theoretically, it encourages the exploration of its possibilities as console, a polymorphous screen platform for a variety of applications and practices. When we separate the *thing* – the DS in its material form – from the *object* – the thing that asks us what it is – we create what is denoted in science by the term theoretical object: a temporary construction. The object – here a particular screen device – is imagined, constructed, in order to interrogate the meaning of the object that is being theorized.

I have proposed that the DS can thus be considered, first as a theoretical object, and more specifically as a theoretical console. The difference between what is called a theoretical object and what I term a theoretical console is that between a thing that is used and considered as object – that is, reflected upon – and a variety of practices performed through that thing – its 'consoleness'. As an object the DS Nintendo already raises questions and suggests ideas about the status, limits and possibilities of the screen. This turns the object into a theoretical object. As a console, it works as a dispositif that compels particular practices, and thus it complicates these questions.

The resulting complications comprise historical and theoretical issues that cannot be disentangled, so that the methodology of visual studies is affected by it. Thus, it becomes a theoretical console. In this guise, we must consider the screen as the surface on which more fundamental issues about media and mediality are sketched. Many of these issues have barely been hinted at here. For example, how can we reflect on medium specificity, even when looking at one aspect, such as the screen, when the notion of a (specific) medium no longer even seems to apply in any simple sense?

For this reason, I contend that the consoleness of the theoretical object can be extended more generally to the notion of theoretical object. This becomes clear, for example, when art historian Rosalind E. Krauss points to this tension between theoretical object and medium specificity. She, too, declares a practice rather than a single thing – in her case, photography – to be a theoretical object. In her article

"Reinventing the Medium" she has this to say about photography in its theoretical function:

> In becoming a theoretical object, photography loses its specificity as a medium. Thus in "The Work of Art in the Age of Mechanical Reproduction," Benjamin charts a historical path from the shock effects courted by futurism and dada collage, to the shocks delivered by the unconscious optics revealed by photography, to the shock specific to the montage procedures of film editing, a path that is now indifferent to the givens of a particular medium. As a theoretical object, photography assumes the revelatory power to set forth the reasons for a wholesale transformation of art that will include itself in that same transformation. (Krauss 1999: 292)

Within the context of the DS, Krauss' remarks on photography as a theoretical object can be rephrased as follows: when we replace the word "object" by the word "console" and we see the transformation, including its own, as a transformation less of art but of the *practice* of photography, including art. This transformation is simultaneously a decisive extension of the cultural domain affected by it. This extension is, thus, a double one – in Krauss' case, of photography and of art, the one re-envisioning the other, so that the two are differently articulated together. Visual culture is seen not as homogeneous but as a *platform* – a term that is central to the Nintendo DS. As such it returns debate, contestation, and differences of opinion to, in Krauss's case, both art and photography. Something like this, by analogy, happens to history and theory through the Nintendo DS.

In addition to the many faces of the console, the specific characteristic of the portable system as a piece of technology, as hardware, the materiality, its thingness raises questions about the gadget status of the apparatus. As such it is also a gateway for *gadget-ivity*, the property of a tool for the user-player to do (other) things with it. This is a performativity of using the object in practice. In Chapter 5 I will examine the performativity implied in gadgetivity. Here, the perspective is on the status of the gadget itself, its materiality and object-status, within this culture of gadget-based practice. In this respect, the console is best understood as a thing, instrument and interface at the same time. It is in this multiplicity that it is perhaps less a medium than a carrier of mediality. Moreover, unlike other (mobile) media players, a console is, in part, an empty interface. The software application determines part of the interface, in dialogue with the hardware elements. The complex of characteristics relevant to the portable console as a versatile object, a thing/medium, demands a theoretical grasp on the phenomenon.

The theory of what the theoretical console compels us to *do*, as Damisch would have it, goes as follows. We wonder what the status of its thing-ness, object-ness, or medium-ness really is. The answer to this question theorizes what a console is. As a console it hovers between three things. It is a material object: the device we hold in our hands. It is also a screen we look *at* as well as *through*, and it is a screen we touch. And thirdly, it is an interface utility, at once an invisible and visible platform – a machine for output of the applications one can play on it. The DS as versatile object thus puts forward the theoretically complex *consoleness* of screen gadgets as material interfaces. It is up to the analyst to approach the console-object with theoretical flexibility.

4. Urban Screens

I ended the first chapter of this book with an injunction to consider the aesthetic qualities of the moving image as guidelines for the design of spatial arrangements as the scripting of perceptual experience. That general point was meant to connect the everyday mobility of people moving through space to a problematic of mobility as an aesthetic practice of performative visuality. Diachronically, this study builds on both continuities and contrasts between historical moments. In this chapter I look at mobility and vision in this combination of everyday efficacy and aesthetic experience, from the other end of that two-way street: the contemporary transformations of space as it is subject to new technologies and media. In terms of the integration of everyday technology and aesthetic experience, it is, moreover, noticeable that mobility receives a different status when it is no longer the subject's doing. When driving on highways, for example, or navigating the screen of a handheld gadget, the subject is to an extent in charge of his own mobility. But this becomes a different experience when the movement comes from the environment to the multi-paced pedestrian, who is distracted or focused, rushed or relaxed. I examine the presence of screens in public spaces, particularly in cities, to understand how these screens function and what they do; how they make hitherto stable architecture mobile, rendering the city-user a participant rather than an initiator of mobility; and how they compel an aesthetic experience infused into the everyday.

Places of Transit

Urban spaces are places of transit of the kind mentioned in Chapter 1, or, as Marc Augé paradoxically calls them, *non-places* that are characteristic of supermodernity and radically different from the spaces of modernity:

> [...] supermodernity produces non-places, meaning spaces which are not themselves anthropological places and which, unlike Baudelairian modernity, do not integrate the earlier places: instead these are listed, classified, promoted to the status of places of "memory", and assigned to a circumscribed and specific position. A world where [...] a dense network of means of transport which are also inhabited spaces is developing; [...] a world thus surrendered to solitary individuality, to the fleeting, the temporary and ephemeral [...]. (1995: 28)

These places are characterized by transience, the preponderance of mobility as Tim Cresswell summarizes. (2004: 45) Generic places of transit, non-places are thus both non-specific (not having "a circumscribed and specific position") and only temporarily inhabited. In calling them non-places, Augé implies that (permanent) residency is a defining feature of 'real' places. These non-places, of which airports, railway stations and bus stations, supermarkets and hotel lounges are the most frequently cited examples, presuppose travel and therefore movement, ephemerality and change. Augé's term is paradoxical because he defines such spaces in the negative, which turns them into the opposite of a spatial category. It is perhaps because of this paradox that his term is often understood to be based on a polarized difference between places and non-places, while in fact, Augé points out that the demarcation between these categories is problematic. As Peter Merriman states:

> Place and non-place are always relational, contingent and continually folded into one another, but academics tend to overlook Augé's statements on the rewriting and relationality of these spaces when they point to the proliferation of non-places in the contemporary world [...]. (2004: 149)

It seems that a focus on the specificity of non-places makes their "relationality" to other places less visible or pertinent.

In general, non-places are not only negatively defined but also evaluated as negative. Political scientist Michael Crozier, for example, is critical when he characterizes our contemporary being at non-places as:

> [...] on motorways, at automatic teller machines, in front of one sort of screen or another; always in transit in a theme-park kind of world where all is packaged, homogenized, and ultimately ephemeral. (1999: 625)

Such sweeping critical judgments seem to me to be a bit hasty. They are anchored in a nostalgic negativity that implicitly situates specificity in the historicity of places – a specificity of not only places but also of people's cultural, social and political place within them. The longed-for stability with which such non-places are contrasted comprises hierarchy and stagnation, protection and exclusion. Seen in this way, Augé's non-places can just as easily be idealized as spaces of freedom, encounter and flexible boundaries. By the same token, I am wary of an overly enthusiastic and uncritical embrace of anything modern, moving, and changing for the sake of the possibilities of newness. Neither nostalgia nor a facile endorsement of innovation for its own sake is very productive for a critical understanding of change and mobility.

Instead, I propose to suspend judgment, and seek to understand both the concept of non-places and its referents outside of such evaluative views. While they are indeed inhabited only temporarily and presuppose the mobility of their temporary dwellers who do not own them, I would like to attribute to such places a specificity of their own. Far from being generic, in this chapter I take them as significant, extremely variable, each time different from another. I make this move because I consider the specificity of these places as temporary; not so much non-places, then, but non-times. With this term I want to refer to a qualitative aspect of time to these places – the temporal and temporary character of these places, rather than an absence of time. In contrast, Augé uses the quantitative aspect of time spent in non-places to underscore the importance of these places in our contemporary culture, or *our time*:

> [...] non-places are the real measure of our time; one that could be quantified – with the aid of a few conversions between area, volume, and distance – by totaling all the air, rail and motorway routes, the mobile cabins called "means of transport" (aircraft, trans and road vehicles), the airports and railway stations, hotel chains, leisure parks, large retail outlets, and finally the complex skein of cable and wireless networks that mobilize extraterrestrial space for the purposes of a communication so peculiar that it often puts the individual in contact only with another image of himself. (1995: 79)

This description of a quantity or volume of such spaces also implies a quantity of time spent in them.

In contemporary urban spaces, people move in and out of particular settings, but these settings are themselves also in a constant mobility and a flux of transformation and subject to time. As such, urban mobility is inherently multi-layered. Augé speaks of a double movement – a movement of the traveler supplemented by the "parallel movement of the landscapes which he catches only in partial glimpses, a series of 'snapshots' piled hurriedly into his memory [...]." (1995: 85-86) The mediated image of the 'snapshot' is used as a metaphor for the temporary visual impressions that remain *after*, as a result of, mobility. Visual experience is thus conceived of as the residue of mobility. This layeredness of perception in mobility does help to understand this double movement as the key feature of perception. Moreover, it also illuminates the idea of visual perception as evidence of mobility. Nevertheless, I think the perception of mobility is more central to spatial experience than this idea of after-image alone intimates. More fundamentally, and contrary to the colloquial expression, I suggest that the event of mobility is performative, not so much *taking* but rather *making* place: a making that includes the aesthetic dimension. The specificity of the making of these places as sites of mobility, or places of transit, is central in this chapter.

People surrounded and enveloped by attractions temporally inhabit these places of transit. In fact, their particularly mobile and temporary presence makes the place into a space of spectacle. But in turn, this mobile dwelling makes place into space. Invoking Maurice Merleau-Ponty, de Certeau underscored this distinction between a *physical* and *geometrical* space on the one hand, and practiced place as the experience of *anthropological* space on the other, so as to bring to the attention the practices of *making* place into space and in particular mobility as a means to do so:

> In short, space is a practiced place. Thus the street geometrically defined by urban planning is transformed into a space by walkers. In the same way, an act of reading is the space produced by the practice of a particular place: a written text, i.e., a place constituted by a system of signs. (1984: 117, emphasis in text)

Augé discusses de Certeau's distinction of place and space in light of his conceptualization of place versus non-place. He concludes that, while his own use of *place* is neither symmetrical nor oppositional to de Certeau's *place*, de Certeau's understanding of what we can call a space-producing effect of mobility is pertinent to non-places:

> Travel [...] constructs a fictional relationship between gaze and landscape. And while we use the word "space" to describe the frequentation of places which specifically defines the journey, we should still remember that there are spaces in which the individual feels himself to be a spectator without paying much attention to the spectacle. As if the position of the spectacle were the essence of the spectacle, as if basically the spectator in the position of a spectator were his own spectacle. [...] The traveler's space may thus be the archetype of non-place. (1995: 86, emphasis in text)

In this quote Augé significantly uses the words "fictional" and "spectacle" and thereby hints at the two aspects relevant here, already pointed out in the previous chapter. The first aspect is the coincidence in mobility of a practice, on the part of the spectator, of making and experiencing vision, so that vision is inherently also fiction. The second aspect is the self-referential nature of the spectacle of mobility which makes the experience of being the mobile spectator itself the main attraction. The self-referentiality of the mobile gaze is crucial to the visual regime of navigation, geared as it is towards finding one's way in a visual field starting from the current location of 'you are here'.[1]

The spectacle of mobility thus turns places of transit into transitory spaces – into specific sites where visual events occur, and where the event of mobile spectating produces space. This connection between mobility, the specificity of place, and the at once creative and experiential potential we can attribute to mobility, makes what I have to say here relevant in terms of a certain form of site-specificity, that is, the paradoxical site-specificity of non-places in non-times. This brings in the aesthetic dimension.

Site-specificity, both as a concept and as an art form, has been around from the mid-1970s on. (Kaye 2000; Kwon 2004) Like the notion of performativity, it evolved from a category of art – art conceived and made in relation to its location of display – to an aspect of all art – once exhibited, the artwork cannot help but addressing its site. In a timely study, Anna McCarthy extends the concept of site-specificity to the object of television. (2001) Television, one can say, is a medial version of a non-place, since television sets can be put and found in any generic setting. And yet, McCarthy's work on the site-specificity of television reverses the Augéan paradox of the specificity of non-specificity of non-places, and is thus helpful in my search for a conceptual grasp of the *spacing* of screens. I use this verb here to point to the spatial arrangements of screens, and the spatial effects of screens in public space, as an inherent aspect of their functioning.

McCarthy writes about television in its different (and changing) shapes and sizes: from giant video walls to mini monitors. In this respect, she develops the concept of *ambient* television, a concept that does justice to the diversity of places where we encounter television screens. Television sets have a great heterogeneity in shape, size and function, but they have in common that they are each site-specific. With ambient, McCarthy means the presence of television "in the routine locations we move through when we leave the house" – the public places of transit. (2001: 1) This notion of ambient television underscores both ubiquity and heterogeneity and through this, specificity of place, materiality and use of television screens. The heterogeneity entails both a multiplicity of forms and functions – a multiplicity that is, paradoxically, specific to the medium as its character lies in the diversity of its form, function and place. McCarthy derives from this not a generic but a site-specific property for television.

Because the specificity implied in her notion of ambient television is this paradoxical heterogeneity, I think this approach can be usefully deployed to interrogate the specificity of practices in relation to the omnipresence and diversity of screens in contemporary urban environments – the urban screenspace we inhabit and navigate. This is how I will be able to substantiate my claim for a site-specificity of screens in alleged non-places (and non-times). Therefore, I am particularly interested in McCarthy's conceptual consideration of the heterogeneity of screen practices in public space.

McCarthy's argument rests on a particular interpretation of space. She can only make this claim because space, in her view, is constructed, produced – therefore, constantly in flux. As a consequence, she foregrounds the material situatedness of screens as part of the complex (of) screening operations that *produce* space, instead of being positioned within it. This production is inevitably subject to mutuality. To put it simply: screens construct space at different stages (production, distribution, reception), and in this operation they are dialectically engaged with the sites in which they are situated that, therefore, also produce them (as specific). Screens are part of a place, but are also produced by their place – a place they also construct.

As such, McCarthy's approach to screens in space is invested in mapping practical differences rather than ontological essences of screens as producers of space. This focus on differences is particularly useful if one is concerned with the multiplicity and diversity of screens. That is, I am concerned with how, in our contemporary moment, space is reconfigured by screen media, made more complex and dynamic, and as such positions and configures us as its inhabitants. Bringing together the argument for site-specificity of screens and the multiplicity of screens within these sites, I propose to consider contemporary public spaces of transit – spaces that are infused by screens in different shapes and sizes and that are constructed for travelers – as hybrid screenspaces within which one navigates.

Screenspace

I locate a *spacecificity* of screens in viewing practices and not in isolated properties of screen content, screen technologies or screen uses. I therefore propose to consider these practices as taking place within particular *screen fields* – the larger terrain constituted by different dispositifs, or spatial and pragmatic arrangements of screens, their content – be it screen content as in moving or still images, or software-based *applications* (in the double sense of the word: use and program) – and their spectators, who are also users. Like Pierre Bourdieu's scientists (1999), who are agents within a competitive field, screens participating in screen fields compete with one another for attention and recognition. Yet, also like scientists, they collaborate as well: they reflect each other, they refer to each other, and they complement each other. Hence, like the intellectual community of my work environment, my analytical field – rather than being a singular object – comprises a diversity of screens, the specificity of these screens, and the production of space that this pervasiveness and diversity of screens in public spaces, specifically spaces of transit, constitutes.

Here, I am concerned with multiplicity, scale and arrangements of screens on site, not with any one screen in particular, even if specific installations and functions of screens must be probed in order to understand the way they work. I approach the use of screens in these public places of transit as a *composite dispositif*: an arrangement that consists of many different screens and composes a navigable screenspace for variously distracted and attracted, mobile, and passing spectators. As such, screenspace is a dispositif of hybridity and transformation. Before, I proposed to define screenspace as the hybrid spatiality that consists of on-screen and off-screen spaces that are fused within the movements of navigation. This entailed the effect of moving in physical, off-screen space for the on-screen space of our navigation devices. Here, the perspective is somewhat reversed: the impact of the presence of screens on our sense of physical space is truly hybrid and consists of both on- and off-screen space.

I will first discuss the exemplary Augéan non-place, the airport, in order to draw from that example insight into the way such a dispositif works on the small scale of one institution. Then I will move my focus to a place that is not *a* non-place but, like the airport, is a micro-model of the city as multi-place. In other words, as non-places have metaphorically stood in for (super)modern urban culture, I want to take what we can see in non-places back to the macro version, which is the city. This metaphoric congruence legitimizes jumping from the specificity of non-places to how we can see something structurally similar in the larger field of the city.

Before being (experienced as) a non-place, an international airport such as Schiphol Airport can be seen as an arrangement that facilitates travel, especially by air. To travel to and from Amsterdam by air, one traverses a great many moments of little necessities, all of which are provided for. If one has a sore throat, Schiphol's pharmacy offers relief. Thirst can be quenched, tired legs rested on benches and chairs, long distances traversed rapidly thanks to the electronically powered moving walkways, and the escalators and elevators are helpful for traveling from one floor to the next. A farewell postcard can be bought, postage stamps purchased for it, then it can be mailed; even those who suddenly feel a craving to document their trip on video will find the electronics store right there. Suitcases, and clothes for the different climate one is soon facing; toys for the children left in care; newspapers and paperback books to suspend the time (and boredom) of the journey. Yet, along with this abundance, this place is also highly regulated: space is divided and controlled, and travelers are constantly monitored, guided, stopped, confined and herded. Put together, all these stores, venues, facilities and regulatory operations condense the different aspects of what it means to travel.

In this jumble of facilities and restrictions, screens take an important place. While traversing the airport, one encounters many moments of choice, selection, admission, guidance and refusal, and the screens are there to help make such decisions. Passing the screens of customs and security, at every turn there is a screen stating which flight takes off from which gate, and when boarding starts for each flight, while other screens show the time it takes to walk there. Taken together, all these elements cohere in the visual regime of navigation so typical for non-places of transit: while each element in a composite dispositif has its own function, they also work together. Navigation in airports entails looking where to go, finding the right gate, taking in clues about times and places, directions and speeds – always alert and searching, having departed but not yet arrived. In my conceptual network, a composite dispositif is indispensable, in combination with mobility – here, of institutionalized and regulated travel – and heterogeneity is indispensable, but it is also inflected. It is in the diachronic and comparative sense discussed in the introduction to this book that I bring the concept of the composite dispositif to bear on the variegated screenspace of airports and other hubs of travel. The specificity of these spaces is that they operate much like a machine: each part or segment has its own function (waiting areas, security sections, shops, restaurants), and has its own screens, but these parts work together as well – these composite spaces process mobility, so to speak.

In *On the Move* (2006), his very insightful account of the multifacetedness and diversity of modern-day mobility, cultural geographer Tim Cresswell concludes with a thorough analysis of Schiphol Airport, providing a rich cartography of the way "architecture, information technology, and signs form a seamless machine with each operating in coordination with each other." For this analysis he discerns a difference between movement and meaningful mobility, which he discusses in a series of essays ranging from photography, dance, the Suffragette movement, to airport spaces. (2006: 247) Moreover, as a popular metaphor for the modern urbanity, this airport-machine functions as a public space, a "miniaturized city", as Iain Chambers sees it, or a "simulated metropolis". (1990: 57-58; quoted in Cresswell, 221)

I do not believe that the microcosm Creswell describes is entirely seamless. Instead, the screens in their multiple but different places are the seams, both interrupting and stitching space together, especially screens displaying departure and arrival information, and instructions for navigating through the airport. And as for Chambers' view, I think it is more useful to reverse the metaphor. The airport is not a miniature city but rather a model for it – an ideal. The city is perhaps also a complex system comprised of parts, presence and traffic. But it is not machine-like in the sense of being primarily oriented at 'processing' this traffic, like an airport does: a 'city' with a *spacecific* purpose.

While allegedly a non-place and, as I suggest, a non-time, Schiphol is both geographically severely delimited and in its temporality, equally severely regulated. If anything goes wrong with the time and place specificity, the schedule collapses, air traffic is halted, and travelers are sleeping on their suitcases, utterly frustrated, and desperate to go home. For air traffic to work, the shops and post offices are dispensable, but what cannot be discarded with impunity are the many screens, some small and discreet, some huge and hard to overlook. Moreover, such ephemeral places of transit constantly change and would, indeed, lose their meaning if they were made stable. My claim, however, goes further than this observation about particular places of transit. My aim is not so much to analyze places of transit themselves, or the role of mobility as such, but rather the way screens operate within them and produce space, or better: *space mobility*. For this analysis, I wish to consider the larger urban public space as a screen field – a field characterized by even more diverse mobilities, forms of transience, and the public anonymity of modern urban culture. As Augé, Cresswell and many others have pointed out, it is of this culture that non-places have become metaphoric models.

Everyday life in cities is increasingly qualified by visual interactions with screens, not only inside, in movie theaters or television and computer screens, but also outside, on streets and buildings, the surfaces of urban space. The urban environment is a screenspace that merges virtual and physical mobility within a realm of mobility and transformation. Therefore, in the following I will reverse the relation between the non-place model and screen fields again and consider how urban space, much like places of transit, has become a screenspace that can be situated somewhere between private and public, inside and outside, present and absent, then and now.

Urban Transformation

It is a commonplace to say that urban life – like contemporary culture at large – is in constant transformation. What I mean by this phrase is something that plays itself out on the large scale of cityscapes as well as the small scale of individual experiences; less the transformation of ever-greater technological innovation than that brought about by specific technological interventions. Emblematic of urban transformation, in the double sense of cities transforming and dwellers or visitors being transformed in the process, is the way architecture, hitherto experienced as relatively stable, has taken to moving. I am referring to the ephemeral architecture of so-called transparent media façades. Transparent screen surfaces comprised of LED technology cover windows or walls of large buildings and allow for constantly changing images and projections. As far as the eye can reach, large buildings change into gigantic screens and show us the result of often commercial and sometimes creative, interactive or reactive programming. These moving-image façades dematerialize the large and stable skylines of our familiar cityscapes by changing static structures of architecture into an entanglement of surfaces of moving images.

The project The Artvertiser by artist Julian Oliver is worth mentioning here, because it deals with the critique of the pervasive occupation of our visual spaces with advertising, colonizing our visual cortex by these images in public space and the possibility to reclaim this visual space for artistic and creative expression. Through the artist's use of augmented reality (which he calls "improved reality") technology, participants can upload alternative content, which is visually overlaid on the billboards and screens that offer commercial content, and can be viewed using a viewing device. In this way, we can hack, or better, squat this colonized public space.[2]

I now consider the phenomenal, experiential and semiotic ins and outs of this phenomenon. The observation of public places of transit such as Schiphol Airport can be extended to the larger urban arena, which can also be considered a place of and in transit. Moreover, while screens in urban space are often related to traditional screens (television and cinema, for example), I think it is more adequate to take into consideration the way they operate in what I have called a composite dispositif. This concept compels attention to the ways screens operate within this larger field. Because the way screens *space* mobility, the spatial operations are at stake here. I see these in the way they produce demarcations of and within that space in terms of domain – between public and private, large and small, individual and networked. They also produce these in terms of demarcation – between inside and outside, real and virtual – and in terms of their programming or curating, in terms of responsiveness and interactivity.[3]

Fig. 4.1: The Artvertiser (Julian Oliver, 2008). Photo: Julian Oliver

The KPN Communication Tower in Rotterdam is a medium in the true sense, as one side of the skyscraper-like building is covered with large monochrome LED 'pixels' used for monochrome texts and animations. Because it creates stylized moving images that cover an entire façade, the *scale* of the screen-façade is challenging: the changing, moving image occupies the entire surface of the building. The sheer size of façades such as these and the resulting prominent covering of buildings allow for a powerful programming of all sorts, ranging from commercial imagery to artistic explorations of interactive possibilities of digital screening. A good example of artistic use of the screen space of the KPN tower is the text and animation installation *Scream* (2006, now part of the KPN Communication Tower animation collection) by artists Karin Lancel and Hermen Maat. In their own words: "Inspired by Edvard Munch we digitalized his screaming man. Visible all over Rotterdam, on the façade of the KPN communication building, his desperate man is looping, haunting the city."[4]

These possibilities for urban screening have come to the attention of architects, media scholars, and other people curious about transformations in urban life, and has thus been added to the agenda of conferences, festivals and other happenings. In 2008, the Media Façades Festival in Berlin artistically and critically explored the contents of media buildings and digital images in public space, which, according to the organizers' statement on the website, "should follow urban necessities," and therefore they "aim to transform the growing number of digital architectural surfaces in our cities into an experimental visual zone on the threshold of virtual and urban public space, contributing to a livable urban society." Their mission statement underscores how the growing number of urban screens not only changes the look of the city, but, more importantly, contribute to a fundamental transformation of the urban experience.[5]

Fig. 4.2: Scream (Karen Lancel & Hermen Maat, 2006) text and animation for the KPN Communication Tower in Rotterdam. Photo: Karin Lancel & Hermen Maat, 2006

While their geneaology can be traced to the advent of the use of electricity in public advertisement in the early twentieth century, or even before, to the arcades of the nineteenth century, media façades that function as large, permanent architectural screens are currently a rapidly growing phenomenon in metropoles – or rather, cosmopoles – around the world. They are part of an extremely varied presence of multi-media in public space. In view of my methodological interest as explained in Chapter 2, I focus the discussion here in particular on self-reflexive screens: on the way screens on site not only transform urban space, but also how they are involved in and comment on screening practices that often have transformation and movement *of* and *within* urban space as their subject. I zoom in on how these screens space mobility or, to be more precise, how screens produce a sense of space that incorporates this double-sided aspect of mobility.[6]

Moreover, screens on site – outdoors and in public spaces – can be considered as architectural elements because of the way they espouse architectural form while transforming it. They embody the specific kind of mobility I analyze here because of their ubiquity and pervasiveness. They are embedded or built-in in constructed spaces, but also open up, make flexible what would otherwise be static, material structures. As screens become integrated in our physical environments, they contribute to an almost literal blending of material and virtual spaces.

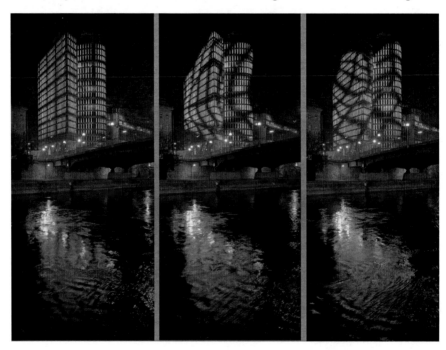

Fig. 4.3: Twists and Turns *(Mader, Stublic, Wiermann, 2007) on the LED façade, Uniqa Tower, Vienna. Photo: Hervé Massard, 2007*

Several terms have been proposed for conceptualizing these gigantic screens. With reference to Paul Virilio, Scott McQuire (2006) calls this phenomenon of screens as architectural surfaces a *dematerialization of architecture*, which recalls Marcos Novak's terminology of *liquid architecture* (1990). Both these concepts attempt to grasp the way material architecture is influenced and transformed by

MOBILE SCREENS

moving images and digital technologies. In a similar vein, Deleuzian spatial concepts such as the rhizome and the fold, smooth versus striated space, and the notion of becoming have inspired thinking about architecture, in particular architecture not based on order and repetition, but on uncertainties and difference. (Marcussen 2008)

These terms are expressions of an interest in transformations of urban space and the role of media technologies in this process of transformation. Visually, the terms make sense. Here is a good example. With the light installation *Twists and Turns* on the media façade of the Uniqa Tower in Vienna, artists Holger Mader, Alexander Stublic and Heike Wiermann morph this rigid tower into a flexible and transforming structure – a time-based structure rather than one based on spatial fixity. At night the silhouette of the tower becomes invisible and the changing lights seem to bring motion to the building.[7]

This transformation is, again, both new and old, and thus historical. Rivaling the effect of sunlight, the installation's oldness brings to mind the solar furnace of Odeillo in the French Pyrenees built thirty-six years ago, long before our LED-screen façades became such a ubiquitous phenomenon. There, a gigantic concave mirror similarly transforms the architecture of the building, making it look unstable, as if collapsing under its own weight. More recently, the furnace has been filmed and the result mounted as an installation in an art exhibition by Belgian artist Ann Veronica Janssens, with the title *Odeillo* (2008).[8]

Figure 4.4: *Solar Furnace at Odeillo. Photo: Ann Veronica Janssens, 2008*

Ironically, the installation at Odeillo captures natural light in order to save energy, while the urban screens are entirely man-made and use large amounts of energy. Another difference is more directly related to my inquiry. Although the solar furnace also changes in the course of the day and in response to the movement of sunlight, and, similar to the Uniqa tower, also transforms the architecture, it is not itself in movement. Nor is the huge mirror an urban screen in terms of the site-specificity of the city, as well as of the specificity of the passing pedestrian as spectator. It is not an urban screen, and not even in the city. Yet, this example, one that predates more contemporary architectural projects for sustainable buildings, suggests loudly that screen façades can also include façades that work like screens in the sense of capturing and redistributing light, making movement, and playing with optical effects.

What we are dealing with in cases of these dynamic façades is a transformation of the urban space through elements of architecture that radiates precisely this transforming power. McQuire gives the contemporary hybrid urban spaces the name *media cities* or *media architecture complex* (2008; 2009). With these terms he refers to spaces with screens as an integral part of architectural structures. These are mixed spaces of media space and urban space. This mixture, I contend, is based on a bidirectional movement that has consequences for social life in public spaces. Taking the impact of pervasive media technologies, connectivity and communication into account, as well as the multiple modes of urban mobility, we can perhaps speak of a *mobile sphere*. This would be a domain between private and public, and infringing upon both. It is characterized by mobility, hybridity and a networked connectivity. In this constellation, individuality – central to the private domain – and communality and exchange – central to the public sphere in a Habermasian sense – are negotiated. These are sometimes in conflict, or they are layered or even disconnected (Habermas 1989 [1962]).

McQuire converses with numerous contemporary scholars whose interest stems from the observation that public space is undergoing transformation in terms of architecture, social structures, modes of mobility and communication. This transformation is manifest in mobile media platforms such as cell phones, portable media players, game consoles or navigation devices in our hands; large public screens, media façades or integrated screens on our architectural surfaces; and a ubiquity of smaller screens and moving billboards. Collectively, they provide a range of screen phenomena that color, permeate and even shape the streets; in short, they transform them. A dominant focus on urban screens looks at their role in the transformation of public space, specifically the political implications of the migration of screens from the private to the public realm.[9]

We can see in this transformation a further commercialization of public space. This being true, we can still wonder why commercial thinking in particular would lead to this specific transformation. The mode in which commerce is realized stems from, and yields reflections on spatiality, mediality and urbanity as much as it taps into the practice of acquiring more customers and increasing consumer addiction. My concern here is not to evaluate commercial rhetoric in urban space, or on urban screens, but rather to examine what ads, art, and archives have in common when we consider that they – literally – share the same screens and the same space.

Of all the alternative angles that could be brought to bear on this transformation, I single out the aesthetic dimension. In this respect, I take my lead from Mirjam Struppek. Complementing the pervasive thinking along the lines of commercialization in discourse on urban screens, Struppek asks how the use of commercial screens can be "culturally curated", using a terminology of artistic practice. With her interest in urban screens she investigates the possible use of digital display technologies for alternative, critical and reflexive content. She considers the urban screens as an "experimental visualization zone on the threshold of virtual and urban public space" (2006: 2).

When taken at face value, the idea of cultural curating seems to be too limited to the analogy with art practice. However, the term is valuable in that it draws attention to the notion that there is inevitably someone who performs these transformations; agency can be neither ignored nor simplified. Moreover, the term also underscores the issue that in the age of participatory culture we have to explore precisely the *nature* of agency: its layeredness, multidirectionality and ambiguity. In short, and paradoxically, I wish to argue that agency is not personal. I return to this issue in the next chapter, where I develop a conceptualization of interactivity as performativity. This also works at the level of interface, not as a machinic processing of input or a communication model of action-response, but as a multi-layered performativity of user, interface and the spaces within which this takes place.

These two complementary views are both important to keep in mind. The overall transformation of public space by screens, for whatever concrete purpose such as commercialization, can be seen against the backdrop of artistic intervention, with the cultural curating of screen content. For this dual reason I endorse the notion that screens in the city transform urban space fundamentally, not superficially. I consider this not so much in terms of social change or a deterioration of public space, however. Instead, I think the transformation primarily concerns a change in cultural practice: a practice where sense experience meets the political of public space in a mobile sphere. And if we recall the etymology of the term *aesthetic* as engagement through the senses (Baumgarten 1970 [1758; 1759]), reckoning with this dimension but not in isolation, is a prerequisite to fully understanding what happens through urban screens.

Screen Practices

The impact of screens in the street can be seen on two interrelated dimensions. Firstly, the screens influence spatial and temporal aspects of mobility. Screens of moving images modify the relationship between the passing individual and the hitherto static structures of urban space. This impact concerns a double movement on two levels, both physical and virtual. As a result, secondly, the screens displace and unhinge previous markers of separation. Walls are no longer walls; beginning and end of available space no longer coincide with visual space. This results in a merging of domains. What we see is a dialectic whole of physical and virtual spaces that have no fixed boundaries, neither between the two categories nor among themselves.

Fig. 4.5: *Video installation Parallel Library by Rob Johannesma at the Special Collections of the University Library on Oude Turfmarkt, Amsterdam. Photo: Nanna Verhoeff, 2008*

Take the screen/window façade of the then-newly renovated building of the library of the University of Amsterdam for the Special Collections division. On the second floor of the building, screens replace two rows of three windows each, forming a rectangular screen space amidst ordinary windows. On the screens we see abstract figures, in a dazzling play of light and colors from a collage of shots of old manuscripts, taking passers-by by surprise and making them stop in their tracks. The light comes from the inside. It gives the illusion we are looking through the windows, instead of into the building. We look at a virtual 'outside'. This simple example already demonstrates several aspects of the new urban screenspace. But the term *virtual* is not quite adequate to describe what happens here.

On the whole, the work of artist Rob Johannesma shows a preoccupation with landscapes and the medium of photography and video, used to provide experiences rather than depictions of landscapes. In an earlier installation, *Inkijk #3* [Looking In #3] Johannesma used moving images of congealed sulfur made from a still slide of a location in Wyoming and projected them on the windows of a small house in the Netherlands. Like the video on the library windows, the artist used abstract details from a still image that are made dynamic. Not only does the installation suggest movement, but the positions of the screens also create a dynamic and layered mobility.[10]

The mobility evoked by the *Parallel Library* installation is layered. First, inside and outside are no longer clearly distinguished; they appear to be reversed. This installation offers a reflection on that simple, seemingly self-evident spatial principle on which so much of our physical orientation and subsequent sense of security is based. This makes the screen self-reflexive, offering reflection on what we don't reflect on because it is too obvious, too 'naturalized'. Second, through this reversal, the installation plays with the conceptual metaphor of the screen as window. It is a window, but it also replaces the window; it is a non-seethrough window, a simulacrum of what it appears to be. Yet, it also reflects, or better: inverses the working of a mirror. Where (interactive) screens in public space are said to reflect, like mirrors, life on the streets before them, these windows-screens display the collection behind them as if they were reversed mirrors or prisms. This work invokes the observation by J. David Bolter and Diane Gromala who point out in their work on digital art: "[...] media and their forms oscillate between being invisible and visible – between being windows and mirrors." (2003: 34)

Third, this uncertainty questions the very notion of public space. The view is outside, but it is also the territorial property of an agent. Thus, the simple loosening of what we tend to take for granted tampers with the foundations of urban, spatial and visual modes of being. This makes the windows attractive as a potential fiction. At the same time, the attraction is extended to the objects the library harbors. This converges with the museal quality of the collection and the (inherently) commercial aspect of display – it is also, simply, an ad. At the same time it is a display window, and thus subject to curating. Note here the similarity between window-dressing and curating. What we see in it is, however, not the collection of objects – the special, old and precious books and manuscripts – but a stylized representation of it that, in fact, consists of details of manuscripts blown up, augmented to abstract proportions – much like the details of the Wyoming excerpt from nature in Johannesma's earlier installation.

The putting into motion of still details can be considered an ephemeral and animated archival gesture. This is what Kaja Silverman focuses on in her analysis of James Coleman's reworking of Leonardo da Vinci's mural *The Last Supper*. In his own words, Coleman offers an "ephemeral memorial" of Leonardo da Vinci's work in a large screen-based installation at the Louvre. As Silverman observes, unlike a conventional archive lifting objects "out of time and making them part of a synchronic system", Coleman actually "provides a space in which a series of images could emerge and disappear." (2009: 139) This archival mobility, repurposing images in a new context, is a significant recurring trope in moving-image installations. The animated display that screens afford is self-reflexively used for transporting, enlarging and depicting in a new light, bits and pieces of our cultural archive. The operations of such screens are the recontextualization, enlargement and animation of the old, the small or the invisible.[11]

Johannesma's installation of the window of the library offers more than a light game. It says something, and it also does something. The simulacrum of a window is not a window, although it says that it is one; instead, it 'does' window. Self-reflexively, it states its own fictionality, and through that statement moves the passerby to live by this uncertain, ambiguous space. There – in moving people to accept the substitution of a real window by a virtual one – lies its performativity. The performativity of screens, as such, points to a self-reflexive gesture of screen practices. Part of what the screens reflect on is their status in the urban setting; their existence as installations. It seems relevant that the window brings together not only inside and outside, and transparency and simulacrum, but also old and new: the reference to and reflection on old manuscripts, precious material things, by means of light alone. This brings me back to the other end of the diachronic slice of the twentieth century.

Installation

In September 2010, EYE Film Institute Netherlands launched the program *Zoomscape*, an exhibition about film, trains and perception. The program took place on platform 2A at Amsterdam Central Station. It consisted of train films from all periods in film history, presented in a program leaflet that listed 'departure' times and film titles as destinations in a train schedule. Early cinema held a distinct and prominent place in the program as one of the four categories included: fiction, experimental, documentary, and silent film. Interspersed with other, later films, early cinema also had its own separate schedule in the program, announced as a "compilation of the archive" with more than twenty titles, ranging from *Arrivé d'un train à La Ciotat* (1895, Lumière), *Conway Castle* (1898, AM&B), *Irish Mail* (American Mutoscope and Biograph, 1898), and bits from the EYE Film Institute's collection of unidentified fragments, *Bits & Pieces*, to *Dans les Pyrénées* (unidentified, 1913) or *A Railroad Wooing* (Kalem, 1913). In Chapter 2, I have discussed some of these train films in light of the self-reflexive gesture in this trope of mobility in early cinema.[12]

Thematically, the program is positioned by the institute as zooming in on the travel trope inherent in the cinematic experience, so that the location is overdetermined by the content of the installation. Or in the curators' words:

> Trains and films go hand-in-hand. When the first trains chugged up to speed around 1835 they changed the way we experience reality. The world became a moving image, the carriage windows an imaginary film screen which new horizons passed by on.[13]

The curators took their inspiration for the title of the exhibition from Mitchell Schwarzer's 2004 book on architecture and the moving image with the same title. The poetic words written on the wall in the exhibition space underscore this thematic ambition:

> Enter a machine that spins out movement, mile after mile.
> Gaze through the window at objects rushing by, out of sync with your body
> Pieces of the landscape move at different speeds
> The foreground is blurred and the background looks like an outline
> Houses and whole cities roll, break apart and recombine
> The world becomes a torrent of images
> The machine eye of Zoomscape burns through space revealing that
> which is usually unseen
> It crosses forbidden thresholds, glimpses private lives
> Encounters feel all the more delightful for their lack of substance
> You can go to places you never dreamed of going
> You are there for the ride

Above I have mentioned the intricate bond between the cinema, as technology of vision, and the train as modern technology of transportation. Congruent to both machines is that the visuality they afford is one of movement and transport, physical movement in the case of the train, and virtual in the optical illusion of moving images of the cinema. The novelty of the moving image and the sensationalism of mechanized travel provided a powerful combination of expanded vision and speed. In this sense, the *Zoomscape* program is not only about train travel; it is about cinema as a medium of virtual transport.

Moreover, I consider this exhibition, its program, and its installation as a historical event. Not because of its monumental status – which it did have, in both senses of the word – but because of its meaning as event both *in* and *about* history. In *Zoomscape*, the historical films are relocated from the cinema (and archival) context to a context of mobility and temporary presence – the station today as a place of transit – and thus do today what they did then. Screening them in this particular location accentuates the key feature of the moving image. These films do what they say: showing transport while doing transport; in moving – as moving images – they move people. Their installation at the train station drives this point home.

Fig. 4.6: Zoomscape installation at Amsterdam Central Station. Photo: Maureen Mens, 2010

Central in the construction of media as a travel machine is, then, the screen. Even if it can represent a temporal mediation, the screen is always also a spatial object, a tool for, but also part of spatial transgression, of mobility. The screen makes both the time of experience and diegetic time into something *spatial* – indeed, it is the locus of that transformation. And with that term 'locus' it draws attention to the point of installation – in situ, site-specific, and in the historical layeredness of the city, also bi-polar in its diachronicity.

As my remarks on the attraction effect of the ride films in Chapter 2 suggest, films were shown in context in early cinema as well. The exhibition format of Hale's Tours is an oft-mentioned example of a traveling exhibition format that reflexively projected cinematic images in a set-up imitating a train compartment. When film was still predominantly a traveling medium and shows were held in temporary locations, the programs often included local views and possibly local people on screen. News event films or *actualités* also provided a strong deictic anchor between the viewer within his/her locative and temporal context and the image on screen. I speculate that these images even framed the other attractions on the screen with an emphatic 'here' and 'now' in their address of the spectator as 'you' and, even if by extension and only as a possibility in most cases, an 'I' as the spectator's cinematic other. The difference of location-based screening then and now is, perhaps, first and foremost the deictic complication of time, as in the case of these archival films. But contemporary screenings can also make use of this deictic aspect.[14]

Fig. 4.7 Hale's Tours exhibition (unidentified photograph, ca. 1906)

I insist on the status of these manifestations as installations to account for their site- and time-specificity in the contemporary city. The space of the frame, established by the deixis of the image, is extended by the space of the screen. In terms of dispositif, the one is encapsulated within the other; the virtual space on screen is *framed* by the external space of the screen. In the case of *Zoomscape*, we see how images of vehicular mobility or train travel is taken up within a cinematic dispositif of virtual mobility, and then thematically positioned within a (contemporary) dispositif of mobility – the metropolitan train station as place of transit *par excellence*. This extends space by adding this layered mobility. Incidentally, the installation recalls the specific spatiality of the alleged non-places of which stations are the emblematic early examples and airports the contemporary ones. Rather than being negatively defined, the station now becomes overdetermined as a historically layered space.

Fig. 4.8: Zoomscape. Photo: Bert Kommerij, 2010

When we look at the spatial arrangement of the installation, we notice the two-sided screen with train benches within an otherwise open space surrounding the screen, which allows people to walk freely around in the space. The open door has an inviting announcement addressing the passerby/spectator in inclusive words: "we are open" and "free entry." You/I can come in. "You are there for the ride" say the words written on the wall. The platform with arriving and departing trains in the background is the entrance and exit to the space. The location as site of installation, as well as its spatial arrangement, emphasize the dialectic of medium and location specific to location-based screening. At the point of arriving and leaving, people can stop in their tracks and linger for a while in this space of virtual transport. The presence of the passing spectator is both positioned 'here' within the image of the ride films and 'here' as visitor of the exhibition space, in spatial relationship to the screen.

It is because of this deictically layered quality of the situation that I speak of 'installation', rather than 'exhibition'. The latter term suggests one-directionality of presenting material to a recipient audience that is itself outside of the display.

Moreover, exhibition is unspecific, while installation, in contrast, suggests location-specificity and the making of meaning through performativity. An installation is activating; 'screening' is, there, not a noun but a verb. Finally, an installation constitutes one 'work', while an exhibition compresses many different works into a single entity. Hence, the term 'installation' is also meant to unify the event.

The setup of the screen in the space at the station, in Zoomscape, proposes a deictic operation outside of the frame of the cinematic image. The presence within the space is visible, if only because of the daylight coming in. People can walk around and even view the screens from both sides. The dispositif of the installation is there to visit, a space to walk around in, emphasizing the spatiality of the dispositif as such. The screening of the films is spatially arranged and the screens are literally 'installed' within the space. This fact of installation, in the strong, artistic as well as the more casual sense of the word, self-reflexively foregrounds the fact that the screening is a performance in a specific location, at a specific time, in the presence of spectators who are addressed and compelled to respond. The space where the films are shown is the site where the installation, literally, takes place. Moreover, the presence of the compilation program invites multiple perspectives. The archival footage, old images in a lively context of urban space where people pass through and possibly stay and sit for a while, creates a sensory domain of temporary presence. This, again, is a situation of installation rather than of exhibition.

Another example of contemporary screening of old films in new contexts is the installation Silent Films, curated by Jennifer Peterson. This was a three-channel (digital) installation of early nonfiction films at The Lab at Belmar in Lakewood, Colorado in 2008. Three screens with images projected from the rear were hanging at about eye level in an otherwise dark and empty space. They ran three separate programs of early nonfiction films – travel images, portraits, and industrial/labor imagery – from the collections of EYE, the Library of Congress, George Eastman House, and the British Film Institute (BFI). Each program ran a slightly different length, so that as the programs looped continuously throughout the day, they were always in different synchronization. Many viewers described the pleasure of the installation to the curator as a puzzle of making associations between the three different images.

This installation is another example of how the medium reflexivity of early cinema can return in contemporary screening practices, at the level of compilation (selecting and combining images), relocation (bringing the screen to new spatial contexts) and installation (spatial arrangement of the screen). The multiple screens looping compilations of films in this installation invoke the fragmentation of early cinema's film programs, by reframing this fragmentation in a culture of "re-using and re-interpreting historical cultural objects," as it was put by the curator in the program leaflet. It is a diachronic gesture, this installation; it not only brings the archival object to a new place of exhibition but also reframes the cultural viewing context of the black box as a site for popular culture to the white-cube gallery space – the conventional space for art. This is a self-reflexive move, even if I use the term 'popular culture' anachronistically, considering that, at the time of its making, the motivation for making this travel imagery was part of attempts to elevate the cultural status of the medium.

Contemporary installations integrate a thematic resonance in the choices made in the selection and compilation of the images, the specific location within which they are shown and the spatial setup of the screen(s): their *spacecificity*. My examples here converge in demonstrating that installation makes for a performative situation. And, as I now wish to put forward, the performativity of these situations requires deixis. Alison Butler suggests as much when she makes use of the specific notion of deixis in theatrical performance to describe film and video screening in gallery spaces as a *theatricalization*:

> The defining role of deixis in theatre arises from the fact that performances, unlike films, actualize meaning in relation to concrete spatiotemporal contexts shared with their audiences. To describe gallery films as deictic in a theatrical sense, then, is to suggest that the "theatricalization" of film in the gallery complicates spectatorship, dividing attention between screen space and screening space and subjecting the spectator's qualified belief in the cinematic illusion to continual – spatial, temporal and discursive – modulation. (2010: 311)

The complication of spectatorship is precisely what makes these appropriate for self-reflexive statements. The selection, relocation and subsequent installation of (archival) early films is a deictic operation. Placing screens for a performative event, then, entails the installation of deixis.

Whether historical resonance and wonder (Greenblatt 1991) or recognition and excess (Casetti 2009) dominate film experience in these exhibition formats, a similar dual structure makes those experiences possible. This is the dualism of the I/you structure. The spectator is hailed by means of deictic address, while simultaneously being given the opportunity to save herself by shrinking back when the train rushes by. The contemporary screening of archival films is not a nostalgic practice of showing images of the past in new context, but it is one that departs from performativity, as a profound present and presence of pastness.

In the age of digitization, the index as a trace of pastness has been endowed with a specifically nostalgic imago, in particular in the case of the photographic image. Due to the alleged ontological loss of indexicality with digital photography, the photograph no longer functions as visual evidence – or perhaps better, we have lost faith in it. But instead of deploring or celebrating this difference between analogue and digital, I prefer to stay with the semiotic working of the index as sign in the making of meaning.

To understand the nature of this semiotic functioning of indexicality (or the indexicality of semiosis), we can look again to the distinction proposed by Mary-Ann Doane, presented in Chapter 2. As I mentioned briefly there, Doane brings together two very different characteristics of the index that we can discern in Charles S. Peirce's writing on the index: the deictic directionality and the temporality of the index as trace. She problematizes the issue of authenticity by proposing a dialectics of these two sides to indexicality: the implied temporality of the index as imprint (what Barthes calls the "this-has-been" of photography) and as indicator: "look here." This indication has a very forceful presence, if not present. In Peirce's own words:

[T]he sign signifies its object solely by virtue of being really connected with it. Of this nature are all natural signs and physical symptoms. I call such a sign an index, a pointing finger being the type of the class. The index asserts nothing; it only says "There!" It takes hold of our eyes, as it were, and forcibly directs them to a particular object, and there it stops. Demonstrative and relative pronouns are nearly pure indices, because they denote things without describing them [...]. (1885: 181)

I seek to implement the temporal aspect of that distinction in the consideration of indexicality as trace, on the one hand, and deixis on the other, in semiotic rather than ontological terms. The trace is a sign of pastness from which the present cannot disentangle itself. The analogue photograph of an object that was once before the lens would be a prime instance of such a trace. Deixis signifies the situatedness of the image in the present of its emergence. The 'here' in 'here was the object' of the photograph – the here which positions the spectator in relation to the image. This is the here that constitutes presence and positions relationality.

The trace and deixis are not mutually exclusive but operate dialectically, framing the present and presence of the image. Working together, however, they unhinge the pastness as an absolute: the situatedness of the image in its emergence is shifted to the situatedness of its presence. The pastness the trace carries is carried over into a bond with the present moment. This is why history remains important: the past is not detached from the present but, bound to it by deixis, informs and intensifies it. In light of navigation, I have called this bond between trace and deixis a 'destination-index', a trace towards the future. But perhaps it is a two-way trace: one that inscribes in our present moment of experience a double temporality.

Alison Butler (2010) points out via Warren Buckland (2000: 68-70) how deixis is brought to the fore in screening as a live *event*. According to Butler, this in particularly clear in the case of site-specific screenings of films:

In the conventionalized setting of the cinema the deictic potential of the cinematic image is minimized, but once prised from its institutional home the

cinematic image discloses "its brazen link with the local and the distant."
(310)

Bringing together the trace in deixis is the historical act of *Zoomscape*. The distinction between the index from the past – the trace – and the index in the present – deixis – is mobilized and its two temporalities are brought in touch with each other whenever the archival or historical becomes an experience in the present. This temporal deixis points to a time with which we have some sort of continuity.

In designing this presentation of the museum's archive in the city's public space, the programmers of *Zoomscape* clearly sought to do something more specific than the general goal of drawing attention to their archive in a larger public space by exhibiting and reframing the collection for the sake of archival visibility alone. They focused their program specifically on films from early cinema that, more than simply being in the movement of the then-new moving image, thematically *represent* movement. This is not simply a topic chosen among many equivalent options. Transportation, as I have argued, is not only a main preoccupation of many early films in terms of thematic content, nor a simple congruence between the moving image and the movement of people, but also a characteristic of the culture of early cinema as such. Both location specificity (the meaning of place) and mobility (movement and the trope of transformation) are also primary preoccupations of today's visual culture. It is this dual track, so to speak, at the intersection of transportation and transformation, that has led me to look at early cinema in the *Zoomscape* film program and its location at a railway station as a structural, rather than only a thematic doubling. The focus on the past is, then, as much a focus on the present. The two cultures meet in the common interest of the two eras in the locomotivity so omnipresent in the two moments.

Programming Hybridity

This temporal bi-polarity brings us back to Johannesma's virtual antiquities in the library window. That example self-reflexively addresses the space-making aspect of screens, specifically with respect to domain, through raising a primary question: 'what is inside and outside?'. The very act of asking this question unhinges a primary distinction between real and virtual, fact and fiction. The installation, a simple ersatz window, performatively does this in the space itself, which is why it must be seen as an installation and not simply an artwork.

Lev Manovich (2006) conceptualizes the uncertainty or mixing of space as *augmented space*, a physical space that is overlain with layers of data. The word *augmentation* emphasizes the extension of space, the 'becoming more' by the use of media technologies. This presupposes a stable essence of something to which a supplement is being added. This brings into tension a sensitivity to the layeredness of space with a fixation of that same space in terms of origin and essence.

The opening up of space, in this conceptualization, is based on hierarchical terms that presuppose a stable domain on top of which a layer can be added, as supplement. While this supplementary thinking can be useful to discern the layers that cooperate, a next step would be to consider this cooperation as establishing a new whole, in which the layers are part of a hybrid entity. As Michiel de Lange asks in his essay on locative media:

> The question is whether this quantitative (by which I mean additive) property of augmentation – an extra layer, more information, multiplying spaces – becomes a qualitative change, and if so, how. (2009: 59)

While his case is pervasive gaming, using mobile media for playful engagement within urban space, to which I will return in the next chapter in relation to location-based and augmented reality applications for mobile screens, I think this question is relevant for urban screens as well.

Taking the literal framing of screens on site, a physical framing of different spatialities, it is perhaps useful to recall an older observation launched by Jacques Derrida in the 1960s. The French philosopher argued for the impossibility to distinguish texts from their "outside", be it literary of visual texts. Everything surrounding the text is itself subject to structuring, interpreting, and connecting. This idea leads to the notion of the *supplement*. Every sign, text, or "interpretable object" (Scarry 1985) is connected to what it lacks to be complete. Hence, the *hors-texte* is also textual in nature. This structure is what Derrida (1976) calls supplementarity. Moreover, the distinctions between one object or text and what surrounds it are never absolute nor stable. The delimitation of the object by its frame is fraught by a two-way permeability. The frame is both part of the painting and its outside. This structure is called *parergon*, a term Derrida (1987 [1978]) borrows from Nietzsche. Very simply put, there is no outside-the-text. But there is more to this Derridean reasoning.

Jonathan Culler points out that supplementarity has the status of an inevitable law. (1997: 11) He quotes Derrida in *Of Grammatology*:

> Through this series of supplements there emerges a law: that of an endless linked series, ineluctably multiplying the supplementary mediations that produce the sense of the very thing that they defer: the impression of the thing itself, of immediate presence, or originary perception. Immediacy is derived. Everything begins with the intermediary. (1976: 226)

This endless series of supplements can be seen in our context as a form of augmentation. And where space is concerned, as it is here, this augmentation of space, or augmented space, is, according to the analogy with supplementarity, by definition unlimited. This makes the stability of space not only unreal, but undesirable. For it is the *hors-texte*, the supplement, that occasions the possibility of a sense of space as here-now, in other words, as delimited. When we consider the layers of augmentation to be supplements in the Derridian sense, it becomes clear that presence is constructed, not ontological in essence; and not fixed, but emerging out of the performance of connectivity that technology allows. This notion of augmenting, which remains ontological, is less relevant here than the performative undermining of spatial certainty and the resulting construction of ambiguity. This, I surmise, is the qualitative change de Lange suggests: the change is in the status of space; the how is in the performance.

Like de Lange, others use *hybridity* for this phenomenon of spatial ambiguity, with an emphasis on building connections. Adriana de Souza e Silva uses the term *hybrid space*, which emphasizes the movements and connections between spatial realms. She defines hybrid spatiality as follows:

> Hybrid spaces are mobile spaces, created by the constant movement of users who carry portable devices continuously connected to the Internet and to other users. A hybrid space is conceptually different from what has been termed mixed reality, augmented reality, augmented virtuality, or virtual reality [...] The possibility of an "always-on" connection when one moves through a city transforms our experience of space by enfolding remote contexts inside the present context. (2006: 262)

In this framing of hybridity, it is essentially in the experience of connectivity that the "enfolding" manifests itself. Or to reverse this: it is the aspect of connectivity that is at the center of the conception of a hybrid spatial *experience*.

Above I considered connectivity at the root of a mobile sphere that takes us out of the obstinately maintained dichotomy of private versus public spheres. This sphere between public space and private sphere is a consequence of individuals being connected, either to other individuals or more diffusely, to an 'online' domain. This sphere in itself has traits of both public space and private sphere. This connected state, and the possibility for communication and traffic between the different realms that together establish our 'reality' exert influence on our experience of physical surroundings. This mobile sphere is a consequence of communication, feedback and interactivity – yet, the feeling that results is neither individual nor communal. It is a paradoxically individual experience of being connected and plugged-in. You are in touch, but not together.[15]

This networked principle makes the mobile sphere not public in the more traditional sense: individual nodes are connected to others, but never simultaneously present either physically or temporally. This notion of a mobile sphere builds on de Souza e Silva's notion of "hybrid space" that is a result of always being connected and online. Of the parasynonyms 'sphere', 'realm', and 'domain', I prefer the term 'sphere' because it refers to an experience as a consequence of this hybrid spatiality, not to the spatiality itself – that just lost its ontological status in the process of this discussion. De Souza e Silva also emphasizes that her notion of hybridity is the result of augmentation of space, to which the practices this involves and makes possible should be added. As a useful concept in this context she puts forward the importance of practices. That is what makes her conceptualization of hybrid space attractive to me. I want to extend this emphasis to my notion of mobile sphere, precisely because it confirms that practice and spatial experience reciprocally constitute each other. In this sense, a notion of mobile sphere works well with ideas of how screens *space* mobility.[16]

This experiential hybridity can be recognized in practices of reactive or interactive programming of urban screens. This involves screen content that responds to passersby or that can be actively modified, for example by using computer terminals, through Internet, or by text messaging. Again in Amsterdam, we can find a contemporary (and temporary) example.

Until 2008, the interior of the restaurant Club 11 on the top floor of the Post CS building in Amsterdam offered a screen situation that, like Johannesma's windows and like most urban screens, played with an inversion of inside and outside. Like virtual windows, screens were mounted above the real windows that show the grand panorama of the city's skyline. While these screens were indoors, I do consider them as urban screens because they are situated in a public place. They were large, and they were visible to a large number of passing or temporary spectators. Moreover, they were silent, like outdoor screens, and had a similar effect of showing images that seemed to subtitle the space that surrounded them. Because they hung above the windows, they reflected, almost literally, the transparent property of glass windows.

Rather than surfaces we can see through, the virtual windows were emphatically opaque, yet showed an array of moving images, entirely unlike the static and distant panorama of the skyline below.

The programming of the twelve screens was varied, but mostly consisted of video art installations. A particularly intriguing aspect was the interactive programming of these screens, like the *Playing Flickr* installation, organized by Mediamatic in 2005. Like photo DJs, visitors could individually call up (public) screen content by sending tags or keywords by text messages, upon which images were selected from the online, public photo archive/database Flickr.[17]

The working of this installation is based on the integration of physical presence, agency of viewers-participants, and access to and display of archival material – in this case an online 'presence' of photographs that is activated in a context of display: the screens in a public space. Whereas Johannesma's Library windows showcase the treasures that are hidden behind the façade of the library's archive, the mesmerizing and partly abstracted play of lights in the still projection of the images of *Playing Flickr* visualize the visitors' picks. The selection itself is what is displayed, self-reflexively highlighting the selection as act.

Fig 4.9: Playing Flickr (Mediamatic, 2005). Photo: Nadya Peek for Mediamatic.

This installation shows us how connectivity as part of programming results in a dialectic binding of spaces: in this case of on-screen space to online space. Screen practices such as these problematize a clear-cut, oppositional distinction between private and public spaces – a dominant dichotomy in debates about the spatial properties of contemporary screen media. Instead, they encourage an active binding by the urban subject of these realms. Specific sites negotiate a certain sense of the relationship between public and private: media shape our experience of sites in these terms, affecting that experience differently from site to site and from time to time. This binding – as procedural activity, not as end result – can be considered as a form of navigation. Navigating screenspace is the continuous construction of space through screens that, in turn, infuse physical space and material architecture. Navigating, then, is not winding your way through a pre-existing space. In the transformed city where such screens occupy more and more visual space, navigating becomes an active construction of spaces that were as yet non-existent, or not quite existent.

Responsive Presence

With these examples, I have tried to discern some aspects that characterize the variety of screens in the streets. I have included the aesthetic dimension in this analysis, in order to be able to establish the performative operations of the different screens that compose the variegated screenspaces of contemporary urban areas. These operations include selection, scale-shifting, display, animation, programming and installation. These screens play with visual attraction, surprise, and the reversal of the domains of 'inside' and 'outside'. In this I see a self-reflexivity in the form of critique of and commentary on urban surroundings, on the virtuality of screen-based 'tele-vision', and mobilization. Screens are programmed with connectivity, based on communication and exchange – for example the *Playing Flickr* event for which the screens were connected with Internet. These aspects make these screens on site part of the spatializing practices of interactivity and performativity, as they facilitate participation and feedback.

In line with the screens that allow for interactive programming, we can see another phenomenon in the development of software-based urban screens – so-called *responsive* or interactive installations. Andreas Broeckmann observes in the screen installation *Sensor* by Carsten Nicolai, a screen in Berlin in 2006 that was responsive to visual and sonic data input from the environment:

> The façade was conceived as an abstracting mirror that reflects light back into the environment as a response to the urban activity in the square – an architecture that "talks back" through the medium of a screen façade. (2009: 114)

This dialogic functioning, the "talking back" of responsive screens, exceeds a communication model of input and output, as well as a conceptualization of interactivity that is built on that mechanic understanding of communication. Moreover, interactivity suggests a possibly infinite interchange back and forth and a suggestion of equality between user and machine, spectator and screen. The idea of responsiveness does not pretend to be more than that: input has *some* kind of output. Its significance is in the possibilities. It is not the "response" per se, but the *responsivity* of the screen that matters. Moreover, this responsivity entails the ability to respond on the part of the spectators, making to their responsibility.

We can see this in a dialogue of presence: the physical presence and occupancy of space that generates particular screen content through contact, and an experience of a bi-located presence on the part of the spectator, much like an avatar. Like mirrors, responsive screens show the effects of presence. The mirroring of these screens can include camera-based mimetic transport – from off-screen presence to on-screen depiction – but it implies more than just a mimetic similarity. It implies an intricate relationship between these spaces. In the next chapter, I will continue my discussion of interactivity or responsivity as a form of haptic engagement and dialogue in case of touchscreens, and more general, as a form of screenic navigation. Here, it is relevant when we consider the working of these responsive screens on site, as part of a location-specific dispositif.

An example is a responsive screen developed by Chris O'Shea for the BBC's Big Screen project, called *Hand from Above* (2009) which premiered in Liverpool and was re-installed in the Dutch city of Utrecht in 2011.[18] The setup of this installation on Clayton Square is inspired by the figure of Goliath in *Goliath and the Land of the Giants*. The screen shows a big hand 'touching' the filmed spectators on screen.

Fig 4.10: Hand From Above (Chris O'Shea, 2009). *Photo: Chris O'Shea.*

The physical presence is doubled: people see themselves on screen and at the same time their 'reflection' is being manipulated, pressed down or tickled or stroked, by the hand on screen. This doubling can be seen as the extension of a communication based on speech or action, to a communication based on located-ness and a material and physical presence.

As screens like these have become consoles for software applications, the dispositif of cinematic projection that is based on the fundamental relationship between, yet also separation of, spectator and screen, has become more complex. Screens allow for – in fact need – a response, which also confers a responsibility on the spectator. Projection implies distance and separation, while responsivity implies a (experience-based) spatial hybridity of a mobile sphere. This is what I called the *spacecificity* of the dispositif: the way the spacing of screens and spectators is performative in that it creates an experience of this spatial relationship. This is the way in which the screens as interfaces transform urban experience, thus not only taking place, but truly making space.

5. Performative Cartography

Throughout this book I am concerned with the visual regime of navigation, that is, a specific mode of interaction at the intersection of visuality and mobility. My ambition has been to use a comparative diachronic perspective to approach various screen arrangements and screen practices, focusing on their hybrid status as part of a dispositif (viewing arrangement) that provides particular rules of engagement in a visual regime of navigation. As I have argued, screens are sites of innovation and change, but also historically constant in that they space mobility, albeit mobilities of different kinds. Unlike forms of historical research that establish continuous genealogies or synchronic epistemes, I adopt a comparative perspective on navigation with shifting, discontinuous bi-polar reference points in the past, in order to grasp the dialectic of oldness and newness in the phenomena I have studied. In this framework, I have treated navigation as a mode of vision that emerges in modernity, part and parcel of modern modes of transportation, fostered in panoramic painting, embedded in urban space, converging in mobile cartographic practices.

In this chapter, I explore digital mapping technologies that allow for active viewing to actually co-create visual representation in mobility. Such interactive practices underscore two aspects of mobile screens: performative cartography and haptic engagement. First, I briefly reflect back on the screen arrangements addressed in previous chapters, establishing the central concepts of screenspace and the mobile dispositif. Second, I briefly position interactive navigation in relation to three scholarly fields in which thinking in terms of cartography has been embedded. I offer this overview in order to outline a conception of performative cartography that does justice to both its traditional background and the innovative potential of interactive navigation. Third, I will address performative cartography in the case of the iPhone, an example of the latest generation of smartphones at the time of writing, a prime example of a hybrid device enabling interactive navigation. Fourth, I explore three principles of performative cartography in locative media practices: tagging, plotting and stitching. The three strands involved in locative media practices then converge in the fifth section, devoted to augmented reality browsing. These practices have in common a solicitation of what I will discuss in the sixth section as haptic engagement. These reflections on navigation with and on screens lead to a view of navigation as a visual regime from the perspective of methodology. Navigating through contemporary as well as historical screen technologies and practices, we not only encounter, but also construct meaning through comparison and in negotiation. In closing, I will reflect on the visual regime of navigation, which provides conceptual coherence to this study.

Mobile Dispositif

As we have seen, a multitude of screens – large and small, publicly visible and privately pocketed – pervades urban spaces, the boundaries of which are permeable. Since they are flexible and open, urban settings produce a space for creativity, possibility and action. The urban screenspace, as a mobile dispositif, invites many different, sometimes mundane, sometimes innovative performative practices. The mobile screens of navigation offer something else in addition: they fundamentally revise the spatial coordinates of hitherto dominant fixed and distancing televisual or cinematic screen dispositifs.

Rather than limiting this discussion to a single phenomenon, several modes of screen-based navigation can be seen to contribute to a fundamentally transformative experience of urban space. Screenspace, as I have argued, is constituted by the screens that surround us, the small screens in our hands, and the relationships between on- and off-screen spaces that we traverse in fluid motions. All these screens foreground dialogic encounters between visual, virtual, material and physical domains, and as such operate as space- and time-binding set-ups, or dispositifs of performative navigation.

In the previous discussions on urban spaces of mobility and the composite dynamic assemblage of screens in places of transit, I have addressed how architectural and interactive screens raise questions about the structural aspects of screen-based *dispositifs*, or screening arrangements. A dispositif that encompasses mobile spectators and architectural screens within an open and accessible space is fundamentally both flexible and permeable, forming a mobile sphere. It is flexible because of the variety in scale, position and programming. As argued in Chapter 1, this dispositif is mobile in the sense that media or mobility technologies bring mobility within the arrangement of spectator and screen. As we have seen in Chapter 3, mobile (touch)screens – or to be more precise, the practices of mobile touchscreening – problematize the distinction between making, transmitting and receiving images. The ambulant and flexible site-specificity of mobile screens generates a fundamentally mobile sphere, a place where viewing and creating images merge in a visual experience of navigation.

Briefly put, screens both *take* space and *make* space: they are positioned within space, but they also produce space. As such, they function both as theoretical console and as historically mutable object, in the sense in which I have explained both functions in Chapter 3. But there is more. Screens are also interfaces, since they mediate images and meanings, and provide experiences within particular places. Moreover, they are connected to other screens. For all these reasons combined, the content that is displayed cannot be approached as 'fixed' texts – which is why methodological innovation, like the gadgets based on an old-new dialectic, is needed to understand them in their full impact. Instead of being static texts, screens provide events in-the-making, or within a flow of becoming. This is why, as my point of departure, I propose to approach screen events as *procedural*.

It is in relation to the conception of a mobile dispositif, a composite of a multitude of screens in a mobile sphere, that this concluding chapter continues my investigation of the performative potential of screening, as both exhibition – or better put, installation – and as interactive practice, through the concept and practice of navigation. Central to this investigation of an expanded field of visuality in urban mobility, which amounts to a hybrid, dynamic mobile sphere, is an analysis of the collapse of making and viewing that is central to navigation, as argued in Chapter 2. This collapse further develops the notion of a hybrid spatiality of a navigable screenspace. Because of the near-collapse of making and receiving, below I will look specifically at the ensuing engagement with screens in which the entire body of the user moves along with the creation of mobile space. This points toward a performative and embodied notion of interactivity as characteristic of navigation as a cultural practice.

As suggested in previous chapters, one of the first theorists of navigation avant-la-lettre was de Certeau with his engaging thoughts about what it means to see a city from within it, walking around inside it, instead of seeing it from above, or from a distance. His thinking about navigational agency, and his cartographic notion of narrative (and vice-versa) have inspired work on navigation in games or other screen-based spaces. Useful and inspiring as his work is, there is some translation to be made when talking not about spatial practices in general, but about how screens space mobility. Moreover, 'walking', whether on- or off-screen, is not the only paradigm of mobility.

Nigel Thrift (2004: 45) takes issue with de Certeau's focus on walking as the paradigmatic practice of mobility that 'speaks' the city. He poses the (rhetorical) question whether the city falls silent when mobility has become primarily vehicular, as is the case with the auto-mobility of car driving in the city. He makes a strong case for interrogating de Certeau's focus on the pedestrian experience, which seems to exclude one of the main forms of transport in today's cities. According to Thrift, de Certeau makes a shift from the incarceration of vehicular (train) mobility, as opposed to walking 'freely', to the panoramic experience of vehicular mobility or vision. We can see this panoramic experience as central to a conceptualization of a mode of vision of moving-image screens as virtual panoramas, as I have argued in the first chapter. Yet in the case of urban screens, we do encounter the spectatorial position of a walker. Virtual mobility, then, meets de Certeau's pedestrian after all.

In the second chapter I indicated how the spatial as well as physical programming urban screens bring about, or perform, invites a deconstruction of both the process of making and of looking, also called 'spectating', with reference to the cinematic role of the spectator. Pervasive and unfinished, these screens come to life in the presence of the mobile, urban spectator, who participates in the constructive work of screening. I consider this co-productivity of screens as architectural (material) interfaces and mobile spectators to be a form of performativity. It is performative in the sense that the practice of this form of screening constructs the spatiotemporal, as well as the experience of urban space in collaboration with the user, without whom the effect would simply not occur. Below I will consider this experience insofar as it is haptic.

This study grew out of a set of core questions about screens of navigation: what is the specificity of mobile screens vis-à-vis their large relatives that cover buildings or stand among them? What forms of urban mobility are we encountering when we trace the practices that these screens afford? And, when looking at a larger and older landscape of screen media, how do mobile screens challenge us to rethink the relationship between spectator-user, on-screen space, and off-screen space, as established by the screen? Here, I take these questions up again, in order to assess the workings of performative navigation in relation to the kind of vision it appears to require for its functioning.

To start with the last question, I proposed in Chapter 3 that one of the main differences between mobile digital screens and larger, what could be called cinematic or televisual screens is that they are application-based. Rather than surfaces of projection or transmission, they are interfaces of complex software applications that combine different technological properties of the hybrid screen device: a camera, an interface for online communication and mobile connectivity, a GPS device, compass, and interface for all kinds of digital input and output.

Other examples that we are looking at today, public screens and locative media projects, show us hybridity or convergence of technologies and examples of networked connectivity. The screen in such installations is an element of what I call a mobile dispositif. There, we see a constellation of technologies rather than one object, one screen that integrates them within one single interface. Moreover, the mobility of the user of the mobile screen does not change the relationship with the screen as material object in their hand, whereas the mobility of the urban flâneur does influence the physical relationship with the screen, even with the possibilities for interactive engagement with the screens they pass or encounter. While the direct, physical or tactile contact between user and a mobile screen establishes a more or less static situation, the relationship to the off-screen space, the world surrounding the screen, is perhaps becoming at once more intimate, more flexible and more mobile.

Because of these characteristics of application-based hybridity and – perhaps intimate – closeness, mobile screens involve practices of a mobile and haptic engagement with the screen that fundamentally revise the spatial coordinates of large, fixed and, paradoxically, distancing televisual, cinematic and architectural screen-dispositifs. When the screen becomes an interactive map, camera and networked communication device all in one, these mobile (touch)screens and practices of mobile screening problematize set boundaries of agency between making, transmitting and receiving images – the formerly clear division of roles between who makes, programs and watches them. Moreover, these devices turn the classical screen as flat and distanced – as well as distancing – window on the world, into an interactive, hybrid navigation device that repositions the viewer as central within that world – a deictic center.

It is because of this transformation and loosening of the division of roles in processes of looking that I think of navigation as a performative cartography. This temporal-spatial navigation is a procedural form of simultaneous making and reading space by exploring a hybrid space of atoms and bits, both the physical and the virtual, through interaction between on- and off-screen navigable space. With the analysis of the performativity of practices of screening, I propose to expand more established notions of one-directional screening as a form of display. After considering how screens contribute to a construction of space, it is in the navigation of the devices and screens themselves that I bring together the three domains central to the visual regime of navigation: screens, space and mobility.

This status of the subject of mobility – either automobilist or pedestrian – has consequences for the cartography at stake in the experience. In order to acknowledge that causal relation as well as bring the specific kind of performativity at issue to the fore, I consider performative cartography here as the *outcome* of navigation. This reversal of the more usual temporal sequence entails a dialectical performativity. An interactive productivity is established between screen and spectator-user, or engager, rather than simply an effect of action-response. This interactive productivity is fundamental to digital input, where interfaces use keys, mouse, touchscreen, motion sensors, webcam, or voice control input. The more complex form of interaction makes the result more strongly performative; the user is more active and, indeed, creative in the process.

In the opening chapter on the panoramic complex – with a particular configuration between mobility, perception, and experience – I pointed out how the panoramic experience, constituted within a panoramic complex, is a procedural and active experience: it is constantly involved in making changes, producing new views through both the mobility of the spectator and the spatial construction of the panoramic view. Panoramic vision is produced by means of a moving panorama through a car windshield, the mobile spectator moving in relation to a visual field, or on a moving-image screen. This panoramic complex proposes a relationship between image and viewer that engages the spectator-subjects with their surrounding – the perceptual surrounding that is perceptually within reach, but paradoxically distanced by speed, motion and the separation through the screen or window.

Here, I continue this idea, but now with another 'complex', one that bears a family resemblance to the panoramic, namely an interactive 'navigational complex'. While equally involving a relation between mobility, perception and experience, two features distinguish interactive navigation from the panoramic complex. First, navigation is directional: the desire is not for an overview but for a destination, a place to go to. Second, it is constructive: the navigator makes the itinerary, and as such constructs the space. Rather than an arrangement to be taken in or to traverse, interactive navigation is a creative act. Making-in-motion is an action – not a result – of cartography. This implies rethinking what cartography is and does. While emerging out of a long tradition both as a map-making practice and an epistemological model, performative cartography nevertheless is radically new, providing a conceptual challenge to the logic of representation and a practical challenge to some of our most basic assumptions regarding the experience of space and time in navigation.

Contesting Cartography

Within the academic field of geography, cartography is a scholarly practice of map-making and map-reading. Traditionally, it is an expertise based on two-dimensional ways of thinking about and representing space. In its analogue tradition, based in centuries-old art of image-based depiction on paper and other surfaces, this can hardly be otherwise. Because a piece of paper is in 2D, even if it allows for a representation of three-dimensional, relative spatiality, the representational map is predicated on an x- and y-axis only: horizontality and verticality. This is also the case when it involves the representation of the breadth of the land, the heights of mountains and the depths of seas and lakes, using contour lines to indicate elevation. The medium in this case dictates the epistemology and, vice versa, the medium suits the logic. The space on the map is represented with principles according to which the observer is at a distance from the observed. This is frequently referred to as a Cartesian way of seeing the world, which Jonathan Crary (1990) has traced to the seventeenth- and eighteenth-century scientific paradigm of 'distant observers' – a paradigm based on the idea of strict separation of subject (observer) and object (observed). Traditional cartography has its roots in this scientific-visual paradigm.[1]

With the advent of what Tristan Thielmann (2010) calls *geomedia* – converging applications of interactive, digital mapping tools and mobile and networked media technologies – the principles of vision, knowledge and the ownership of these in analogue cartography are challenged. The interactive possibilities of digital information, or Geographic Information Systems (GIS), uproot the Cartesian principle of a cartography based on a fixed coordinate-system. Mapping practices such as GPS, geobrowsers like Google Earth, map hacking, social-network applications linked to geotagged image databases, locative media projects, or the more ludic pervasive or ubiquitous games that use maps to explore and interact with (urban) spaces wreak havoc with these principles. They not only present space differently, but also provide tools to modify maps, to create mash-ups, to fill maps with different kinds of knowledge. Mapping has become interactive, social, creative or ludic, and the making and using of maps is no longer limited to professional cartographers. Amateurs can make or modify maps, and collaborative, social mapmaking gives communities and networks a platform for exchange. Moreover, due to technological innovation in the tools of map-making and map-using, this representational change signals a different way of thinking about maps and what maps tell us.

Valérie November, Eduardo Camacho-Hubner and Bruno Latour evaluate digital cartography, or cartography A.C. (after computers), as compared to cartography B.C. (before computers), as what they call a navigational definition of the map, which includes anticipation, participation, reflexivity and feedback. This yields a differentiation between a navigational versus mimetic interpretation of the map:

> Why the use of the word navigational? Because our argument is that the common experience of using digital maps on the screen, and no longer on paper, has vastly extended the meaning of the word navigation. In effect, we are led back to the earliest use of the map-making impulse (Jacob, 1992), not only in the maritime sense of the word but in the vastly enlarged meaning that is now familiar through digital worlds (Cartwright, 1999). The users of the platforms are engaged into receiving and sending information to allow other agents to find their way through a maze of data: it could be data about the yacht's trajectory [...] or in a digital library [...], or through a social network, or through a city. It does not matter: everyone has now the experience of navigating through successive sign posts on screen. The A.C. and B.C. meaning of navigation taken literally or figuratively are thus in continuity with one another. The whole history of cartography would show, if it is taken as a practical activity, all the explorers, navigators, cartographers, geometers, mathematicians, physicists, military personnel, urban planners, tourists that have "logged in", so to speak, on those "platforms" in order to feed the "data banks" with some piece of information, or to draw the maps, or to use them in some ways to solve their navigational problems. (2010: 586)

And they conclude: "In all those cases, there is indeed a correspondence but it works precisely *because it is not mimetic*."

Representation as characteristic of traditional cartography entails *fixed* outcomes of the creative production processes: results such as images, statements, models, materials can be distributed, transmitted, stored or tagged. I consider the view of cartography as representation insufficient, however, especially for mobile navigation, but even retrospectively for traditional cartography. Our contemporary mapping interfaces foreground and, precisely, process mutability, flux, simulation, remediation and mobility. As I have suggested above, this makes the assumption of stability implied in the concept of representation less adequate to account for navigation and the cartography that supports it. Instead of foregrounding the prefix 're' in repetition, I prefer to conceptualize the 'pre' in *pre*sentation. This is not only the pre- of making present (pre-sent-ation) but also in the temporal dimension of the processes *before* (pre-) representation, or better yet, the process through which representation comes into being. This is why Deleuze uses the gerund becoming (devenir). The coincidence of critical thinking about maps, the political power of cartography, and the radical change in the tools of the trade, so to speak, show us the intricate relationship between meaning and practice, knowledge systems and cultural forms.[2]

As geographer Jeremy Crampton poetically asks in his consideration of locative art projects and artistic interventions using GIS for a critical cartography:

> These "map events" challenge the commensurability of Euclidean space, a basic assumption of much GIS. [...] If you break from Cartesian space what new perspectives are thrown up? What strange conjunctions and serendipitous new knowledges? Like the surrealist map the answer to these questions is not a distorted map, but an impossible one, yet one that exists and can be created. Perhaps it is better to say it is a paradoxical map. (2010: 22)

Crampton's somewhat hyperbolic choice of words to make his readers realize how dramatic the break from hegemonic mapping can turn out to be, points to a search for an alternative view, or paradigm, to representation, which he locates in what he calls critical cartography. When traditional cartography – or any kind of cartography for that matter – is said to be inherently political, in the sense that it structures and as such produces space, a change in its paradigm is inherently critical in its potential. This we can hear in Crampton's words as well:

> Critical cartography assumes that maps make reality as much as they represent it. [...] Maps are active; they actively construct knowledge, they exercise power and they can be a powerful means of promoting social change. (18)

GIS and the spread of mapping tools, in effect, have transformed not only mapmaking as a practice, but also the thinking about maps as technologies of visualization. Moreover, the intricate relationship between epistemological principles and technologies of cartography has become clear with the fundamental change in digital, interactive and widely-accessible map-making technologies. While I do not want to equate digital cartography with critical cartography, the interactive possibilities for mash-ups, mutation and remixing open up a fundamentally critical potential. This critical potential is due to the fact that the fixating fundament and epistemological regime of representation has changed.

In digital cartography, both the representation of the world in another material medium – drawing on paper – and even its presentation through arrows and other road signs, for example, are made redundant. Digital cartography substitutes Cartesian *presence* – or (re)presentation, in line with what Derek Gregory (1994) calls the "world-as-exhibition" model for cartography – for a model of *process* in multiple senses of the word. This model comprises a procedural collecting or data-gathering, a procedural networked data management, and interactive applications that process this data for different purposes, different contexts, and different uses. The change is dramatic: flexibility and availability of data for implementation in different contexts allows for possibly endless creative, critical, or plain practical repurposing.

In a very optimistic rhetoric, Janet Abrahams and Peter Hall proclaim that

> [...] mapping technology has split the interface from the database, a split comparable to the liberating effect photography had on the development of painting. Before the advent of aerial photography, satellite tracking, and computerized data-gathering, a map was expected to represent its territory with comprehensive accuracy. Freed of that responsibility, cartographers can manipulate their data into any number of visual representations – an act so potent it has attracted the attention of other disciplines. (2006: 12)

The twice-mentioned idea of the freedom this technology affords exalts the perceived liberation, even while words such as "manipulate" and the idea of multiplicity of possibilities can just as well give a cultural hypochondriac reason to worry, especially when the celebrated freedom is predicated by the phrase "of responsibility". Moreover, what is not made explicit here but implied in the technology, and suggested by the freedom "of responsibility", is the idea that anyone can now be a cartographer. To somewhat temper this jubilant tone and mitigate too stark an opposition between past and present that threatens to obliterate history and flatten the present, I will explore below this shift from map to screen as precisely the place where a media-historical perspective becomes pertinent.[3]

Cartography is also a methodological staple within epistemology, the branch of philosophy concerned with the question of knowledge. Here, cartography is the label – perhaps I should say, conceptual metaphor – of one out of two conceptions of knowledge, or paradigms, that tend to be compared and opposed. Epistemology works traditionally along the lines of roughly two paradigms, namely the classificatory and the cartographical. Classification is a traditional approach based on distinction, usually along lines of binary opposition. For a historiography of thought, such an approach involves charting schools of thought in terms that establish one school as central, others as pre- or post- that central one. For example, the division of historical time in eras comprises such divisions as pre-modern, modern and postmodern. This practice is based on a dualist mindset that frequently entails evaluative views, for example when postmodernist thinkers are opposed to modernist ones. Moreover, the linearity and the assumption of continuity this view implies are at odds with my approach to history through diachronic comparisons, which simultaneously bring to light the oldness and newness of the phenomena in question – both continuity and breaks.

Epistemological approaches based on the model of cartography shift the fixity and linearity, and move in the direction of a relational approach based on fluctuating relations between philosophers. These shifts are also based on a theory of time that conceptualizes revolutions in thought as disrupting a progressive narrative. For example, the postmodernist can be seen as not opposed to, but ambivalently re-confirming the modernist, via a relation of opposition that cannot help but also remain within what it criticizes. The cartographical in philosophy, then, is a mode of thinking in which theme-based groupings of philosophers and concepts are constructed instead of relying on streamlined charts of predetermined schools of thought.[4]

We can discern an embedding of cartographical principles in media archaeology. Media archaeology has found directions in the consideration of changing paradigms or dispositifs that can very well be considered cartographic in their perspective. Much work has been done on 'mapping' the screen-based, mediated experience in three dimensions. The screens studied are still in 2D, but the viewing arrangement adds a third dimension. The mapping of spatial arrangements concerns x-, y-, and z-axes, positioning objects within a space. A media-archaeological thinking in terms of dispositifs, as I have implemented in this comparative study of screen arrangements, implies a focus on these multiple axes. Moreover, in an explicit effort to refrain from teleological historical narratives of progress, the archaeological project itself is often very self-reflexively concerned with a cartographic endeavor of mapping relationships *between* media dispositifs, multiplying the points of reference in comparison.

In this schematic way I wish to suggest how cartography cuts across these domains: *cartography*, conceived as the geographical practice of two-dimensional map-making, is supplemented by, if not grounded in, epistemology. *Epistemology* is structured along the lines of either a classificatory or a cartographical logic, with its practices of mapping thinkers, thoughts and concepts, based on historical, conceptual and epistemological relations. In media *archaeology*, the focus is on media dispositifs as a three-dimensional mapping of the mediated experience itself with an emphasis on (spatial) relations between technology and spectator-user on the one hand, and a historical-comparative mapping perspective on the relationship between different (historical) media dispositifs on the other.

I propose that a possible way of *doing* cartography yields a productive integration of these three categories of space, time and thought. This is to say that, from the point of view of an inverted temporal logic, I aim to conceptualize a shift from *representational* cartography to navigation as a *performative* cartographic practice. This new type of performative cartography taps into non-Newtonian thinking, breaking with a Euclidean model of space. Put simply and succinctly, according to the Newtonian paradigm, time and space are absolute and measurable phenomena that work along the lines of a predetermined mechanical, progressive logic. A Euclidean model of space can constitute a basis for thinking in terms of multiple dimensions. Yet, this model still assumes an immobile grid in which all objects take place within a fixed system of (Cartesian) coordinates.[5]

Representation entails more or less fixed outcomes of creative production processes. The results, such as images, statements, models and materials can, for example, be transmitted or stored. This would be an insufficient understanding for some contemporary media practices and approaches to these practices that foreground process, mutability, flux, simulation, remediation, notions of becoming, and mobility. These characterize the 'pre' to representation – the processes *before* representation in which representation comes into being, in its performativity.

Christian Jacob, in his seminal study on the semiotics of maps throughout history, addresses precisely this question of the conceptual status of the map as representation, as medium, and as interface:

> An effective map is transparent because it is a signified without a signifier. It vanishes in the visual and intellectual operation that unfolds its content. The map spreads out the entire world before the eyes of those who know how to read it. The eye does not see; it constructs, it imagines space. The map is not an object but a function. Like a microscope, a telescope, or a scanner, it is a technical prosthesis that extends and refines the field of sensorial perception, or, rather, a place where ocular vision and the "mind's eye" coincide. As a mediation, an interface, it remains hidden. (2006 [1992]: 11)

This double-sidedness of the map as object and function brings about a paradoxical status, if not a "conceptual vacuum" as Jacob calls it. He continues:

> And yet, paradoxically, what defines the map is the mediation of representation, a mediation that is a signifier with its own codes and conventions (symbolization, schematization, miniaturization, colors, nomenclature, vertical overview, etc.). (12)

We can thus discern the materiality of the map, the interfacing operation of the map in terms of mediation, and the content it is supposed to mediate while being transparent.

Because representational maps work according to a Cartesian dualistic logic, a certain phenomenon *is being mapped*. From the perspective of representation as Western cultural and scientific (historical) tradition, Karen Barad stresses the epistemological implication of separation as the logic of representation:

> Representationalism takes the notion of separation as foundational. It separates the world into the ontologically disjunct domains of words and things, leaving itself with the dilemma of their linkage such that knowledge is possible. (2007: 137)

This separation implies difference and distance, operation and (the making of) meaning. The map is the result of the mapping *of* a certain phenomenon. We can take the common practice of geographical map-making as a first example of a representational map: land is being mapped along the lines of an x- and y-axis, and the changes through time are represented by subsequent maps – e.g. polar ice before and after the twenty-firstcentury's climate change, or patterns of migration as a result of the spread of mobility technologies such as trains and cars. The dualism is to be found in the relation between the phenomenon and the map, but also between the spatial element and the element of time. Talking about the mapping of the cinematic experience is not fundamentally different: adding another axis to an analysis does not shift the dualist logic: there is e.g. the movie-theatre experience as a phenomenon and the map thereof on the one hand, and there is time and space as measurable and measured on the other hand, separately.

The same goes for the classificatory approach that is common in a classical historiography of philosophy: classifying schools of thought works along the lines of the predetermined spatiality of the chart or matrix, and the time element is nothing but progressive. The conceptualization of this methodology is straightforward: time and space are not only measurable (they consist of certain elements) but also disconnected, and map-making has fixed characteristics. Whether land, a media experience, or schools of thought, the approach is always already there for the scholar to put into practice. Coupling time and space, thus "inserting duration into matter", encourages a qualitative shift away from dualism.[6]

What does a map look like when it is itself in movement, in flux, and when we talk about practices of mapping and navigating instead of the map as an object? Then the map itself is a spatial and temporal *event*. It is spatial, because it does not map a pre-existing height, breadth and depth; and temporal, because it does not map a pre-existing spatiality through time. Focusing on the map as a navigational tool and on navigating as a practice that occurs in time and space enforces a rethinking of the dualist frame of the representational map.

As a consequence of this, in each and every case the cartographical experience of navigation needs to be conceptualized anew. Spacetime is non-linear; it is not measurable along predetermined lines. Since space and time unfold in practice, experiences do not happen in space and time but are themselves events. This is why these experiences themselves constitute an immanent spatio-temporality. This makes it necessary to think immanent dimensionality, hence, pre-representationality.

With this in mind, we can productively investigate the hybridity of screens as interface for interactive navigation – a perspective on both object and practice that steers cartography away from representation and towards performativity. Performative cartography is where pervasive presence, embedded pasts, and evolving futures can intersect in screenspace.

Performative Cartography

Performative cartographies emerge during movement, as a particular form of interactive navigation: fixed maps do not dictate the itinerary, but rather maps and views evolve and emerge along the way. In performative cartography there is a timespace collapse between making images and viewing them, a creative cultural practice also at play in other screen arrangements discussed in previous chapters. Creative, in this context, indicates the activity of making; I do not posit an inherently artistic connotation involved in creation, rather a performative generation through the embodied motion of the navigator interacting with digital mapping devices.

Performative cartography can be seen as a 4D operation, a dynamic model of the 3D world set in motion. This posits a problem of using representation of four-dimensionality within a 3D world. (Fisher 2000: 106) As feminist philosoher Karen Barad puts it, critiquing the constraints that a Euclidean imaginary puts on a traditional epistemology within this paradigm:

> The view of space as container/context for matter in motion – spatial coordinates mapped via projections along axes that set up a metric for tracking the locations of the inhabitants of the container, and time divided up in evenly spaced increments marking a progression of events – pervades much of Western epistemology. (2001: 76)

In order to avoid this problem, a notion of performative cartography assumes that it is not so much *time* but rather *spacetime* that is the fourth dimension. We have already seen in the previous chapter that time and space are not easily distinguishable: space is temporal and time needs space to unfold.

Instead of the traditional divide between space and time in representational cartography, performative cartography is a procedural experience, implying a thorough rethinking of relative and positional dimensionality itself as more fluid than fixed spatio-temporal positioning. Moreover, time and space unfold in practices and consequently do not work along predetermined lines.

Performative cartography is a cartography of multi-directionality and best conceptualized as the practice of a theoretical cartography in 4D, which challenges some basic conceptualizations of cartography to be found in geography and media archaeology, and to some extent epistemology – the three domains I deem to be relevant to the cases at hand. The objects of my investigation are cultural practices and technologies that are concerned with meaningful and significant intersections of space and time; as such, they require a cartography of (cultural) practice.

The concept of 4D signifies change, difference and, to some degree, unpredictability. Performative cartography postulates the need to understand cartography as an activity, as a form of navigation, signifying change and difference rather than aiming to produce representational cartographic products such as maps. Perhaps mobile technology operates within Euclidean space; but the experience of it does not.

We are faced with a demand to rethink cartography in light of screenspace and performative screen practices. The corporeality constitutive of the engagement with screens of navigation changes the nature of cartography. This is so because it shows how a cartographic practice is spatio-temporal and, specifically, involves duration as a non-linearity. This is to be understood through an immanent approach to the devices. Such an approach can only be practical, and pre-representational.

Performative cartography is a creative practice, but not a creation ex nihilo. I want to end this section with giving a larger perspective on what this could mean for today's cultural practices. To this end, I draw some connections with other conceptions of cultural practice that also foreground creativity in this more modest sense. Performative cartography can be seen, for example, as modeled on what Claude Lévi-Strauss (1966 [1962]) and in his wake Gérard Genette (1982), called long ago "bricolage": creation by recombining ready-made bits and pieces; not from scratch. But this view, devised in the high days of structuralism, was not meant in a critical way. Genette instead argued that literature – which was his field of study – is always by definition a bricolage, since the bits of language – words, syntax, and cultural clichés – always pre-exist any new formation.

Before Genette and in a similar vein, Mikhail Bakhtin famously contended that the word never forgets where it has been. This view inspired Julia Kristeva to formulate her concept of intertextuality as a mosaic: "any text is constructed as a mosaic of quotations: any text is the absorption and transformation of another." (Kristeva 1980: 66) While perhaps not central to Kristeva's development of the concept of intertextuality, the word "forgets" suggests a collective memory of language use, which indeed, seems an important aspect of the interactive practices of bricolage we have seen in the discussion of navigation, such as geotagging, caching and stitching. The collaborative aspect is central to the ever-expanding archive of tags.[7]

From this point of view, bricolage is a structural property of all texts. However, it also has an inherent subversive or critical potential, particularly when the text – in the broadest sense of the word – is in the hands of the consumer, reader, or, in the case of interactive media, the user:

> As a cultural practice, bricolage refers to the activity of taking consumer products and commodities and making them one's own by giving them new meaning. This has the potential to create resistant meanings of commodities. (Sturken and Cartwright 2001: 350)

This view of resistance has been developed from a cultural studies perspective, for instance in the work of Dick Hebdige (1979) who understands bricolage as a personal remixing and subversion of fashion and style of commodity culture by subcultures. Also, de Certeau's notion of textual poaching as the struggle of authorship or control over text gives the idea of bricolage a political slant. This fits with his conception of strategies as dominant structures and means of control and tactics as individual, possibly random, negotiational or oppositional poaching of texts at the level of interpretation or production. The latter is particularly relevant here, although obviously closely related to the former.

To continue with de Certeau's term: Henry Jenkins (1992) appropriates the term textual poaching for fan culture and participatory culture from the perspective of fluidity between oppositional or hegemonic practices. This fluidity stems from a reading and interpretative positioning of, in Jenkins' case, media fans within popular culture. This reading of dominant culture matches this new age of participatory culture and what Jenkins calls convergence culture (2006a and 2006b):

> Patterns of media consumption have been profoundly altered by a succession of new media technologies which enable average citizens to participate in the archiving, annotation, appropriation, transformation, and recirculation of media content. Participatory culture refers to the new style of consumerism that emerges in this environment. (2006b: 554)

Returning to the formal cutting and pasting – to summarize Jenkins' "archiving, annotation, appropriation, transformation, and circulation" –, in locative media practices it seems useful to see the fluidity of convergence culture not only as a cultural phenomenon, but also as a perspective on culture. A perspective that can have critical potential. The concept that binds cartography to performativity is agency.

When we are concerned with (and about) the possibilities for agency within dominant discourse and societal structures, I wish to advance the idea of a critical and political potential in appropriation and bricolage as property of the process of creation. High expectations and idealizations of digital media and interactivity notwithstanding, appropriation is not always critical, and agency and creativity are not necessarily democratic, emancipating, or essentially political. It is therefore relevant to position these allegedly new forms of creativity and authorship from a historical perspective. Formally, there is nothing new about this sense of a creativity made of pre-used bits and pieces. However, appropriation and bricolage are cultural production, and in the case of locative media they are very much at the center of our conception of location and of our position in the world. What is new, and potentially problematic, is the combination of this making as bricolage with a sense that the bits, because they emerge from geotagged locations, are themselves anchoring us to the world. Instead of cutting up reality and thus transforming it into fiction, they appear to augment the former and obliterate the latter.

As a creative practice in the sense of bricolage, augmentation implies changing by adding and combining information. Moreover, it entails an analytic and associative practice – cutting up and making links. Since the advent of Photoshop we have learned to deconstruct the image, not only in flat (horizontal/vertical) sections or cut-outs, but also in different 3D layers, adding layered surfaces to a flat image. With sections and layers combined, tagging provides a *mash-up logic* to our understanding of the spaces surrounding us. It fuses layers of information that create a hybrid space, and paradoxically it also teases this space apart: it makes visible the exchangeability, and hence the design of these information layers.

This brings me back to the central part that navigation and the cartography it needs and makes plays in this consideration of creativity as (simply) making, of performativity as undermining the distinction between making and using, or spectating. *Navimation* is the term Eikenes and Morrison (2010) propose, to bring navigation and animation together. They introduce that term to characterize the "the intertwining of visual movement with activities of navigation" in (interactive) screen-based interfaces. For this reason they propose to discern temporal navigation, spatial manipulation, and motional transformation. To me, their argument combines two perspectives. On the one hand, it implies a perspective on the layering of spaces when dealing with interfaces. This integrates space on screen and space of interaction with the screen. On the other hand, the argument implies an ambition to develop analytical tools for the design of interactive, screen-based interfaces. They try to grasp such interfaces as both machines that one interacts with and which produces spaces/visuals, and as product: the resulting 'production' or mediation of the interface. This seems helpful for analyzing interface design precisely as something that *is* (textual level) and something that *does* (mediational level). I have suggested something of the same order in Chapter 3 when analyzing the status of gadgets. In the next section I will return to gadgets, shifting from this more conceptual level to the iPhone as an interface for performative cartography.

Cartographic Interface

With touchscreen, camera, compass, GPS, network connectivity and the divergent mapping applications that are being developed for it, the smartphones such as Android devices and the iPhone can be considered a fundamentally cartographic interface. The hybrid interface of the gadget not only allows for navigation within the machine, and on the screen, but also within the physical space surrounding the device. It provides an interface for navigating bits, pixels, and spatial coordinates.

A wide range of innovative navigation software is being developed for the handheld devices such as the iPhone, enabling new ways of navigating urban space. Interactive tours, augmented reality, social locative media, and mobile navigation contribute to an expanding and transforming field of cartographic screen practices that not only represent space, but also truly make space – operating as performative cartography by generating a hybrid screenspace.

The hybridity of the interface compels us to investigate the complexity of navigation as it is taking shape as a prominent cartographic and epistemological model, or a visual regime of navigation in today's culture of mobility. This navigational model, as I argue, entails a shift in cartography. Originating in the art of making maps, but as such putting forward a regime of understanding and representing space, a new mobile cartography infuses spatial representation with a temporal and procedural dimension: a performative cartography, a dynamic map which emerges and changes during the journey. Moreover, divergent spatial categories of information or data space and physical space are connected in the map as a hybrid screenspace. The physical engagement of the user-navigator with the iPhone in this temporally dynamic and spatially layered process of making maps while reading them entails a collapse of making images and viewing them. This brings forward the co-operation of the device's (hardware) specifications, the applications' (software) affordances and the user's activity (the interfacing) in processes of connectivity, participation and mobility.

The iPhone – a handheld, mobile and hybrid device, and a console for multiple uses – invites us to interrogate the characteristic of the screen gadget as interface for mobile use. However, simply asserting that smartphones such as the iPhone are hybrid devices glosses over the complex and layered structure of characteristics and affordances of the interface of the device, as well as the different interactive practices involved in this hybridity. The iPhone raises questions about the specificity of this type of screen gadget as a *hybrid object*. In this sense, it is just as much a theoretical object as the Nintendo DS I alleged as such in Chapter 3. To be specific, because it is a mobile device, questions about the iPhone's hybridity are intrinsically related to movement, touch, and the process of spatial transformation. This is situated in an entanglement of technologies, applications, and interactive practices that iPhone *interfacing* entails.

Handling the iPhone takes place within what we have called a *mobile* screening arrangement or dispositif. As a hybrid object, the device is embedded within a mobile dispositif that encompasses both the perceptual positioning of the (mobile) user, and the physical (interactive) interfacing with the screen. The screening arrangement in motion, taking place within public space and making connections with this space, establishes a *mobile sphere*: a space that is marked by mobility and connectivity, and constructed within the (mobile) arrangement of the user, location, and device.

This mobility in space is intricately bound to the mobility, or flexibility, of the on-screen space itself: the interactive touchscreen that in fact requires physical manipulation for its operation. Considering the use of the iPhone as machine for navigation, the mobility of the device makes it a visceral interface: the entire body of the user is incorporated in mobility and making space.

The iPhone has a cartographic interface for the simultaneous navigation of both on- and off-screen space. As a machine, it enables navigation within the machine itself, as well as the navigation within physical space with the machine in hand. This makes the screen use of the iPhone distinct from historical screen uses such as televisual or cinematic viewing. The multi-touchscreen and the divergent practices of mobile touchscreening problematize the distinction of making, transmitting, and receiving images. Moreover, characteristic of the mobile screen is positioning within a mobile sphere – or dispositif – implying an ambulant locatedness and, hence, flexible site-specificity.

This mobility and physicality, I argue, points toward a performative and embodied notion of interactivity as characteristic of navigation, not only as a spatial decoding of map information, orientation and mobility, but as a cultural trope structuring our sense of (spatial) presence – as well as (temporal) present – as hybrid and flexible categories. This establishes a new spatial category, screenspace, which is activated by the simultaneous construction of on- and off-screen spaces when traversing in fluid motions with navigation devices in our hands. (Verhoeff 2008)

As a device for navigation, the iPhone comprises a layered interface. While phenomenally intricately connected and hard to separate or isolate, conceptually we can discern three (non-hierarchical) levels that are all essential for navigation. First, it encompasses the level of the *internal interfacing* of applications: the back-end operating system and software. This includes so-called application programming interfaces (API), making communication between applications possible, as well as the communication of the software with the graphical user interface (GUI) that enables the human user of the applications to 'read', or understand, and use them.

The Google Maps API is a good example here. The fact that it is open source makes Google Maps a highly adaptable framework for all kinds of implementations. This is very suitable for mapping applications, because it provides the tools for mash-ups, or web-application hybrids: the integration of data from different sources within, in this case, the mapping environment of Google Maps. This level is the *processing* of data.

The second layer of the interface is the spatial positioning and connectivity of the apparatus in relation to physical as well as data space: the interface of internal instruments of the iPhone that connect with the external space. This entails the digital camera, GPS, Wifi/G3 connectivity, compass, and motion sensor or accelerometer, calculating the position, orientation and velocity, and the screen. This level of the interface communicates between the hardware of the device and 'the world'.

It includes what is called an *inertial* navigation system, defined by Oliver J. Woodman as follows:

> Inertial navigation is a self-contained navigation technique in which measurements provided by accelerometers and gyroscopes are used to track the position and orientation of an object relative to a known starting point, orientation and velocity. (2007: 4)

This inertial positioning system is combined with the *absolute* positioning system of GPS which is based on triangulation of geographical coordinates (which currently only works outdoors). This ability to calculate position and orientation is necessary for e.g. gravimetric (rather than marker-based) augmented reality applications as interface for location-based data, or *ambient intelligence*. Moreover, Internet connectivity also positions the device via wireless connection. The second layer of the interface, then, concerns *connecting* and *positioning* the interface, whether based on inertial, absolute, camera-based or wireless technologies.[8]

This positioning, then, is communicated to the user who might, for example, see the on-screen image tilt, or find a representation of position and movement signified by an arrow-shaped icon in the on-screen maps, and can then read this orientation and subsequently act or move. This is taking place on a third level of the interface of *user interaction*, enabling the communication between the user and the internal operation of the device (first level) as it is connected to the space surrounding it (second level). The first level of the applications interface also includes software operation of the graphical user interface (GUI). However, the way in which this data is visualized and made understandable, its output, operates at this third level of user interaction. This level contains the user feedback input options such as the touchscreen, buttons, the 'shake control' (making use of the inertial system), but also representational conventions of the GUI. In the case of navigation, this means the way that spatial information is represented on the screen and interacted with by the user.

Significant for the touchscreen of the iPhone is that at the level of user interaction it is both an instrument for input and for output. This is the level of 'access' (to data) and of the 'experience' of it. Where the action takes place is, literally, on the screen. Moreover, it is a multi-touchscreen in a technological and practical sense: multi-touch technology allows for multifarious ways of touching such as swiping, virtual scrolling or swirling, and two-fingered pinch movements for enlarging or shrinking. Moreover, the dynamic horizontal or vertical scrolling of screen content establishes a connection between the image on the screen and its off-screen spaces: the frame is always a detail of a larger whole. The map is always larger than the part that is displayed on screen. Objects can be moved outside and brought into the frame by the swipe of a fingertip. Moreover, tapping the screen to give commands make more buttons, keys, sticks or a mouse controller redundant. For example, pressure can make the screen image zoom in, simulating a virtual camera lens.

Seen within a layered constellation of the interface, the iPhone requires a triple perspective: it is a machine that processes and combines data, it is a sensor that connects and positions data, and it is a medium that produces perception. Within this constellation, its products, results, or yields received as visuals on screen by the user, cannot be approached as fixed entities, or 'texts', both in a temporal sense and in terms of authorship, or better, of agency. While walking and using the iPhone for an interactive tour, for example, the different layers of the interface operate together: location-based information is processed and communicated to the user via the screen. This complex layering of the interfacing process is not experienced as such because it is filtered by the user interaction interface. However, the integration of these processes (data processing, spatial positioning and connectivity, and the communication with the user) is the condition of possibility for creative navigation: an integration of the mechanisms and affordances that underlie our actions, but that are not experienced as discrete layers. As such, the hybridity of the iPhone interface provides the conditions for creative navigation of screenspace as a performative cartography.

These creative practices that make use of the affordance of the (layered) interface of the iPhone as navigation device involve different interactive engagements with an array of cartographic applications. We can discern three different ways in which the broad concept of interactivity becomes specific for navigation, as the point where interface and agency meet and where performativity is actualized: navigation understood as a constructive form of interactivity, as a participatory form of interactivity, and as yielding a haptic engagement with screenspace.

Let me explore briefly how this performative cartography constructs an urban space in which pervasive presence, embedded pasts, and evolving futures intersect, according to my triple interpretation of the index. I take locative media, or geomedia practices, and augmented reality navigation as popular and (at the moment of writing) innovative uses of mobile screens and sketch the way they revamp some cartographic principles. I first address the three aspects of tagging, plotting and stitching in the following section before elaborating on augmented reality navigation.

Tagging, Plotting, Stitching

Interactive tours using online connectivity, GPS navigation, and interactive maps show us how both space and time unfold in the practice of navigation. The basic principle of screen-based navigation is that we see how we move, while how we move enables vision. This mutually constitutive, discursive relationship between seeing and moving is a new principle in real-time, digital cartography. It is the movement that establishes the map; reading space requires navigation, rather than the other way around. Digital maps make use of the logic of tagging, plotting, stitching as forms of interaction.

Tagging is essentially labeling objects or locations with metadata. Tags are clusters of digital data and primarily operate on the interface level of internal applications. Usually we refer to 'tags' in relation to the way they appear: as textual or visual information or visual on our screen. It is, however, important to distinguish the tag as data and tag as symbol (visual or in words). The different levels on which tagging works correspond to levels of interfacing incorporated in the map: as metadata linked to objects, as inserts on screen providing information in relation to specific objects or locations, or as a visual layering of hybrid screenspace.

This warrants a precise terminology when analyzing how tagging is a central principle of digital cartography. Although tags primarily operate on the level of data processing, when visualized as clickables, they activate the level of user interaction. On maps they often function as geotags: location-specific hyperlinks that make a connection between data/objects and location.

The specific practice of tagging objects in space, and inserting tagged objects in the map, we can call the *plotting* of space. This entails marking locations and giving them a layered presence and hence, an added meaning. When these are 'read' and used for navigation, we can call this *tracing*. When integrated into a navigable whole, this process I call *stitching*. While originally a term used for the montage of separate images into a seamless panoramic image, a more horizontal (two-dimensional) stitching, it also applies to a broader practice of 'sewing together' visual layers in digital cartography. In similar terms, the developers of the AR browser Junaio speak of "glue" for this practice:

Junaio has extended its capabilities beyond the usual location based internet services. Not only may the user obtain information on nearby POIs such as

shops, restaurants or train stations, but the camera's eye is now able to iden-
tify objects and "glue" object specific real-time, dynamic, social and 3D information onto the object itself. Enrich your packaging, books, posters, flyers,
magazines or whatever you can think of with junaio glue.[9]

Tagging, plotting, and stitching operate on the multiple levels of the interface:
tagging on the level of software communication (data connecting to data), the
spatial positioning (spatially connecting the objects) of plotting, and stitching,
become effective on the screen, where the user actually perceives the connections
as a navigable space.

Locative media activate different temporal layers within a set of spatial coordinates, which can be activated by tags. Dots on the map unfold, like spatio-temporal hyperlinks. The city becomes a clickable screenspace, a terrain of pop-ups
that are triggered by real-life avatars in the physical world whose movements are
tracked on-screen by GPS. In contrast to two-dimensional maps, which are a flat
and still representation of space within a fixed frame, based on a fixed scale, and
a fixed, abstract perspective, the digital tour-map is dynamic, layered, expandable,
mutable, and flexible. It is now possible to attach geographical coordinates (geotags) as digital information, placing data back on a map of physical space, as well
as tracking one's current location. Geotags bring together all levels of the hybrid
interface: they combine data, they are locative and activated by positioning and/or
connection, and they are perceived and activated on the screen.[10]

Geotagging photographs – attaching GPS coordinates of the time and place of
photographing – underscores the geographical as well as a temporal aspect of
tagging. It allows for a mnemonic mobility by placing (plotting) and tracing of
digital footprints. We can understand this implication of memory as reinstating
indexicality that digital photography is said to have lost when we can attach geographical coordinates as digital information: adding data about the exact location
from where the picture was taken. This location is not necessarily close to what is
photographed, to the object of the image – the GPS tag marks the location of the
camera, locating the object as well as the photographer in reality. These coordinates constitute the digital footprint of the image-making: its trace.

But it is also its deictic positioning in the present. The main use of this is in
applications that integrate geotagged objects or images in mash-ups or in navigation software. Navigation systems like TomTom or Garmin, or smartphone applications using GPS maps, enable downloading POIs (points of interest) uploaded
by other users, marked by geotagged images. Online one can find a lot of so-
called 'POI collections' or applications that make use of them. Geotags make it
possible to retrace these digital footprints and turn the past into a destination: a
deixis to the future.

The constructive quality of tagging, plotting and stitching as several aspects of
the making of locative, semiotic connections entails possibilities for participatory

engagement. People can make their own personal archives or use them for exchange or for the building of a collective archive. Tagged "mobile mementos" (de Vries 2009) make a subsequent (online) exchange of data, or a collective image gathering or stitching possible. This is essentially collecting information from large social databases.

Photosynth is an example of an online collaborative image collection, also providing the software to stitch together multiple photographs of the same object, space, or event taken from slightly different points of view into a navigable, panoramic whole. In the company's words, it is a "viewer for downloading and navigating complex visual spaces and a 'synther' for creating them in the first place. Together they make something that seems impossible quite possible: reconstructing the 3D world from flat photographs."[11]

Fig. 5.1: Photosynth of Panorama Mesdag (Serge van Schie, 2008)

The company's slogan is, in fact, "use your photos to stitch the world." Images can be stitched together and users can navigate by scrolling through the interactive panoramic rendering of the image. The website offers pre-fab collections, showing buildings, animals, natural reserves, or interiors – basically anything that works in an interactive panoramic image, and gives space to upload one's own synths to the database. The application iSynth takes this navigational model and database logic of stiching to the iPhone. The iPhone screen interface, then, allows for a touch-controlled visual navigation in a composite stitched image field. In the company's words:

Capture, upload, share, and view Photosynth panoramas wherever you go with our new Photosynth app for iOS. These panoramas, which are the same as the ones created using our desktop panorama tools, can be created anywhere, from your favorite restaurant, a space station, or wherever inspiration strikes. From just a few stitched photos up to full spherical panoramas, the Photosynth app allows you to take Photosynth on the go and use it anytime.[12]

Stitching is a useful term for the activity of connecting individual elements to create a larger whole, a cooperative collage. Large databases such as Photosynth, much like the online photo-sharing site Flickr, serve the double purpose of creating and sharing one's own, individual archive, and using the network as a larger repository. This makes longer-running events or games possible. Geocaching, for example, is a treasure-hunt game that uses GPS coordinates tagged to 'real' containers that hold objects. This is a clear case of tagging and plotting, and the user's reading of the map as a form of tracing. Moreover, when found, these may be taken if they are replaced by new objects. The user thus becomes a participant. Waymarking is based on a similar concept, to "share and discover unique and interesting locations on the planet," but does not use 'real' containers for treasures. It only offers POIs, marked by other users.[13]

Yellow Arrow is a famous and long-running project that is a cross between a game, a database, a map, and a locative art project:

Yellow Arrow is a global public art project of local experiences. Combining stickers, mobile phones and an international community, Yellow Arrow transforms the urban landscape into a "deep map" that expresses the personal histories and hidden secrets that live within our everyday spaces.[14]

Geocaching is an example of a similar, yet slightly different and also very popular formula: it is a treasure-hunt game that uses GPS for treasure hunts or other tours that involve the search of real-world objects using GPS software.[15]

These examples of locating the (physical) object of the image and the possibility of retrieving it (as image), and subsequently repositioning, collecting or sharing it – or better: tagging, plotting and stitching – have consequences for our conceptions of time and space. The integration of photography in applications on hybrid devices contributes to a cut-and-paste worldview: a being in the world that consists of endless possibilities. It makes it possible not only to practice limited ways of framing pictures, to crop and thus make cut-outs, but also to transpose, translate, transform and paste these cuts into new contexts. As such, the world becomes a digital, clickable scrapbook that consists of different forms of data, overlapping information, connected dimensions, and multidirectional navigation. This transforms our sense of how we can engage in and with the world.

In an analysis of contemporary digital image-making practices, Uricchio (2011) proposes to distinguish an "algorithimic turn" exemplified by software applications like Photosynth and augmented reality, which, as I will discuss below, point towards a performative cartography. This turn in visual culture entails a radically new relationship between the image of the world and the viewing subject. He clarifies how we should on the one hand recognize the algorithimic operation in the constructing of images, but on the other hand also recognize the activity of the beholder of that image, as co-constructor. He states:

> Although of a different order than the clearly defined subject-object binary that characterized the modern era for the last few hundred years, the algorithmic turn remains rooted in human experiential and semiotic practices. (34)

Here, I am particularly interested in the creative activity as the co-operation of the different levels of the interface and the user as navigating agent in this semiotic practice. Tagging, plotting and stitching constitute a networked and temporally expanding cartography, based on a "cooperative connected performativity" (de Vries 2009), or as I call it in the context of spatial practices, performative cartography. As such, the constructive aspects of this creativity, as I will argue below, are also inherently participatory. While practices in their own right, tagging, plotting and stitching also converge in layering in augmented reality applications, which I will discuss next.

Layering in Augmented Reality

In the hybrid interface of mobile screens, tagging, plotting and stitching converge in augmented reality browsing. Augmented reality is a container term for the use of data overlays on real-time camera view of a location, a term coined by Claudell and Mizell (1992). Originating from developments in virtual reality, using bulky head-mounted displays and later backpacks with equipment, the use of augmented reality is currently taking off in applications for mobile phones. This is a fast-developing field at the moment of writing: from marker-based augmented reality (Rekimoto 1996) and QR codes, to image recognition technologies and experiments with haptic feedback to create a sensation of material depth of objects. AR browsers Layar and Wikitude and, more recently, Junaio are rapidly expanding the possibilities of (consumer) AR browsing for smartphones such as the iPhone. They offer browser applications on devices that have a video camera, GPS, a compass, and an orientation sensor, entailing a new way of engaging with screenspace and navigation of digital space, by effacing the map representation and using direct camera feed with a layer of data superimposed. AR browsing entails a new way of engaging with screenspace that converges the practices of touring, tagging and navigation of digital maps.

Augmented reality browsers make it possible to browse data directly within 'reality' as it is represented on the screen, showing objects within their spatial context. The camera eye on the device registers physical objects on location, and transmits these images in real time on the screen. On-screen this image is combined with different layers of data in different media: still image, text, moving image. These layers have various scales and dimensions within one master frame. We see information superimposed on a real-time image on screen.

Fig. 5.2: Flashmob in augmented reality. Image: Sander Veenhof, 2010

The screen is not actually transparent, but in effect, through real-time, simultaneous display of the camera feed, it seems to be. It looks like and functions as a transparent window, framed only by the edges of the screen. This framing is temporary and directly changeable by the user wielding the screen. As such, in terms of screen-based representation, augmented reality browsing provides a complex sort of framing of this 'reality'. We could say that the screen itself frames the video image on screen, yet the information is layered on the image, and in a sense frameless. The frame is the camera image that brackets off the contours of the world-as-image. With this new mode of 'reality browsing' by means of camera feed, the map on the screen has been rescaled to the same proportion as our vision through the camera lens. Like that vision, it depends on the relative distance between ourselves and the objects seen, and the perspective changes according to our movements.

AR browsers such as *Layar*, *Wikitude* and *Junaio* offer platforms with different uses for this layering, ranging from commercial applications of location-based services showing where restaurants, banks or shops are located, or what real estate is for sale, to more artistic interventions such as virtual expositions, galleries on location, or museum tours. Augmented reality offers a new platform for exhibition in public space, as is being discovered by museums, archives and other cultural institutions. *ARtours*, for example, is an initiative by the Stedelijk Museum in Amsterdam to develop an AR infrastructure for art tours.

Fig. 5.3: ARtotheque, a virtual gallery on location at the Lowlands music festival, organized by the AR project of the Stedelijk Museum, 2010. Image: Stedelijk Museum/Tabworld-media.

In the summer of 2010, the Stedelijk Museum collaborated with the MediaLAB to hold a virtual exhibition of AR art on the Museumplein. The first augmented reality flashmob was organized in April 2010, also in Amsterdam. There and then, people could 'encounter' all kinds of virtual statues or other characters on the street by wielding their mobile phones. These initiatives explore ways to bring AR applications to the public space for (scheduled) public events that can be shared.

There is, however, a tension between the size of the individual screen, and the space available for multiple participants.[16]

The location specificity of augmented reality based on the tagging and plotting of space is, paradoxically perhaps, highly transportable to other locations. Tags can be moved easily. Time- and space-specific events – like festivals – can be used as settings for temporary virtual exhibitions, as ARtours experimented with such concepts at a music festival. In augmented reality, exhibitions can travel, infinitely multiplying and coexisting in space.

Fig 5.4: Can You See Auras? by artist Marieke Berghuis at the Stedelijk Museum virtual art exhibition Ik op het Museumplein [Me on the Museumplein]. Image: Hein Wils, 2010

A less time-based programming of augmented reality tours, but dealing with time nonetheless, is the Urban Augmented Reality (UAR) application launched by the Netherlands Architecture Institute (NAi). The tour shows large 3D buildings that were either once there in the past, will be there in the future, or were designed but were never actually built at all. In the hybrid screenspace this tour establishes, the present, past, future, and even the 'past future' do in fact coincide.

MOBILE SCREENS

Fig. 5.5: *Urban Augmented Reality (UAR) in Rotterdam. Image: Netherlands Architecture Institute (NAI), 2011*

Using the reality browsing property of real-time camera vision, the navigation software Wikitude Drive shows new directions in consumer navigation. The map has disappeared in favor of direct on-screen visual and acoustic feedback. While this application uses the mobile screen of phones for live camera vision layered with data, this combination of real-time video feed and on-screen layering on transparent screens has been developed in the military and aviation, much like the integration of data-layering into special glasses or contact lenses, and *heads-up display* (HUD) layering of information on the windshield of our cars. The possibilities for commercial applications of this type of on-screen navigation are readily apparent. In boasting rhetoric, CEO of Mobilizy (developers of *Wikitude Drive*) Philipp Breuss-Schneeweis suggests:

> [Wikitude Drive] is a light-weight navigation system which takes a different approach than all other navigation systems: You see the real street on your mobile phone, instead of 2D or 3D maps. [...] There is a lot of room to grow in this area when you imagine the possibilities by having access to the huge number of mobile services and points of interest that are already available on mobile devices. Imagine driving by virtual billboards of your favorite fast food chain, or simply having an alert when one of them is nearby. This is going to happen within Wikitude Drive. The Wikitude platform offers [...] a fantastic base to sell premium content or to display location based ads."[17]

According to this rhetoric, the device will be a true competitor, rivaling for first place with spatial reality itself. This disregards the question of whether anyone really needs "millions of POIs".

Despite the commercial nature of the latter application, these examples generally demonstrate that augmentation is a form of creative contribution, which not only adds to space but inherently also modifies it. It creates hybrid space. I wrote above that this use of the word *creative* does not always imply artistic creation, but simply the act of making. Nevertheless, the word also suggests that the categories are porous. The possibility of activating the more traditional sense of creativity has the advantage of debunking an exalted, romantic vision of art that traditionally accompanies the qualifier 'creative' and bringing out the participatory potential of creation. Margriet Schavemaker (2010), Head of Research and Collections at the Stedelijk Museum in Amsterdam and initiator of the earlier mentioned ARtours, the museum's project for AR tours for modern art, has pointed this out. She intimates that augmentation itself is at the core of art in general.

The mash-up logic we can recognize in the navigation of a layered reality entails mnemonic, temporal and experiential aspects of mobility. First of all, it engages with objects in their specific place, while adding temporal layers: a form of mnemonic spacing. This logic requires some sort of spatial stability: objects need to be in their place for some time in order to function as markers for their tags. As such, the logic relies on archival information attached to a spatial presence. AR applications are built on databases (archives) of metadata attached to geospatial information. Secondly, the mash-up logic provides means to experience a 'different' city. It adds, changes, enhances and constructs a city of difference. The augmented reality navigator is an interactive performer, erecting a city of difference.[18]

These AR browsers and applications construct a particular kind of cartography. Like any kind of cartography they are information-based, but this information can be modified and personalized. Moreover, it is an interactive cartography in that it is responsive to input. The navigator operates it individually on a small, handheld touchscreen and the cartography activates a subjective perspective on the directly surrounding space, unlinking the abstracted bird's-eye view of space in traditional paper maps. The layeredness of the augmented-reality image is a superimposing of different spatial representations: one based on photographic/filmic framing, and the other a dataspace.

Discussing new-generation AR navigation systems for cars, Tristan Thielman makes the comparison with Edward Soja's (1996) conception of first, second, and thirdspace:

> In accordance to [Soja] the new generation of navigation systems that project the travel route onto the windscreen can also be described as the rise of the perspective of a third space. The driver is himself in the first space and

through the windscreen sees a first space that can be experienced physically. Via the head-up display, a second space is simultaneously projected before his eyes as a mental concept of space. These spaces, when overlaid and integrated into each other, represent something like a "both/and" instead of an "either/ or" through this hybridity, mobility and simultaneity. Such a complex understanding of space opens up new spaces. (2007: 70)

The analogy with Soja's thirdspace is that of a conceptual and experiential category. As Thielmann seems to suggest here, this spacing is a quality of the experience of hybridity. Augmented reality thus brings about not the sum of layers, but a whole new dimension to the experience of space.[19]

Like cartography in de Certeau's sense, augmented reality provides a practiced narrative in that it tells spatial stories in the making: it makes experiences unfold in space at the moment of their occurrence. Hence, it is procedural, in the sense that movement through space and interaction with on-screen layers of digital information to off-screen geographical and material presence unfolds in time. But not only does it take time, it becomes over time. A conception of time that includes the productive, or literally creative aspect of time, is relevant here; it includes change in time.

This puts us with our historical feet back on the ground. This new technology has much in common with the age-old habit of walking, and in this links back to, say, Baudelaire's flâneur as leisurely stroller. The cartographic principle of (AR) browsing is a synthesis of the two other models, that of touring and tagging. Incorporating geotagging as a principle, the spatial logic is that of cut-outs and layers of information. Being structured as tours, the engagement is not visual, fixated and distanced, but haptic, fluid and procedural.

Haptic Engagement

One particular aspect of interactive navigation in performative cartography is the successive rendering of changing positioning in physical space which is, in turn, used for reading and traversing this space. I propose to consider this the *haptic* aspect of engagement. Engagement brings together the aspects of agency – the doing – and the experiential – the seeing and feeling. It is the haptic engagement, understood as form of interactivity and as experience, which is significant for mobile screen gadgets. I will briefly explore here how a conceptualization of haptic experience addresses precisely the intersection of touch and physical interaction with the experience of the device, on the one hand, and the agency in and experience of spatial unfolding on the other. It is in haptic engagement that the creative meets the cartographic.

Brought into currency in the wake of Deleuze's work on aesthetics, the term haptic has become quite popular in recent film and media theory – so much so that its meaning is at risk of becoming diffused, and as a consequence lost. 'Haptic' comes from the Greek verb *aptô*, which means to touch. The term is currently widely used in three fields of study – art, cinema, and interface studies. The term is used to qualify a certain kind of looking, a specific gaze. In that sense, it exists in opposition to another kind of gaze, namely the optical one.

Aloïs Riegl introduced the term in 1901 in a distinction between haptic and optic art. In distinction from the optical gaze, which is limited to the eye that sees at a distance, haptic looking means that the look can graze the object, caress it with the touch, and by extension, experience it with all the senses. This potential entails close proximity.[20]

Deleuze discusses the haptic primarily in relation to painting. This is the first of three fields that exploit the haptic in today's culture. In Deleuze and Guattari's various entries in *A Thousand Plateaus* (2004 [1980]), where they discuss the haptic quality of primarily abstract painting, the attempt to circumscribe the non-optical quality of haptic looking, figures and forms are replaced with flux, movement, forces; continuous variations most pointedly characterized by the sea or the desert with ever-moving, fleeting constellations. For example, instead of connecting points, lines move between points.[21] For a painter, this means that the artist is so close to the object to be depicted that it is no longer possible to distinguish discrete features; the object within a smooth field without fixed points. For the viewer, such looking entails the loss of the distinction between form and background, as well as, in its wake, that between form and content. Hence, Deleuze's interest in abstraction.

In film theory the idea of the haptic has come to stand for an engaged look that involves, and is aware of, the body – primarily that of the viewer. Vivian Sobchack (1992 and 2004) has developed this perspective on haptic perception of cinema in her phenomenological theory of cinematic spectatorship with the ambition to bridge the theorized gap between viewer and screen. This gap had been put forward in the psychoanalytical film theory of Metz and Baudry. This theory gives the spectator a passive position, written into the dispositif of classical cinema. Laura Marks (2002) also makes a claim for haptic visuality as a way of looking within a more intimate and dialogic relationship between screen and image on the one hand and the spectator on the other. In her view, haptic perception is less based on mastery than optical visuality, allowing for a more intimate form of criticism. This is considered a direct consequence of spatial difference: the proximity of touch is considered more intimate and less controlling than the distancing gaze (2000; 2002).[22]

These perspectives on the haptic as an overlooked aspect of the experience of viewing are ultimately focused on visuality. Touch, then, becomes "folded into optic tactility" as David Parisi critically remarked (2008: 65). In his project, Parisi is concerned with the actual 'touching' of interfaces. Marks purports that her main objective is with the construction of subjectivity in the haptic, but she nevertheless emphasizes the haptic within the context of visual perception. When she points out how a haptic quality can be attributed not just to the way of looking but to the object of the gaze, she argues how this relationship changes because of this reciprocity of the haptic:

> The term haptic visuality emphasizes the viewer's inclination to perceive hapti-
> cally, but a work itself may offer haptic images. Haptic images do not invite
> identification with a figure so much as they encourage a bodily relationship
> between the viewer and the image. Thus it is more appropriate to speak of the
> object of a haptic look than to speak of a dynamic subjectivity between looker
> and image. (3; emphasis in text)

A third notion of the haptic is pertinent for interface studies in a derived but different sense. There, it indicates the presence, activity and role of other senses than vision alone. The attention for the haptic has increased awareness of the pervasive presence in cultural artifacts of synesthesia – the trope of the different senses merging, or rather, of transferring meaning from one sense domain to another. There is, moreover, an obvious attraction to a haptic perspective because of the senses implicated in using interface devices, primarily the actual physical touch. However, from a perspective of haptic interfaces, touch is embedded within an extended sensory perception, which not only includes the entire body with all its other senses, but also the extension of them by the handheld device; the interface itself is incorporated in the haptic.

Interfaces such as touchscreen and tactile feedback, as well as the interactivity such devices require, easily lead to an assumption that the resulting gaze is haptic. This is not necessarily the case, but for that very reason, they have made thinking about agency, materiality, subjectivity, but also the status of the 'text' urgent. For my argument here about the cartographic gesture of interactive, and as I argue, creative navigation, my concern is not so much with the 'touching' of the interface – which I addressed in previous chapters, in particular in Chapter 3 on the touchscreen – nor with the question if the result is a haptic way of looking, but with the procedural and unfolding creation of space in navigation. It is there that the haptic can take its place.

Here, the notion of haptic space allows a useful distinction from representational regimes of space. Yet, with performative cartography I propose to find a convergence between these regimes: the haptic and the optical visual converge in navigation. This convergence renders the image or map always already pre-representational. Supplementing these views of the haptic, here I wish to draw attention to the consequence of such a look for the object. The object of haptic vision is in movement, in flux; it has lost all fixity. This is precisely what characterizes the practice of screens of navigation, in particular in relation to location, something we traditionally see as fixed. In contrast to this traditional conception of location, haptic screens of navigation put forward a practice that incites us to rethink the notion of locating as a fixating gesture. This gesture is not necessarily fixating, since such screens enable a mobile engagement with the screen.

The haptic is part and parcel of the trends in mobile, digital cartography I have discussed above – tagging, plotting, stitching and (AR) browsing – which establish the practice of navigation as performative construction: a practice of *making* space. This construction takes time and is hence also temporal. Multi-dimensional, performative navigation is a cartographic practice in that it is constructive, flexible, open-ended. Moreover, because it makes the space the user then enters, it is pre-representational. Instead, it is physical and experiential. In this thinking about navigation, a different notion of cartography is being unfolded. Cartography is not a precondition only, but a *product* of navigation, and as such, cartography is more than a systematic representation of space. It is a performance of space in a true sense: a making and expressing of space in the collaboration of the device and its user. This practice is a truly haptic performance of cartography.

With the analysis of the performativity of the practices of screen-based navigation, I propose to reconsider notions of one-directional screening practices of display, including older ones, whether this display is based on storage, transmission, or even interactive feedback. This perspective develops the notion of a hybrid spatiality of a 'navigable' screenspace. Contrary to a common-sense idea about screens, media and technology as distancing and alienating facets of modernity, such a notion in fact foregrounds a fundamentally corporeal, or embodied experience of space this technology makes possible. This is the creative potential, I would say, of mobile screen cartography in its relationship with the haptic: the ensuing haptic and productive engagement with screenspace. Interacting with screens in a mobile dispositif not only implies a full-bodied experience, it is a performative act.

Epilogue: You Are Here!

From navigation as a screen practice to navigation as an analytical practice: the project of a comparative analysis, both historical and theoretical, of screen media compels us to rethink not only present-day media practices but our way of thinking about these practices in terms of what they mean. When our focus is more on the movements and inscriptions of media than on particular texts, our thinking about the issues entails different questions, concepts, and perspectives: a different epistemology. In other words, not only does the location or site-specificity of screens and the locating of screens affect media practices, but also the way we understand them. In this study, I have suggested that we can productively investigate the intersection of space and mobility as site and practice – a perspective on both object and analysis. This shifts our attention away from representation to navigation.

For this argument, I have been looking at both artistic and commercial screens in public spaces, most prominently in places of transit such as airports and stations. These screens play with the tension between mobility – of trains and travelers – and locatedness: the stillness of situated objects, surfaces, material structures embedded in architecture, the fabric of our cities. Therefore, I would like to conclude with a short reflection on an example of 'still' screens – the works or installations of art or advertisement that suggest, create or reflect on the movement surrounding them, or the movement in their spatial presence.

In the Vuosaari Metro Station in Helsinki, among a labyrinthine mass of constructivist metal pipes, a series of concave polycarbonate semi-translucent abstract sheets block and at the same time encourage the view of the sky through the glass ceiling. With the eleven pieces, Finnish artist Jussi Niva challenges the distinction between still and moving vision. Passengers on the trains arriving, as well as people waiting to board the train, see their vision of the outside blocked by the computer-controlled airbrushed sheets of the series entitled *Expose*, from 1998. By virtue of their function, we can call the sheets *screens*.

The imagery on the screens is unstable. Not frontally positioned, they are semi-transparent, and reflect light differently, at each particular moment offering images of the ever-changing sky. The width of the intervention in the skeleton of the building, and the curves of the screens, suggests panoramic vision. The movement is brought in by the spectators in the installation of screens: the people passing the screens, who, after first sitting still in moving trains, suddenly get up and move onto the platforms, through the station, switching platforms, perhaps into the mall adjoining the station. The arrangement suggests the panoramic complex discussed in the first chapter of this book. As an intervention in urban public space, specifically a place of transit, the composition also connects to my second chapter. Yet, the staggered movement of passing spectators and the waiting or halted passengers brings movement and change into the setup. How is this positioned at the intersection of the panoramic complex and the performative cartography on which Chapter 5 ends?

Fig. 6.1: Expose (Jussi Niva, 1998) at Vuosaari Metro Station, Helsinki. Computer controlled airbrush, acrylic on polycarbonate, 7 pieces of 180 x 600 cm, 4 pieces of 180 x 160 cm. Photos: Jussi Niva

The artist seems aware of the dilemma of movement and locatedness, and boldly states his refusal to make this an either/or choice, when he says:

> A panorama is a short wipe into a view, and instead of a single-point perspective, it always accommodates several vanishing points. It constantly strains towards motion, or perhaps it would be more accurate to say, it is a depiction of the viewer's motion. The eye grazes its undulating expanses [...] All clear signs of a perspective are at their minimum. The impression must be as if all convexity were pressed into a flat sheet, where the directions take on an exquisite curve and everything flees from the centre. (Jussi Niva quoted by Inkamaija Iitä 2010: 29)

While "the eye grazes its undulating expanses" is an adequate phrasing of the haptic gaze, this statement gives the highway panorama a mobility that takes it out of its nineteenth-century beginnings and helps bring it in close proximity to the cartographic devices the final chapter has brought to the fore. Thus, Niva demonstrates the need to think theoretically and historically; to merge seeing and making, grasping and moving, thinking and doing. Expose, then, closes the circle this book has been sketching. As a true performative, by way of a concrete intervention in urban space, it does what it says. This performativity contributes to an understanding of *interfaces*, not so much as technologies, as objects, or as tools, but as sites of practice, and of *interfacing* as a performative and corporeal event. In this sense, in its appeal to an essentially mobile gaze, *Expose* can be seen as an emblem of what this book has explored.

This performativity lies at the heart of the visual regime of navigation. It is not only performative, but also haptic, constructive, flexible, open-ended, non-representational and experiential. In this study of screens and navigation, a different notion of cartography has been unfolded. With the analysis of performativity of the practices of screen-based navigation, I have reconsidered notions of one-directional screening practices of display, and complicated the locatedness and site-specificity of screens. The collapse of viewing and making develops the notion of a hybrid spatiality of a navigable screenspace that enables a fundamentally haptic engagement in viewing. This firmly positions the viewer as an active agent within the visual regime of navigation.

This agency, however, while offering possibilities for a dialogic and reflexive stance, does not necessarily lead to a critical engagement. I do not wish to end this book with a judgment on the success or failure of our current uses of mobile technologies and innovative screen dispositifs for 'meaningful' content and participatory ideals. However, an uncritical, jubilant endorsement also seems premature. The relatively unstable nature of innovative technologies and practices that are changing rapidly, together with the enthusiastic embrace of their possibilities for public engagement, call for a critical interrogation. We must examine not only the possibility of access and the participatory potential of locative, screen-based projects, but also consider the convergence of and conflicts between the ambitions of initiators (i.e. heritage institutions), of media designers, and the media competencies required from the public.

Locative media provide interactive platforms for museums and archives in public space, enabling new modes of engagement. Moreover, the use of interactive technologies also generates new content for cultural collections: co-creation, user-generated content, new connections to other data, and other forms of annotation are enabled through open access to digital archives. Locative media function as interfaces to the digitized collections, meeting the archives' ambitions for open access and interaction with their audience. This raises questions about the functioning of these technologies for interaction with cultural heritage, with present-day co-habitation, and, simply, with the act of looking. The transition from in-house collection, access and exhibition to the use of mobile platforms entails challenges for both archival institutions and media designers involved with developing interactive digital platforms. But is access the same as engagement, and seeing identical to looking? While I refrain from speculating on how these questions should be answered, their presence in our reflections on our contemporary culture is of great importance. Without such reflections, a cultural vision is impossible.

A historical and theoretical understanding of how a visual regime of navigation is taking shape in our screen practices reveals the tensions as well as synergies between media ideals, the status of technology in cultural practice, and the performativity implied in practices. This synergy, of course, entails players. Among these, museums, archives and educational institutions, but also commercial companies, work in collaboration with developers and designers on behalf of a broad and often unspecified population of users. These groups do not necessarily have the same skills, the same ambitions, nor do they speak the same language. Heritage, media literacy, innovation – both technical and creative – and the pleasures of media use do not always converge. Neither an uncritical embrace nor a nostalgic reluctance can help evaluate the social effects of these projects, especially in the longer term. Moreover, the status of these projects challenges media theory: what are our objects (installations, screens, images, public participation?); how do we deal with historicity and innovation, and how do we include performative practices in our analyses?

This book has not only suggested what the questions are, but has proposed an approach to these issues, which are characteristic of a screen culture that embraces a visual regime of navigation; a perspective that provides a conceptual framework for further analysis of this culture in transition.

Notes

1. Panoramic Complex

1. Francien Houben (1999). For a presentation of the project, see Francien Houben and Luisa Maria Calabrese (2003).
2. In 2006, I participated in a research project on highway panoramas with the Netherlands Institute for Spatial Research, culminating in a publication intended to provide tools for the design and direction of highway panoramas. See Piek et al. (2007).
3. See, for example, Barker (2009); Bruno (2002); Sobchack (2004); Marks (2000) and (2002); and Patterson (2007).
4. Quoted in http://www.tii.se/mobility/projects.htm (accessed October 2011); emphasis added.
5. See also Oskar Juhlin (2005).
6. Vivian Sobchack defines syneasthesia succinctly as the "exchange and translation between and among the senses" (2004: 69).
7. About the advent of cinema and in particular the representation of the landscapes of the American West in the context of emerging technologies of both transport and visuality, see Verhoeff (2006). Lynne Kirby (1996) writes about the cinema as "mechanical double" for the train.
8. The cultural historic role of "machines of the visible" is discussed, for example, by Jonathan Crary (1990) and Martin Jay (1988). Vanessa Schwartz (1998) has argued that this period just before the advent of cinema saw a rapid rise of popular (visual) sensations and spectacles as part of the process of modernization and the advent of mass culture. About the relationship between popular sensationalism and the late-nineteenth-century 'shock' of modernity, see Ben Singer (2001).
9. Svetlana Alpers' article on the "mapping impulse" in Dutch painting is interesting in this light. She compares pictorial traditions and cartographic principles. She distinguishes two types of mapping in painting: the panoramic, which she calls "mapped landscape view", and the cityscape or "topographical city view" (1987: 72).
10. For an elaborate study on the Panorama, see Stephan Oettermann (1997). In his very thorough discussion on the history of the moving panorama, Erkki Huhtamo clearly establishes how the first use of the term 'panorama' is dated differently in studies on the history of panoramic paintings (2004). On immersive panoramic spectatorship in comparison to interactive entertainments, see Alison Griffiths (2008).
11. Emphasis added. A facsimile of the original patent can be found at the Edingburgh Virtual Environment Centre, http://www.edvec.ed.ac.uk/html/projects/panorama/barker.html (accessed October 2011), and the website Adventures in Cybersound on http://www.acmi.net.au/AIC/PANORAMA.html (accessed October 2011). For a reproduction see also Laurent Mannoni, Donata Presenti Campagnoni, David Robinson

(1995: 157–158). It is striking how the text almost only addresses the manner of disposition where great concern is reserved for the illusion and attaining the effect of immersion.

12. Eliminating the frame is explicitly emphasized in the patent applied for by Barker, when he writes that it is necessary "to prevent an observer seeing above the drawing or painting" and "to prevent the observer from seeing below the bottom of the painting or drawing, by means of which interception nothing can be seen on the outer circle, but the drawing or painting intended to represent nature." This goes to show that the borders of the screen are considered a representation.

13. For more about the history of this unique panorama, see http://www.panorama-mesdag.com/ (accessed October 2011).

14. Hence Ralph Hyde's book title Panoramania!: The Art and Entertainment of the "All-embracing" (1988) and the exhibition with the same name at the Victoria & Albert Gallery in London.

15. Angela Miller compares the stationary and moving panoramas and traces the characteristic of the medium of film in both traditions (1996).

16. For a comparison between the panorama and the diorama, see Friedberg (1993): 25-29. The effects of the diorama are also described in Van Eekelen (1996): 19. The technology and formation of the diorama are described with great precision and with illustrations and the original patent in the online version of the article on "The Diorama in Great Britain in the 1820s" by R. Derek Wood (1993) at: http://www.midley.co.uk/diorama/Diorama_Wood_1_1.htm (accessed October 2011).

17. For a clear explanation of the technical aspects of the panoramic photo and the consequences this has for perspective, see Rombout, ed. (2006).

18. Huhtamo compares the stereoscope with the virtual traveler (1995).

19. For a comprehensive discussion of the early phantom rides, and how the film archetype was connected to other visual spectacles and cultural practices such as travel and tourism, see Verhoeff (2006: 282-295). Giulliana Bruno (1997) discusses at length the way in which visual transport of these panoramic films offer a way in which urban space should be visually designed. For an example of the deployment and probing of phantom rides in contemporary art and popular culture, see Stan Douglas' installation Ouverture from 1986 or Michel Gondry's video clip of Star Guitar by the Chemical Brothers (2001).

20. Performance is not the same as performativity. The first term is derived from the theater and other aptly named 'performing arts', the second from the philosophy of language. Performance refers to the stage of a public setting. Performativity refers to the notion that acts bring about effects that are not reducible to meaning. For a discussion of the distinction as well as the similarities between performance and performativity, see Mieke Bal (2002: 147-212) and Marvin Carlson (2004).

21. A useful overview of the discussion can be found in Sturken and Cartwright (2001).

22. The French philosopher and art historian Hubert Damisch has analyzed the theory and practice of linear perspective in great detail (1994). About perspective in light of modernity's regime of visuality and inextricably linked scientific paradigm based on the logic of Cartesian thinking, see Martin Jay's landmark text "Scopic Regimes of Modernity" (1988).

23. The American art historian Jonathan Crary discusses this in relation to stereoscopic viewing (1990). See also Kaja Silverman (1996), who discusses Crary at great length. Silverman herself develops the forms of dialogic viewing in greater depth, with the purpose of articulating what she calls an "ethics of looking".

24. Friedberg suggests replacing the panoptic model with this mobilized and virtual visual regime (2006). Within media studies, the integration of mobility and virtuality is an important adjustment in the conceptualization of visual perception.

2. Self-Reflection

1. About the relationship between automobility of cars and television see for example Urry (2004) and Featherstone (2004). Lisa Parks examines how, instead of using notions of 'weightlessness' in online navigation, we should understand the material and political realities of virtual mobility: "I use the term 'epistemologies of movement' to suggest that there are different ways of signifying and interpreting (or seeing and knowing) movement at a web interface. I do not mean to suggest that all web-users experience movement in the same way; rather, I want to develop a way to understand the meanings of online navigation in more material and semiotic terms." (2004: 37). This caution is relevant for my discussion in Chapter 5.

2. About simultaneity as ambition in a new medium, see Uricchio's argument about the wish for simultaneous 'tele-vision' that predates the invention of cinema as a storage medium. (Uricchio 2004) Seen from a slightly different perspective, 'liveness' as an aspect of new media technologies has been reinvented in the course of history. About the concept of liveness in different media technologies from a comparative view point, see e.g. Auslander (2008), Caldwell (1995), Couldry (2004), McPherson (2002), and White (2004), and more specifically with a focus on television, Feuer (1983).

3. For an excellent overview of the ins and outs of deixis, see Stephen C. Levinson (2004). Levinson considers deixis as coextensive with indexicality, which he considers a larger category of contextual dependency and reserves deixis for linguistic aspects of indexicality. (97-98) Below I will return to the deictic quality of certain forms of indexicality, specifically in relation to the index as trace, when considering the specifically layered temporality at work in the screening of early cinema today. About focalization, see Mieke Bal (2009).

4. Thanks to Karin van Es for her suggestion to use the term screen *engager* to conceptualize the active and dialogic relationship between the screen and its user or spectator. In the absence of a single, sufficiently precise term, I will use the term spectator, engager-spectator, or navigator when appropriate. For a more elaborate discussion about terms for spectatorship, in particular in relation to the 'user' of computer screens, see also Michele White's excellent introduction to her book on Internet spectatorship. (2006: 1-16)

5. For a discussion of the difference between what Doreen Massey (1994) calls space/time (with slash), spacetime, and timespace, see Lammes and Verhoeff (2009). Spacetime, as a fourth-dimensional quality of time-in-space, will be discussed in the next chapter. Not coincidentally, timespace refers to the Bahktinian notion of chronotope. About Mikhail Bahktin's terminology, see Peeren (2007). In short, 'timespace' is what

is constructed in 'spacetime'. See also May and Thrift (2001) for their considerations in using the word TimeSpace as their book title to connote the inseparability of time and space and the multiplicity of space-times they want to address. Their main focus is on multiple "senses of time" that are spatially constructed in social practices. (3-5)

6. Among some valuable studies of the trope of mobility in early cinema, in relation to turn-of-the-century culture and the shock of modernity, are Lynne Kirby (1996) who writes about the cinema as "mechanic double" for the train; Ben Singer (2001) on cinema and the sensations of modernity; and Lauren Rabinovitz (1998a) on the perceptual experience of travel, in particular in the case of Hale's Tours. Rabinovitz (1998b) also argues for a lineage between early cinema's phantom rides and modern ride films. Stephen Bottomore (1999) provides a thorough analysis of the so-called 'train effect' and the myth of the early-cinema audiences panicking by watching approaching trains. Tom Gunning (1990) examines the relationship between cinematic visuality and the culture of modernity and positions the phantom ride as emblematic of early cinema as a cinema of attractions.

7. Brooks Landon (1992: 94). Scott Bukatman (1999: 254) quotes Landon when he summarizes his argument concerning the affects of special effects in science fiction cinema that go beyond narrative. The phrase "ways of seeing" alludes to John Berger's book with that title.

8. This view of narrative and attraction as different but not opposing categories is put forward by Frank Kessler (2006) as well, who argues that there is no exclusive opposition between narration and attraction, as attractions can be narrativized. In his view, that is why one should rather distinguish between modes of address and functions in terms of narrative integration versus attractional display.

9. For the link between cinema of attraction and contemporary screen culture, see Strauven, ed. (2006). I borrow the qualifier "heteropathic" – but not its specific meaning – from Silverman (1996).

10. About the chase film as proto-genre in early cinema, see Tom Gunning (1984) and Jonathan Auerbach (2000). About early cinema's train films, phantom rides, chase films, and the relationship between these and other genres as based on family resemblances (Wittgenstein), see Verhoeff (2006).

11. *Conway Castle* is part of the Biograph 68mm collection; the films in that collection have a particularly bright and sharp image due to their wide gauge. The spectacular visuals of the ride film are enhanced by the strikingly beautiful use of color in this film.

12. For a background to this terminology, see Jean-Louis Comolli's 1971 essay "Machines of the Visible" in which he positions cinema not as (strict) technology but as a cultural dispositif: "It was necessary that something else be constituted, that something else be formed: the *cinema machine*, which is not essentially the camera, the film, the projector, which is not merely a combination of instruments, apparatuses, techniques. Which is a machine: a *dispositif* articulating between different sets – technological certainly, but also economic and ideological." (108, emphasis in original) In line with this, Maaike Bleeker approaches theater as a critical vision machine in her book *Visuality in the Theater* (2008). About visual tropes in early cinema, particularly in train films, see Nanna Verhoeff and Eva Warth (2002).

13. Watch the commercial at: http://nl.youtube.com/watch?v=Im4PToAJvqU (accessed October 2011).

14. Jenkins' line of thinking can be seen in conjunction with an older view expressed by Stephen Heath about narrative space in cinema. (1981)

15. For the narratological terms used here, see Bal (2009).

16. Elsewhere, I have pointed out the way in which landscape depiction in photography and cinema entails a deictic framing of 'elsewhere' for a viewer who is the focal point of the deictic constellation (2006: 191-192) using Benveniste's terminology. See Benveniste (1971).

3. Theoretical Consoles

1. Digitally animated games are not the only applications that can be played on the DS. An Internet browser, movie players and music players have been developed – both by Nintendo, by official software developers, and as *home brew* by the user community – with which it is possible to browse the web, watch movie files, listen to audio files, view maps, or read e-books on the DS.

2. Without referring to the concept of dispositif, Erkki Huhtamo (1997) makes explicit how a media-archaeological approach can uncover the historical life of the topos of mobility that structures these dispositifs.

3. Although I do not wish to suggest that the DS is explicitly targeted by Nintendo as a retro console. As Melanie Swalwell (2007) has pointed out, the nostalgic recuperation of 'early' videogames and consoles is a remarkable recent trend.

4. http://www.nintendo.com/consumer/systems/ds/faq.jsp (accessed October 2011), emphasis added.

5. Originally posted at http://www.nintendo.com/overviewds.

6. Parikka and Suominen (2006) point out this rhetoric of generation in the presentation of the DS gaming platform by Satoru Iwata, Nintendo president: "We have developed Nintendo DS based upon a completely different concept from existing game devices in order to provide players with a unique entertainment experience for the 21st century." Quoted from Kristian Reed (2004).

7. Here, I use symptom in a semiotic sense, as a sign emitted unwittingly, unintentionally – not referring to the word as used in medicine. The symptom is in this case a reference to a past that can be recognized, not a surfacing sign of disease, which in (Peircian) semiotic terms would be called an index.

8. Tips and Tricks for the DS Browser originally posted at: http://www.opera.com/products/devices/nintendo/tips/. See also http://www.game.co.uk/en/nintendo-ds-web-browser-22497 (accessed October 2011). To give an example of the old/now discourse: both scrolling and browsing hark back to rolls of paper and leafing through a book.

9. Although very different in terms of technique and technology, this experimenting with the game console as moving picture-making machine is reminiscent of machinima: films made with the option that most game consoles have to save gameplay. We can consider both uses as artistic experiments with technology that modify dominant uses of the commercial apparatuses. In this way, these inventive uses of the 'original' technology play with the remediating possibilities that these new tools offer.

10. To avoid misunderstanding: I do not equate tactility with the haptic nor does touch automatically lead to haptic vision. More on this issue in Chapter 5.

11. See http://cs.nyu.edu/~jhan/ftirtouch/index.html (accessed October 2011).

12. Originally posted at http://www.apple.com/iphone/technology/ (2007).

13. The button-less interface comes in more versions. Something similar in its goal, although different in its means, is the technology of what are known as Laser, Projector, or Virtual Keyboards, which allow you to type on a projected, virtual and immaterial image of a keyboard while the movements of your fingers are registered by a camera device which translates these movements into actions.

14. The (French) term *mise en abîme*, or *mise en abyme* has been first proposed by André Gide, (who spelled it with a y) and has been further theorized by Lucien Dällenbach (1989) for literary studies. In painting the phenomenon has been studied by Victor Stoichita (1996) and in cinema by, for example, Thomas Elsaesser (2000).

15. This may remind us of the separate, yet connected spaces of navigation devices. In the next chapter I discuss further the idea that in those cases the on-screen *representation* of navigation is, in fact, the means for navigating off-screen space. This simultaneous on- and off-screen navigation can be conceptualized as the construction of *screenspace*: a hybrid space between on- and off-screen space.

4. Urban Screens

1. John Urry uses this understanding of mobility as visual experience expressed by Augé to signal a larger trend that makes *land* into *landscape*: "The notion of landscape prescribes a visual structure of desire to the experiences of different places [...]." (2007: 102)

2. About this project, see http://selectparks.net/~julian/ (accessed October 2011).

3. On the incorporation of technology in architectural infrastructure, see Nigel Thrift and Shaun French (2002: 314, 317) cited in Nick Couldry and Anna McCarthy. (2004: 2)

4. See http://www.lancelmaat.nl/content/scream (accessed October 2011).

5. See the Media Architecture Institute at http://www.mediaarchitecture.org (accessed October 2011).

6. For an archaeology of urban screens as part of a longer history of what he calls, "public media displays", see Erkki Huhtamo (2009).

7. For this and more installations by the artists, see http://www.webblick.de/ (accessed October 2011).

8. Janssens has made several pieces on this furnace-façade in photography and video, exhibited in various places. In 2011, she exhibited several videos derived from this building in the show *unExhibit* at the Generali Foundation, Vienna. See Folie and Lafer (2011).

9. *The Urban Screens Reader* (McQuire, Martin, Niederer 2009), for example, provides a selection of writings on the politics of public space and strategies for participation in locative media. A pervasive question concerns the possibilities for interaction and the space for art and counterculture in the public domain.

10. About Johannesma's work, and in particular his approach to landscape, see Bloemheuvel and Guldemond (eds.), 2001. About *Parallel Library*, see http://classic.skor.nl/

artefact-3109-en.html (accessed October 2011). About *Inkijk #3*, see http://stichting-
kunstenopenbareruimte.nl/eng/archive/item/inkijk-3 (accessed October 2011).

11. Elsewhere, I have considered the archival poetics of bits and pieces in film archives.
    (2006: *Bits & Pieces*) Part of my argument there was that the archival context suspends
    the distinction between the fragment and the whole; a distinction that in this archival
    showcasing is questioned yet again.

12. The *Bits & Pieces* collection of EYE is unique in its kind, and consists of unidentified
    fragments that the archive finds beautiful and enchanting enough to not only preserve
    but also to exhibit, in spite of, or perhaps because of their 'incomplete' status.

13. From the program description, EYE Film Institute, 2010. Many thanks to Anna Abra-
    hams, project manager of experimental programming at EYE, for giving me back-
    ground information about the project.

14. The touring show *Crazy Cinématographe*, curated by Vanessa Toulmin (National Fair-
    ground Archive) and Nicole Dahlen and Claude Bertemes (Cinémathèque Luxem-
    bourg) in 2007 recreated the celebrated early cinema's traveling years as fairground
    attraction for a contemporary audience. The films were projected in a tent completed
    with a cast of performers bringing back the tradition of the fairground shows. Their
    programming comprised titles from European film archives and featured many re-
    gional and location-specific titles. This screening turned the contemporary and local
    audience into the deictic 'you' of the archival films. The show was organized as a
    public event to accompany the academic conference Traveling Cinema held at the Uni-
    versity of Trier, the proceedings of which were edited by Martin Loipedinger (2011).

15. The permeability of the now obsolete distinction of private and public space is the
    starting point of e.g. the volume edited by Mark Shepard (2011), in particular Martijn
    de Waal's contribution.

16. The consequences of mobile communication technologies for participation in and
    connectivity between private and public domains and the convergence of these realms
    are discussed by Zizi Papacharissi (2010). Raymond Williams (1997 [1974]) writes
    about a *mobile privatization*, a term that suggests a similar role of mobility in the con-
    nection between private and public (or not-private) domains. Williams used this term
    more in the sense of virtual transport – for example by television in the home – which
    is centered in the private sphere, rather than constitutive of a hybrid and simultaneous
    presence that has become mobile in itself.

17. About *Playing Flickr* ("public space installation"), see http://www.mediamatic.net/
    attachment-8946-en.html (accessed October 2011).

18. About this installation, see http://www.chrisoshea.org/hand-from-above/gallery
    (accessed October 2011). About the Big Screens project, see http://www.bbc.co.uk/
    bigscreens/ (accessed October 2011).

5. Performative Cartography

1. See Christian Jacob (2006) for a study of the history of map-making as a permanent
   attempt to achieve a 3D representation on flat paper.

2. J. Brian Harley is often credited for opening up the academic discipline for topics such
   as ideology, discourse and power, and surveillance as aspects of cartography that is

traditionally, in Tom Conley's words, "a teleological discourse that reifies power." (2007: 220) See, for example, Harley (1988) and (1992).

3. Sybille Lammes (2009) makes use of Bruno Latour's work on scientific artifacts (2005) for her approach of maps as material interfaces and differentiates digital maps from Latour's category of "immutable mobiles" (1990), a category that is more easily applicable to analogue maps. This shift from maps as objects to maps as interfaces opens up a way to consider the literal 'working' of maps. This is a shift from maps as 'objects' to maps as 'machines', one which aligns with my approach to theoretical consoles (Chapter 3) in the sense that our screen-based objects are objects, interfaces, and dispositifs, all in one.

4. Feminist philosophers, among others, have critiqued the classificatory principle of epistemological thinking for a long time now. A few examples can be found in Alcoff and Potter, eds. (1993), a representative collection; Code (1991) for a neo-Kantian alternative, and (1995) for the consequences in thinking about place in relation to language; Keller (1999), an article also relevant for the discussion of touch.

5. Jeremy W. Crampton locates a performative turn in cartography and understands maps as performative practices rather than as objects, in his essay 'Cartography: Performative, Participatory, Political'. (2009)

6. For this Bergsonian understanding of time, or duration, and materiality, see Elizabeth Grosz (2005: 11). I am indebted to Iris van der Tuin who pointed out Grosz's phrasing to me in relation to non-dualist thinking. See also van der Tuin (2010) for her deployment of Barad's use of *diffraction* (2007; via Donna Harraway) as a method for refraining from an oppositional reading of Henri Bergson's philosophy, based precisely on the non-dualistic framework inherent in Bergson's thinking.

7. Bakhtin's line is indirectly rendered in Bal (1999: 100). For the relevance of Bakhtin's work for cultural analysis, see Peeren (2007).

8. About ambient intelligence see Aarts, Harwig and Schuurmans (2001) and also Crang and Graham (2007).

9. http://dev.junaio.com/publisher/junaioglue (accessed October 2011)

10. Tuters and Varnellis speak of two kinds of cartography in the broader 'genre' of locative media: annotative (based on tagging) and phenomenological (tracing movement) (2006: 359). This is close to my terminology here, although I wish to analyze the merging of these two forms in performative cartography, as it is made possible by the hybrid of interface.

11. http://photosynth.net/about.aspx (accessed October 2011).

12. http://photosynth.net/capture.aspx (accessed October 2011).

13. From the perspective of an outsider making use of the assembled database, this is also called, like a business model and with a different and more top-down connotation, crowdmining or crowdsourcing. The use of multiple amateur image feeds can also create a new, cooperative 'YouTube aesthetic'. In 2010 rock band Radiohead supported a fan initiative to make and distribute online a movie made by about 50 cellphone cameras of their 2009 concert in Prague. It shows a do-it-yourself concert movie compiled from a multitude of low-resolution camera views. See http://stereogum.com/495031/download-radioheads-prague-concert-film/video/ (accessed October 2011). Jer-

emy Crampton discusses crowdsourcing as part of the digital transformation of carto-graphy in his essay "Cartography: Maps 2.0" (2008).

14. http://yellowarrow.net/v3/ (accessed October 2011).

15. See, for example www.geocaching.com (accessed October 2011). Geocaching is a treasure-hunt game that uses GPS coordinates tagged to 'real' containers that hold objects. When found, these may be taken if replaced by new objects. Waymarking is a similar concept, to "share and discover unique and interesting locations on the pla-net", but does not use actual physical containers to hold treasures, instead offering points of interest that have been marked by other users. www.waymarking.com (accessed October 2011).

16. About the exhibition, see http://ikophetmuseumplein.nl/ (accessed October 2011). For the flashmob, see http://sndrv.nl/ARflashmob/ (accessed October 2011).

17. Philipp Breuss-Schneeweis, CEO of Mobilizy. Quoted in "Winning the Navteq Chal-lenge 2010 Grand Prize with Wikitude Drive" on http://www.wikitude.org/en/demobi-lizy-gewinnt-den-hauptpreis-der-navteq-challenge-2010enwinning-navteq-challenge-2010-grand-prize-wikitude-drive (accessed October, 2011).

18. An analogy can be made between locative media practices and pervasive games, and the project of the Situationists International, led by Guy Debord between ca. 1957-1972. From a more radical and political perspective, the Situationists' ambition was to provoke a new urbanism with their psychogeography of drift, or *dérive*, and cartogra-phy of experience. For this comparison, see e.g. Nieuwdorp (2007), McGarrigle (2010), and Tuters and Varnelis (2006). About the Situationists, see Sadler (1998).

19. In her study on what she terms nomadic theater, Liesbeth Groot Nibbelink also uses Soja's ideas about thirdspace as a lived space – in addition to a first (perceived) and second (conceived) spatiality. For her analysis of the 'cartography' of nomadic perfor-mances, she uses Soja for a rethinking of presence, performance and representation as layers rather than categories in the theater (in preparation).

20. Patterson (2007) provides a broad-ranging multidisciplinary history of touch in art, philosophy, science, medicine, digital design, and other areas of human experience, including the everyday.

21. For this summary rendering of Deleuze's idea of the haptic, see Buydens (2005: 124-128).

22. Building on Sobchack and her use of Merleau-Ponty, Jennifer M. Barker (2006) con-tributes to phenomenological film theory with her examination of the structural corre-spondence between touch and the cinematic experience. This she considers to be a haptic encounter between spectator and film. In line with Laura Marks and Giuliana Bruno (2002), she envisions a more sensuous scholarly approach to cinema.

Bibiliography

Aarseth, Espen
  1997 *Cybertext: Perspectives on Ergodic Literature*. Baltimore, MD: Johns Hopkins University Press

Aarts, Emile, Rick Harwig and Martin Schuurmans
  2001 "Ambient Intelligence." 235-250 in Peter Denning (ed.), *The Invisible Future: The Seamless Integration of Technology in Everyday Life*. New York: McGraw-Hill

Abrahams, Janet and Peter Hall
  2006 "Where/Abouts." 12-17 in Janet Abrahams and Peter Hall (eds.), *Else/Where: Mapping. New Cartographies of Networks and Territories*. Minneapolis, MN: University of Minnesota Press

Alcoff, Linda and Elizabeth Potter (eds.)
  1993 *Feminist Epistemologies*. New York: Routledge

Altman, Rick
  1992 *Sound. Sound Practice*. New York: Routledge

Alpers, Svetlana
  1987 "The Mapping Impulse in Dutch Art." 51-96 in David Woodward (ed.) *Art and Cartography: Six Historical Essays*. Chicago, IL: Chicago University Press

Appleyard, Donald, Kevin Lynch and John R. Myer
  1964 The View from the Road. Cambridge, MA: MIT Press

Auerbach, Jonathan
  2000 "Chasing Film Narrative: Repetition, Recursion, and the Body in Early Cinema," Critical Inquiry 26, 4: 798-820

Augé, Marc
  1992 Non-lieux. Introduction à une anthropologie de la surmodernité. Paris: Seuil

Auslander, Philip
  2008 *Liveness: Performance in a Mediatized Culture*. 2nd edition. London, New York: Routledge

Austin, J.L.
  1962 How to Do Things with Words: The William James Lectures delivered at Harvard University in 1955 In J.O. Urmson (ed.) Oxford: Clarendon, 1962.

Bal, Mieke
  2009 Narratology: Introduction to the Theory of Narrative. Toronto: The University of Toronto Press
  2002 "Performance and Performativity." 147-212 in Travelling Concepts in the Humanities: a Rough Guide. Toronto: The University of Toronto Press
  1991 *Reading Rembrandt: Beyond the Word-Image Opposition*. New York: Cambridge University Press

Barad, Karen
  2007 Meeting the Universe Halfway. Quantum Physics and the Entanglement of Matter

and Meaning. Durham, NC: Duke University Press

2001 "Re(con)figuring Space, Time, and Matter." in Marianne DeKoven (ed.) Feminist Locations: Global and Local, Theory and Practice. New Brunswick, NJ: Rutgers University Press

Barker, Jennifer M.

2009 *The Tactile Eye: Touch and the Cinematic Experience.* Berkeley: University of California Press

Barthes, Roland

1981 *Camera Lucida* New York, NY: Hill and Wang

Baudrillard, Jean

1996 *The System of Objects.* Translated by James Benedict. London, New York: Verso

Baudry, Jean-Louis

1986 "Ideological Effects of the Basic Cinematographic Apparatus" and "The Apparatus: Metapsychological Approaches to the Impression of Reality in the Cinema." 286-318 in Philip Rosen (ed.) *Narrative, Apparatus, Ideology.* New York: Columbia University Press

1978 *L'effet cinéma.* Paris: Albatros

Baumgarten, Alexander Gottlieb

1970 [1758; 1759] *Aesthetica.* Frankfurt am Main, 1750 [vol. 1], 1758 [vol. 2]; reprint, Hildesheim: Olms, 1970

Bazin, André

1967 "The Myth of Total Cinema." 17-22 in *What is Cinema? Vol 1.* Translated by Hugh Gray. Berkeley, CA: University of California Press

Benjamin, Walter

1999 *The Arcades Project.* Translated by Howard Eiland and Kevin Mc Laughlin. Cambridge, MA: Harvard University Press

Benveniste, Émile

1971 *Problems in General Linguistics.* Translated by Mary Elisabeth Meek. Coral Gables: University of Miami Press

Bleeker, Maaike

2008 *Visuality in the Theatre: The Locus of Looking.* Basingstoke: Palgrave Macmillan

Bloemheuvel, Marente and Jaap Guldemond (eds.)

2001 *Post-Nature: Nine Dutch Artists.* Rotterdam: NAi Publishers, 2001

Bois, Yve-Alain et al.

1998 "A Conversation with Hubert Damisch," *October* 85 (Summer): 3–17

Bolter, J. David and Diane Gromala

2003 *Windows and Mirrors: Interaction Design, Digital Art, and the Myth of Transparency.* Leonardo Books. Cambridge, MA: MIT Press

Bolter, J. David and Richard Grusin

2000 *Remediation: Understanding New Media.* Cambridge, MA: MIT Press

Boomen, Marianne van den et al. (eds.)

2009 *Digital Material: Tracing New Media in Daily Life and Technology.* Amsterdam: Amsterdam University Press

Bottomore, Stephen

1999 "The Panicking Audience: Early Cinema and the 'Train Effect'," *Historical Journal of Radio, Film and Television* 19, 2: 177-216

Bourdieu, Pierre

1999 [1975] "The Specificity of the Scientific Field and the Social Conditions of the Progress of Reason." 31-50 in Mario Biagioli (ed.) *The Science Studies Reader.* New York: Routledge

Broeckmann, Andreas

2009 "Intimate Publics: Memory, Performance, and Spectacle in Urban Environments." 109-120 in Scott McQuire, Meredith Martin and Sabine Niederer (eds.) *Urban Screens Reader* (INC Reader #5) Amsterdam: Institute of Network Cultures

Brown, Bill

2004 "Thing Theory." 1-22 in Bill Brown (ed.) *Things.* Chicago: The University Of Chicago Press.

Brown, Richard and Barry Anthony

1999 *A Victorian Film Enterprise: The History of the British Mutoscope and Biograph Company, 1897-1915.* Trowbridge: Flicks Books

Bruno, Giuliana

2006 *Altlas of Emotions: Journeys in Art, Architecture, and Film.* New York: Verso

1997 "Site-Seeing: Architecture and the Moving Image," *Wide Angle: A Film Quarterly of Theory, Criticism, and Practice.* 19, 4 (October 1997): 9-24

Buck-Morss, Susan

1989 *The Dialectics of Seeing: Walter Benjamin and the Arcades Project.* Cambridge, MA: MIT Press

Buckland, Warren

2000 *The Cognitive Semiotics of Film.* Cambridge: Cambridge University Press

Buisseret, David

2003 *The Mapmaker's Quest: Deciphering New Worlds in Renaissance Europe.* New York: Oxford University Press

Bukatman, Scott

1999. "The Artificial Infinite: On Special Effects and the Sublime." 249-275 in Annette Kuhn (ed.) *Alien Zone II: The Spaces of Science Fiction Cinema.* New York: Verso

Burch, Noël

1973 *Theory of Film Practice.* Translated by Helen R. Lane. New York: Praeger

Butler, Alison

2010 "A Deictic Turn: Space and Location in Contemporary Gallery Film and Video Installation," *Screen* 51, 4: 305-323

Buydens, Mireille

2005 *Sahara. L'esthétique de Gilles Deleuze.* Paris: Vrin 2005

Carlson, Marvin

2004 *Performance: A Critical Introduction* (2nd Edition). New York/London: Routledge

Cartwright, William

1999 "Extending the map metaphor using web delivered multimedia," *International Journal of Geographical Information Science* 13, 4: 335-353

Casetti, Francesco

2009 "Filmic Experience," *Screen* 50, 1: 56-66

Chambers, Iain

1990 *Border Dialogues: Journeys in Postmodernity.* New York: Routledge

Chion, Michel

1994 *Audio-Vision. Sound on Screen.* New York: Columbia University Press

Claudell, Thomas and David Mizell

1992 "Augmented Reality: An Application of Heads-Up Display Technology to Manual Manufacturing Processes," *Proceedings of 1992 IEEE Hawaii International Conference on Systems Sciences:* 659-669. http://ieeexplore.ieee.org/search/srchabstract.jsp?arnumber= 183317&isnumber=4717&punumber=378&k2dockey=183317@ieeecnfs [retrieved August 2010]

Code, Lorraine

1991 *What Can She Know? Feminist Epistemology and the Construction of Knowledge.* Ithaca/ London: Cornell University Press

1995 *Rhetorical Spaces: Essays on Gendered Locations.* New York: Routledge

Comolli, Jean-Louis

1996 [1971] "Machines of the Visible." 108-117 in Timothy Druckrey (ed.) *Electronic Culture: Technology and Visual Representation.* New York: Aperture

Conley, Tom

2007 *Cartographic Cinema.* Minneapolis, MN: University of Minnesota Press

Cooley, Heidi Rae

2004 "It's All About the Fit: The Hand, the Mobile Screenic Device and Tactile Vision," *Journal of Visual Culture* 3 (2): 133-155

Couldry, Nick

2004 "Liveness: Reality and the Mediated Habitus from Television to the Mobile Phone," *The Communication Review* 7:4: 353-361

Couldry, Nick and Anna McCarthy

2004 "Introduction: Orientations: Mapping MediaSpace." 1-18 in Nick Couldry and Anna McCarthy (eds.) *MediaSpace: Place, Scale and Culture in a Media Age.* London, New York: Routledge

Couldry, Nick and Anna McCarthy (eds.)

2004 *Mediaspace: Place, Scale and Culture in a Media Age.* London, New York: Routledge

Crampton, Jeremy

2010 *Mapping: A Critical Introduction to Cartography and GIS.* London: Wiley-Blackwell

2009 "Cartography: Performative, Participatory, Political," *Progress in Human Geography* 33, 6: 840-848

2008 "Cartography: Maps 2.0," *Progress in Human Geography* 33: 1 (2008): 91-100

Crang Mike and Stephen Graham

2007 "Sentient Cities: Ambient Intelligence and the Politics of Urban Space," *Information, Communication & Society* 10, 6: 789-817

Crary, Jonathan

1990 *Techniques of the Observer: On Vision and Modernity in the Nineteenth Century.* Cambridge, MA: MIT Press

Cresswell, Tim

    2006 *On the Move: Mobility in the Modern Western World.* New York: Routledge

    2004 *Place: A Short Introduction.* Oxford: Blackwell

Crozier, Michael

    1999 "After the Garden?" *The South Atlantic Quarterly* 98, 4 (Fall): 625-631

Culler, Jonathan

    2006 "The Performative." 137-165 in *The Literary in Theory.* Stanford, CA: Stanford University Press.

    1997 *Literary Theory: A Very Short Introduction.* Oxford, New York: Oxford University Press

Dällenbach, Lucien

    1989 *The Mirror in the Text.* Translated by Jeremy Whitely with Emma Hughes. Chicago, IL: University of Chicago Press

Damisch, Hubert

    1994 *The Origin of Perspective.* Translated by John Goodman. Cambridge, MA: MIT Press

De Certeau, Michel

    1984 *The Practice of Everyday Life.* Berkeley, CA: University of California Press

De Souza e Silva, Adriana

    2006 "From Cyber to Hybrid: Mobile Technologies as Interfaces of Hybrid Spaces," *Space and Culture* 9, 3 (2006): 261-278

Debord, Guy

    1994 *The Society of the Spectacle* (1967) Translated by Donald Nicholson-Smith. New York: Zone Books

Deleuze, Gilles and Felix Guattari

    2004 [1980] *A Thousand Plateaus.* Translated by Brian Massumi. London, New York: Continuum

Derrida, Jacques

    1987 [1978] *The Truth in Painting.* Translated by Geoffrey Bennington and Ian McLeod. Chicago, IL: University of Chicago Press

    1976 *Of Grammatology.* Translated by Gayatri Chakrovorty Spivak. Baltimore, MD: Johns Hopkins University Press, 1976

Doane, Mary Ann

    2007 "The Indexical and the Concept of Medium Specificity," *Differences: A Journal of Feminist Cultural Studies* 18 (1): 128–52

Eekelen, Yvonne van

    1996 "The Magical Panorama." 11-26 in Yvonne van Eekelen (ed.) *The Magical Panorama: The Mesdag Panorama, an Experience in Space and Time.* Translated by Arnold Pomerans and Erica Pomerands. Zwolle: Waanders

Eikenes, Jon Olav H. and Andrew Morrison

    2010 "Navimation: Exploring Time, Space & Motion in the Design of Screen-based Interfaces," *International Journal of Design* 4, 1: 1-16 http://www.ijdesign.org/ojs/index.php/IJDesign/article/view/622/284 [retrieved august 2010]

Elsaesser, Thomas

    2000 *Weimar Cinema and After: Germany's Historical Imaginary.* London: Routledge

Featherstone, Mike

    2004 "Automobilities: An Introduction," *Theory, Culture & Society* 21, 4-5: 1-24

Feuer, Jane

1983 "The Concept of Live Television: Ontology as Ideology." 12-22 in E. Ann Kaplan (ed.) *Regarding Television: Critical Approaches – An Anthology*. Los Angeles: American Film Institute

Fisher, Kevin

2000 "Tracing the Tesseract: A Conceptual Pre-history of the Morph." 103-130 in Vivian Sobchack (ed.) *Meta-morphing: Visual Transformation and the Culture of Quick-Change*. Minneapolis, MN: University of Minnesota Press

Flynn, Bernadette

2003. "Languages Of Navigation Within Computer Games." Paper presented at the 5th *International Digital Arts and Culture Conference*, RMIT, Melbourne. Also available at http://hypertext.rmit.edu.au/dac/papers/Flynn.pdf [retrieved August 2010].

Folie, Sabine and Ilse Lafer

2011. *Un-Exhibit*. Vienna: the Generali Foundation

Foster, Hal

1988 *Vision and Visuality*. Dia Art Foundation. Discussions in Contemporary Culture, 2. Seattle: Bay Press

Foucault, Michel

1980 *Power/Knowledge. Selected Interviews and Other Writings 1972-1977*. Colin Gordon (ed.) New York: Pantheon Books

[1979] 1995 *Discipline & Punish: The Birth of the Prison*. Translated by Alan Sheridan. New York: Vintage Books

Freud, Sigmund

1940 [1925]) "A Note Upon the 'Mystic Writing Pad'." *International Journal of Psycho-Analysis*, 21: 469-474

Friedberg, Anne

2006 *The Virtual Window: From Alberti to Microsoft*. Cambridge, MA: MIT Press

1993 *Window Shopping: Cinema and the Postmodern*. Berkeley, CA: University of California Press

Fuller, Mary and Henry Jenkins

1995 "Nintendo® and New World Travel Writing: A Dialogue." 57-72 in Steven G. Jones (ed.) *Cybersociety: Computer-Mediated Communication and Community*. Thousand Oaks: Sage Publications

Gaudreault, André

1990 "Film, Narrative, Narration: The Cinema of the Lumière Brothers." 114-122 in Thomas Elsaesser and Adam Barker (eds.) *Early Cinema: Space, Frame, Narrative*. London: BFI Publishing

Genette, Gérard

1982 *Figures*. Vols. 1-3. English Selections. Translated by Alan Sheridan. New York: Columbia University Press

Gitelman, Lisa

2006 *Always Already New. Media, History, and the Data of Culture*. Cambridge, MA: MIT Press

Gledhill, Christine and Linda Williams (eds.)

2000 *Reinventing Film Studies*. London: Arnold

Greenblatt, Stephen

1991 "Resonance and Wonder. 42-56 in Ivan Karp en Steven D. Lavine (eds.) *Exhibiting Cultures – the Poetics and Politics of Museum Display*. Washington & Londen: Smithsonian Institution Press

Gregory, Derek

1994 *Geographical Imaginations*. Cambridge, MA and Oxford, UK: Blackwell

Griffiths, Alison

2008 *Shivers Down Your Spine: Cinema, Museums, and the Immersive View*. New York, NY: Columbia University Press

Groot Nibbelink, Liesbeth

(in preparation) *Nomadic Theatre. Movements in Contemporary Performance* (working title). PhD Dissertation Utrecht University

Grosz, Elizabeth

2005. *Time Travels: Feminism, Nature, Power*. Durham, NC: Duke University Press

Gunning, Tom

1990 "The Cinema of Attractions: Early Film, Its Spectator and the Avant-Garde." 56-62 in Thomas Elsaesser and Adam Barker (eds.) *Early Cinema: Space, Frame, Narrative*. London: BFI Publishing

Habermas, Jürgen

1989 [1962] *The Structural Transformation of the Public Sphere: An Inquiry into a Category of Bourgeois Society*. Translated by Thomas Burger and Frederick Lawrence. Cambridge: Polity Press

Harbord, Janet

2007 *The Evolution of Film. Rethinking Film Studies*. Cambridge: Polity Press

Harley, J. Brian

1992 "Deconstructing the Map." 231-247 in T. J. Barnes and J. S. Duncan (eds.), *Writing Worlds: Discourse, Text and Metaphor in the Representation of Landscape*. London: Routledge

1988 "Maps, Knowledge, and Power." 277–312 in Denis Cosgrove and Stephen J. Daniels (eds.) *The Iconography of Landscape: Essays on the Symbolic Representation, Design and Use of Past Environments* . Cambridge: Cambridge University Press

Hayles, N. Katherine

2002. *Writing machines*. Cambridge, MA: MIT Press.

Heath, Stephen

1981 "Narrative Space." 19-75 in *Questions of Cinema*. London: McMillan

Hebdige, Dick

1979 *Subculture: The Meaning of Style*. London: Methuen

Houben, Francine

1999 "Ingenieurskunst en Mobiliteitsestetiek." 20-41 in *De dynamische delta 2. Architectuur en de openbare ruimte*. Den Haag: Ministerie van Verkeer en Waterstaat/Mecanoo Architects

Houben, Francine and Luisa Maria Calabrese (eds.)

2003 *Mobility: A Room with a View*. Rotterdam: NAi Publishers

Huhtamo, Erkki

2009 "Messages on the Wall: An Archeology of Public Media Displays." 15-28 in Scott McQuire, Meredith Martin and Sabine Niederer (eds.) *The Urban Screens Reader*. INC

Reader #5. Amsterdam: Institute for Network Cultures

2004 "Peristrepic Pleasures: The Origins of the Moving Panorama." 215-248 in John Fullerton and Jan Olsson (eds.) *Allegories of Communication: Intermedial Concerns From Cinema to the Digital*. Rome: John Libbey Publishing

1997 "From Kaleidoscomaniac to Cybernerd: Notes Toward an Archeology of Media." 297-303 in Timothy Druckrey (ed.) *Electronic Culture: Technology and Visual Representation*. New York: Aperture

1995a "Armchair Traveler on the Ford of Jordan. The Home, The Stereoscope, The Virtual Voyager," *Mediamatic* 8: 2/3 http://www.mediamatic.net/article-5910-en.html?lang=en

1995b "Encapsulated Bodies in Motion: Simulators and the Quest for Total Immersion." 159-186 in Simon Penny (ed.) *Critical Issues in Electronic Media*. Albany: SUNY Press

Hyde, Ralph

1988 *Panoramania!: The Art and Entertainment of the "All-embracing" View*. London: Trefoil in association with Barbican Art Gallery

Iitä, Inkamaija

2010 "The Space of Representation and the Postmodern Stage: Jussi Niva's Exposes." 22-57 in *Jussi Niva: Timely Remains*. Helsinki: Parvs Publishing

Jacob, Christian

2006 [1992] *The Sovereign Map: Theoretical Approaches in Cartography Throughout History* Edited by Edward H. Dahl. Translated by Tom Conley. Chicago, IL: University of Chicago Press

Jay, Martin

1993 *Downcast Eyes: The Denigration of Vision in Twentieth-Century French Thought*. Berkeley, CA: University of California Press

1988 "Scopic Regimes of Modernity." 3-23 in Hal Foster (ed.) *Vision and Visuality*. Seattle: Bay Press

Jenkins, Henry

2006a *Convergence Culture: Where Old and New Media Collide*. New York: New York University Press

2006b "Quentin Tarantino's Star Wars? Digital Cinema, Media Convergence, and Participatory Culture." 549–76 in M. Durham and D.M. Kellner (eds.) *Media and Cultural Studies: Keyworks*, revised edition. Malden, MA: Blackwell

2004 "Game Design as Narrative Architecture." 118-130 in Pat Harrington and Noah Frup-Waldrop (eds.) *First Person: New Media as Story, Performance, and Game*. Cambridge, MA: MIT Press

1992 *Textual Poachers: Television Fans & Participatory Culture*. New York, NY: Routledge

Juhlin, Oskar

2005 "Beyond Just Getting There: The Interactive Road," *Receiver* #12, http://www.vodafone.com/flash/receiver/12/articles/pdf/12_05.pdf [accessed 8/1/10]

Kaye, Nick

2000 *Site-Specific Art: Performance, Place and Documentation*. London: Routledge

Keller, Evelyn Fox

1999 "The Finishing Touch." 29-43 in Mieke Bal (ed.) *The Practice of Cultural Analysis: Exposing Interdisciplinary Interpretation*. Stanford: Stanford University Press

Kessler, Frank

2010 "Ostranenie, Innovation, and Media History." 61-79 in Annie van den Oever (ed.) *Ostranenie* (The Key Debates. Appropriations and Mutations in European Film Studies). Amsterdam: Amsterdam University Press

2007 "Notes on Dispositif" unpublished seminar paper, http://www.let.uu.nl/~frank. kessler/personal/Dispositif%20Notes11-2007.pdf [retrieved August 2010]

2006 "The Cinema of Attractions as *Dispositif*." 57-69 in Wanda Strauven (ed.) *The Cinema of Attractions Reloaded*. Amsterdam: Amsterdam University Press

Kirby, Lynne

1996 *Parallel Tracks: The Railroad and Silent Cinema* Durham, NC: Duke University Press

Kittler, Friedrich

1999 Gramophone, Film, Typewriter. Stanford, CA: Stanford University Press

Klein, Norman M.

2004 *The Vatican to Vegas: The History of Special Effects*. New York: The New Press

Krauss, Rosalind E.

(1999) "Reinventing the Medium," *Critical Inquiry* 25 (2): 289-305

Kristeva, Julia

1980 *Desire in Language: A Semiotic Approach to Literature and Art*. L.S. Roudiez (ed.), translated by T. Gora, A. Jardine, and L.S. Roudiez. New York: Columbia University Press

Kwon, Miwon

2004 *One Place After Another: Site-specific Art and Locational Identity*. Cambridge, MA: MIT Press

Lammes, Sybille

2009 "Transmitting Location: Digital Cartographical Interfaces as Transformative Material Practices." Paper delivered at MiT6 at MIT, Cambridge, MA. http://web.mit. edu/comm-forum/mit6/subs/abstracts.html

Lammes, Sybille and Nanna Verhoeff

2010 "Landmarks: Navigating Spacetime and Digital Mobility," *ISSEI: Language and the Scientific Imagination* 2008. http://helda.helsinki.fi//handle/10138/15294

Landon, Brooks

1992 *The Aesthetics of Ambivalence: Rethinking Science Fiction Film in the Age of Electronic (Re) Production*. Westport, CT: Greenwood Press

Lange, Michiel de

2009 "From Always-On to Always-There: Locative Media as Playful Technologies." 55-70 in Adriana de Souza e Silva and Daniel M. Sutko (eds.) *Digital Cityscapes: Merging Digital and Urban Playspaces*. New York: Peter Lang Publishing

Latour, Bruno

2005 *Reassembling the Social: An Introduction to Actor-Network-Theory*. Clarendon Lectures in Management Studies. Oxford, New York: Oxford University Press

1990 "Visualisation and Cognition: Drawing Things Together." 19-68 in Michael Lynch and Steven Woolgar (eds.) *Representation in Scientific Activity*. Cambridge, MA: MIT Press

Lévi-Strauss, Claude

1966 [1962] *The Savage Mind*. Chicago, IL: University of Chicago Press

Levinson, Stephen C.

2004 "Deixis." 97-121 in Laurence R. Horn (ed.) *The Handbook of Pragmatics.* Oxford: Blackwell Publishing

Loipedinger, Martin (ed.)

2011 *Early Cinema Today: The Art of Programming and Live Performance.* KINtop Studies in Early Cinema. Frankfurt am Main/Basel: Stroemfeld Verlag

Lynch, Kevin

1960 *The Image of the City.* Cambridge, MA: MIT Press

Mannoni, Laurent, Donata Presenti Campagnoni, David Robinson

1995 *Light and Movement: Incunabula of the Motion Picture 1420-1896.* Gemona: Le Giornate del Cinema Muto

Manovich, Lev

2006 "Interaction as an Aesthetic Event," *Receiver* (17) http://www.receiver.vodafone. com/17/articles/pdf/17_09.pdf [retrieved August 2010]

2001 *The Language of New Media.* Cambridge, MA: MIT Press

Marcussen, Lars

2008 *The Architecture of Space –The Space of Architecture.* Copenhagen: Danish Architectural Press

Marks, Laura U.

2002 *Touch: Sensuous Theory and Multisensory Media.* Minneapolis: University of Minnesota Press

2000 *The Skin of Film: Intercultural Cinema, Embodiment, and the Senses.* Durham: Duke University Press

Massey, Doreen

1994 *Space, Place, and Gender.* Cambridge: Polity Press

Massumi, Brian

2002 *Parables for the Virtual: Movement, Affect, Sensation.* Durham: Duke University Press

May, Jon and Nigel Thrift

2001 "Introduction." 1-46 in Jon May and Nigel Thrift (eds.) *TimeSpace: Geographies of Temporalities.* London: Routledge

McCarthy, Anna

2001 *Ambient Television: Visual Culture and Public Space.* Durham: Duke University Press

McGarrigle, Conor

2010 "The Construction of Locative Situations: Locative Media and the Situationist International, Recuperation or Redux?" *Digital Creativity,* 21, 1 (March): 55-62

McKenzie, Jon

2001 *Perform or Else: From Discipline to Performance.* London, New York: Routledge

McLuhan, Marsall

1964 *Understanding Media: The Extensions of Man.* New York: McGraw Hill

McPherson, Tara

2002 "Reload: Liveness, Mobility and the Web." 458-470 in Nicholas Mirzoeff (ed.) *The Visual Culture Reader,* 2nd Edition New York: Routledge

McQuire, Scott

2009 "Mobility, Cosmopolitanism and Public Space in the Media City." 45-64 in Scott McQuire, Meredith Martin and Sabine Niederer (eds.) *Urban Screens Reader* (INC Reader

#5) Amsterdam: Institute of Network Cultures, 2009

2008 *The Media City: Media, Architecture and Urban Space*. London: Sage

2006 "The Politics of Public Space in the Media City," *First Monday* Special Issue 4 (2006)

McQuire, Scott, Meredith Martin and Sabine Niederer (eds.)

2009 *Urban Screens Reader* (INC Reader #5) Amsterdam: Institute of Network Cultures, 2009

Mecanoo Architects

2003 *Holland Avenue, Research Road Atlas; Holland Avenue, Design Road Atlas*. Ministry of Transport, Public Works and Water Management, The Hague

Merriman, Peter

2004 "Driving Places: Marc Augé, Non-places, and the Geographies of England's M1 Motorway," *Theory, Culture & Society* 21, 4/5 (2004): 145–167

Metz, Christian

1982 [1977] *The Imaginary Signifier: Psychoanalysis and the Cinema*. Celia Britton et al. (translation) Bloomington, IN: Indiana University Press

Miller, Angela

1996 "The Panorama, the Cinema and the Emergence of the Spectacular," *Wide Angle* 18, 2 (April): 34-69

Mitchell, W.J.T.

1994 *Picture Theory: Essays on Verbal and Visual Representation*. Chicago: University of Chicago Press

Mulvey, Laura

2006 *Death at 24X a Second: Stillness and the Moving Image*. London: Reaktion Books

Murray, Janet H.

1997 *Hamlet on the Holodeck: The Future of Narrative in Cyberspace*. Cambridge, MA: MIT Press

Nieuwdorp, Eva

2005 "The Pervasive Interface: Tracing the Magic Circle." Proceedings from the International DiGRA Conference *Changing Views: Worlds in Play*. Vancouver, Canada. www.digra.org/dl/db/06278.53356.pdf [retrieved August 2010]

Novak, Marcos

1991 "Liquid Architectures in Cyberspace." 225-54 in Michael Benedikt (ed.) *Cyberspace: First Steps*. Cambridge, MA: MIT Press

November, Valérie, Eduardo Camacho-Hubner, Bruno Latour

2010 "Entering a Risky Territory: Space in the Age of Digital Navigation," *Environment and Planning D: Society and Space* 28, 4: 581-599
http://www.bruno-latour.fr/articles/article/117-MAP-FINAL.pdf

Oettermann, Stephan

1997 *The Panorama: History of a Mass Medium*. Cambridge, MA: MIT Press/Zone Books

Paech, Joachim

1997 "Überlegungen zum Dispositiv als Theorie medialer Topik," *Medienwissenschaft* (14): 400-420.

Papacharissi, Zizi

2010 *A Private Sphere: Democracy in a Digital Age*. Cambridge, UK: Polity Press

Parikka, Jussi and Jaakko Suominen

2006 "Victorian Snakes? Towards a Cultural History of Mobile Games and the Experience of Movement," *Game Studies* 6 (1), December. URL (consulted October, 2008): http://gamestudies.org/0601/articles/parikka_suominen

Parisi, David P.

2008 *Touch Machines: An Archeology of Haptic Interfacing*. Ph.D. dissertation New York: New York University

Parks, Lisa

2004 "Kinetic Screens: Epistemologies of Movement at the Interface." 37-57 in Nick Couldry and Anna McCarthy (eds.) *MediaSpace: Place, Scale and Culture in a Media Age.* London, New York: Routledge

Patterson, Mark

2007 *The Senses of Touch: Haptics, Affects and Technologies*. Oxford: Berg

Peeren, Esther

2007 *Intersubjectivities and Popular Culture: Bakhtin and Beyond. Cultural Memory in the Present.* Stanford: Stanford University Press

Peirce, Charles S.

"On the Algebra of Logic: A Contribution to the Philosophy of Notation," *The American Journal of Mathematics* 7 (1885): 180 – 202. Reprinted in *The Writings of Charles S. Peirce.* Volume 5. Compiled by the Editors of the Peirce Edition Project (Bloomington: Indiana University Press, 1993): 162-190

Piek, Maarten, Marnix Breedijk, Willemieke Hornis, Manon van Middelkoop, Niels Sorel and Nanna Verhoeff

2007 *Snelwegpanorama's in Nederland*. Rotterdam: NAi Publishers

Poster, Mark

2006 *Information Please: Culture and Politics in the Age of Digital Machines.* Durham, NC: Duke University Press

Rabinovitz, Lauren

1998a "From *Hale's Tours* to *Star Tours*: Virtual Voyages and the Delirium of the Hyper-Real," *Iris* 25: 133-152

1998b *For the Love of Pleasure: Women, Movies and Culture in Turn-of-the-Century Chicago.* New Brunswick: Rutgers University Press

Reed, Kristian

2004 "Nintendo Unveils Dual Screen Handheld," *Gamesindustry.biz* 21 (January) http://www.gamesindustry.biz/content_page.php?section_name=pub1998 "Matrix: A Real-time Object Identification and Registration Method for Augmented Reality," *Proceedings of Third Asian Pacific Computer and Human Interaction:* 63-68 http://ieeexplore.ieee.org/xpl/freeabs_all.jsp?arnumber=704151 [retrieved December 2010]

Richardson, Ingrid

2005 "Mobile Technosoma: Some Phenomenological Reflections on Itinerant Media Devices," *Fibreculture* (6) http://journal.fibreculture.org/issue6/issue6_richardson.html [retreived August 2010]

Richardson, Ingrid and Rowan Wilken

2009 "Haptic Vision, Footwork, Place-making: A Peripatetic Phenemenology of the Mobile Phone Pedestrian," *Second Nature: International Journal of Creative Media* 1, 2: 22-41

Riegl, Aloïs

    1995 [1901] "Late Roman Art Industry." 116-126 in Eric Fernie (ed.) *Art History and Its Methods: A Critical Anthology*.Translated by Rolf Winkes. London: Phaidon

Rombout, Ton (ed.)

    2006 *The Panorama Phenomenon: The World Round!* The Hague: Panorama Mesdag/ PF/ Kunstbeeld

Sadler, Simon

    1998 *The Situationist City*. Cambridge, MA: MIT Press

Saldwell, Melanie

    2007 "The Remembering and the Forgetting of Early Digital Games: From Novelty to Detritus and Back Again," *Journal of Visual Culture* 6, 2: 255-273

Scarry, Elaine

    1985 *The Body in Pain: The Making and Unmaking of the World*. Oxford, New York: Oxford University Press

Schavemaker, Margriet

    2010 "AR(t): Learning from the Paradox." Lecture given at AR: *Artistic Explorations*. Rotterdam, The Netherlands: V2: Institute for the Unstable Media, June 4

Schivelbusch, Wolfgang

    1986 *The Railway Journey: The Industrialization of Time and Space in the Nineteenth Century*. Berkeley, CA: University of California Press

Schwarzer, Mitchell

    2004 *Zoomscape: Architecture in Motion and Media*. Princeton, NJ: Princeton Architectural Press

Schwartz, Vanessa R.

    1998 *Spectacular Realities: Early Mass Culture in Fin-de-Siècle Paris*. Berkeley: University of California Press

Shepard, Marc (ed.)

    2011 *Sentient City: Ubiquitous Computing, Architecture, and the Future of Urban Space*. Cambridge, MA: MIT Press

Silverman, Kaja

    2009 *Flesh of My Flesh*. Stanford, CA: Stanford University Press

    1996 *The Threshold of the Visible World*. New York: Routledge

Singer, Ben

    2001 *Melodrama and Modernity: Early Sensational Cinema and Its Contexts*. New York: Columbia University Press

Sobchack, Vivian

    2004 "What My Fingers Knew: The Cinesthetic Subject, or Vision in the Flesh." 53-8 in *Carnal Thoughts: Embodiment and Moving Image Culture*. Berkeley: University of California Press

    2000 "Introduction." xi-xxiii in Vivian Sobchack (ed.) *Meta-Morphing: Visual Transformation and the Culture of Quick-Change*. Minneapolis, MN: University of Minnesota Press

    1992 *The Address of the Eye: A Phenomenology of Film Experience*. Princeton, NJ: Princeton University Press

Sobchack Vivian (ed.)

2000 *Meta-Morphing: Visual Transformation and the Culture of Quick-Change.* Minneapolis, MN: University of Minnesota Press

Soja, Edward

1996 *Thirdspace: Journeys to Los Angeles and other Real-and-Imagined Places.* Oxford: Basil Blackwell

Steward, Garreth

2007 *Framed Time: Toward a Postfilmic Cinema.* Chicago, IL: The University of Chicago Press

Stoichita, Victor

1996 *The Self-Aware Image: An Insight into Early Modern Meta-Painting.* Cambridge University Press

Strauven, Wanda (ed.)

2006 *The Cinema of Attractions Reloaded.* Amsterdam: Amsterdam University Press

Struppek, Mirjam

2006 "Urban Screens: The Urbane Potential of Public Screens for Interaction," *intelligent agent* 6, 2 (2006) Special Issue: Papers presented at the ISEA2006 Symposium, August 2006

Sturken, Marita and Lisa Cartwright

2001 *Practices of Looking: An Introduction to Visual Culture.* New York: Oxford University Press

Swalwell, Melanie

2007 "The Remembering and the Forgetting of Early Digital Games: From Novelty to Detritus and Back Again," *Journal of Visual Culture* 6 (2): 255-273

Thornburn, David and Henry Jenkins

2003 "Introduction: Toward an Aesthetic of Transition." 1-16 in David Thornburn and Henry Jenkins (eds.) *Rethinking Media Change: The Aesthetics of Transition.* Cambridge, MA: MIT Press

Thrift, Nigel

2004 "Driving in the City," *Theory, Culture & Society* 2, 4/5: 41–59

Thrift, Nigel and Shaun French

2002 "The Automatic Production of Space," *Transactions of Visual Anthropology Review* 10 (1): 94-102

Tuters, Marc and Kazys Varnelis

2006 "Beyond Locative Media," *Networked Publics Blog* http://networkedpublics.org/locative_media/beyond_locative_media [retrieved August 2010]

Uricchio, William

2011 "The Algorithmic Turn: Photosynth, Augmented Reality and the Changing Implications of the Image," *Visual Studies* 26, 1 (March): 25-35

2004 "Storage, Simultaneity, and the Media Technologies of Modernity." 123-138 in John Fullerton and Jan Olsson (eds.) *Allegories of Communication: Intermedial Concerns from Cinema to the Digital.* Eastleigh: John Libbey Press

1999 "Panoramic Vision: Stasis, Movement, and the Redefinition of the Panorama." 125-133 in Leonardo Quaressima, Alessandra Raengo, Laura Vichi (eds.) *La nascita dei generi cinematografici / The Birth of Film Genres.* Udine: Forum

Urry, John

   2007 *Mobilities*. London: Polity Press

   2004 "The 'System' of Automobility," *Theory, Culture & Society* 21, 4/5: 25–39

Thielmann, Tristan

   2010 "Locative Media and Mediated Localities: An Introduction to Media Geography," *Aether* 5a Special Issue on Locative Media (Spring): 1-17 http://130.166.124.2/~aether/volume_05a.html [retrieved August 2010]

   2007 "'You Have Reached Your Destination!' Position, Positioning and Superpositioning of Space Through Car Navigation Systems," *Social Geography* 2: 63-75 www.soc-geogr.net/2/63/2007/ [retrieved August 2010]

Tuin, Iris van der

   2010 "'A Different Starting Point, a Different Metaphysics': Reading Bergson and Barad Diffractively," *Hypatia* http://onlinelibrary.wiley.com/doi/10.1111/j.1527-2001.2010.01114.x/pdf   [published online April 2010, retrieved August 2010]

Verhoeff, Nanna

   2008 "Screens of Navigation: From Taking a Ride to Making a Ride," *Refractory* 12 http://blogs.arts.unimelb.edu.au/refractory/2008/03/06/screens-of-navigation-from-taking-a-ride-to-making-the-ride/ [Published March 2008]

   2006 *The West in Early Cinema: After the Beginning (Film Culture in Transition)*. Amsterdam: Amsterdam University Press

Verhoeff, Nanna and Eva Warth

   2002 "Rhetoric of Space: Cityscape/Landscape," *Historical Journal of Film, Radio and Television* 22, 3: 245-251

Vries, Imar de

   2009 "Mobile Mementos: Expanded Archives, Fragmented Access." Paper delivered at MiT6 at MIT, Cambridge, MA. http://web.mit.edu/comm-forum/mit6/subs/abstracts.html

Waal, Martijn de

   2011 "The Urban Culture of Sentient Cities: From an Internet of Things to a Public Sphere Centered Around Things." 190-195 in Mark Shepard (ed.) *Sentient City: Ubiquitous Computing, Architecture, and the Future of Urban Space*. Cambridge, MA: MIT Press

White, Michele

   2006 *The Body and the Screen: Theories of Internet Spectatorship*. Cambridge: MIT Press

White, Mimi

   2004 "The Attractions of Television. Reconsidering Liveness." 75-91 in Nick Couldry and Anna McCarthy (eds.) *Mediaspace: Place, Scale and Culture in a Media Age*. London: Routledge

Williams, Raymond

   1997 [1974] "Mobile privatization." Reprinted in Paul du Gay, Stuart Hall, Linda Janes, Hugh Mackay and Keith Negus (eds.) *Doing Cultural Studies: The Story of the Sony Walkman*, Sage, London

   1975 *Television: Technology and Cultural Form*. New York: Schocken Book

Wood, R. Derek

   1993 "The Diorama in Great Britain in the 1820s," *History of Photography* 17, 3 (1993):

284-295. Reprinted with added material at: http://www.midleykent.fsnet.co.uk/diorama/Diorama_Wood_1_1.htm

Woodman, Oliver J.

2007 "An Introduction to Inertial Navigation," *Technical Report* 696. University of Cambridge

Zielinski, Siegfried

2006 *Deep Time of the Media: Toward an Archaeology of Hearing and Seeing by Technical Means*. Translated by Gloria Custance. Cambridge, MA: MIT Press

1999 *Audiovisions: Cinema and Television as Entr'actes in History* (Film Culture in Transition). Amsterdam: Amsterdam University Press

Art, Exhibitions, Video and Installations

ARtotheque (Stedelijk Museum, 2010)

Artvertiser, The (Julian Oliver, >2008)

Auras (Marieke Berghuis, 2010)

Crazy Cinématographe (National Fairground Archive, Cinémathèque Luxembourg, 2007)

Expose (Jussi Niva, 1998)

Hand From Above (Chris O'Shea, 2010)

Ik op het Museumplein. Me on the Museumplein (Stedelijk Museum, 2010)

Inkijk #3 (Rob Johannesma, 2001)

Odeillo, (Ann Veronica Janssens, 2008)

Ouverture (Stan Douglas, 1986)

Parallel Library (Rob Johannesma, 2007)

Playing Flickr (Mediamatic, 2005)

Scream (Hermen Maat & Karen Lancel, 2006)

Silent Films (Jennifer Peterson, 2008)

Star Guitar (music video for the Chemical Brothers) (Michael Gondry, 2001)

Twists and Turns (Holger Mader, Alexander Stublic, Heike Wiermann, 2006)

Zoomscape (EYE Film Institute Netherlands, 2010)

Films

2001: A Space Odyssey (Stanley Kubrick, 1968)

Arrivée d'un train à La Ciotat (Lumière, 1895)

Avatar (James Cameron, 2009)

Bits & Pieces (miscellaneous fragments, EYE Film Institute Netherlands)

Conway Castle (British Mutoscope & Biograph, 1898)

Dans les Pyrénées (unidentified, 1913)

Eternal Sunshine of the Spotless Mind (Michel Gondry, 2004)

eXistenZ (David Cronenberg, 1999)

Fast and the Furious, The (Rob Cohen, 2001)

Fast Mail, Northern Pacific Railroad (Edison, 1897)

Hold-Up of the Rocky Mountain Express (American Mutoscope and Biograph, 1906)

Irish Mail (American Mutoscope and Biograph, 1898)

Inception (Christopher Nolan, 2010)
Matrix (Andy & Larry Wachowski, 1999)
Matrix Reloaded (Andy & Larry Wachowski, 2003)
Minority Report (Steven Spielberg, 2002)
Railroad Wooing (Kalem, 1913)
Railway Tragedy (British Gaumont, 1904)
Romance of the Rail (Edison, 1903)
Speed (Jan de Bont, 1994)
Star Wars (1977, George Lucas)
Strange Days (Kathryn Bigelow, 1995)
Toy Story 3 (Lee Unkrich, 2010)

Index of Names and Titles

Index of Terms

television theory 18

theoretical object 23, 71, 73-75, 79, 95-96, 149

theoretical console, *see* console

thirdspace 162-163, 179n19

three-dimensional, *see* 3D

time 16-19, 21, 23, 29, 32-33, 40, 43, 46-49, 52-53, 55, 57, 59, 62-63, 65, 67-70, 74-77, 79, 82, 89-90, 92, 95, 101-103, 105-106, 111, 116, 118-119, 121-122, 124, 129, 134, 138, 142-147, 153-154, 156-163, 166, 173n5, 178n6

timespace 18, 21, 57, 59, 62, 145, 173n5

see also spacetime

touch 24, 29, 41, 65, 67, 69, 77-79, 82-89, 97, 134, 150, 152, 155, 163-165, 176n10, 178n4, 179n20, 179n22

see also tactile

touchscreen 13, 23-25, 56, 65, 67-68, 73, 77-79, 82-89, 91, 130, 134, 137, 149-152, 162, 165

tour 56, 69, 92, 94, 149, 152-154, 156-157, 159-160, 162-163

versus map, *see also* map

tourism 28, 46, 61-62, 139, 172n19

trace 25, 65-66, 82, 122-124, 154, 173n3

tracing 153, 154, 156, 178n10

train 29, 32-33, 41, 44-46, 52, 56, 58, 60-64, 67, 71, 77, 116-120, 122, 135, 144, 154, 167, 171n7, 174n6, 174n10, 174n12

see also railway

transgression, spatial 57, 65, 118,

transition, transitional 17, 23, 40, 51, 53-54, 70-71, 80, 169-170

transmediality 18

transparent, transparency 2 1, 48, 82-85, 107, 116, 127, 143, 158, 161, 167

transport, transportation 13, 16, 21, 25, 27, 29-30, 32-33, 41, 44-48, 52, 56, 59-60, 67, 77, 89-92, 99, 101, 116-118, 120, 124, 130, 133, 135, 160, 171n7, 172n19, 177n16

trope, troping 13, 16-17, 50-53, 56, 58-59, 63-64, 70, 90, 116-117, 124, 150, 165, 174n6, 174n12

two-dimensional, *see* 2D

Uniqa Tower 110, 111-112

Urban Augmented Reality (UAR) 160, 161

urban screen 14-15, 23-24, 103, 108-109, 112-113, 115, 125, 127, 129, 134-135, 176n6, 176n9

see also façade

user (as distinct from spectator) 22, 24, 41, 51, 53, 55-57, 66-67, 71, 76-78, 81-82, 84-87, 89-92, 96, 99, 104, 113, 126, 129, 135-137, 139, 142, 147, 149-158, 166, 169-170, 173n4, 175n1, 179n15

see also engager or navigator

vantage point 25, 35, 39, 58, 71

vehicular 21, 47, 49, 52, 91, 119, 135

virtual, virtuality 13-15, 18, 20-22, 24, 28-30, 32, 37, 44-46, 49, 51-54, 56, 58-59, 63, 68, 70, 76, 82, 84, 86, 90-92, 94, 107-110, 113-117, 119-127, 129, 134-135, 137, 152, 157, 159-161, 171n11, 172n18, 173n24, 173n13, 177n16

virtual reality 37, 45, 86, 126, 157

visceral 14, 16, 25, 150

visual culture 13, 17, 19-20, 22, 50, 51, 71, 77, 95-96, 124, 157

visual regime, *see* regime

visual turn 13

visuality 13-17, 19-21, 24, 25, 29-30, 34, 45, 59, 68, 70, 99, 117, 133, 135, 164-165, 171n7, 172n22, 174n6, 174n12

haptic visuality 14, 16, 19-21, 24, 164-165, 176n10

voyeurism, voyeuristic 42-43, 46

Vuosaari Metro Station 167-168

walking 19, 52, 135, 152, 163

Waymarking 156, 179n15
weightless, weightlessness 14, 52, 64,
    173n1
West, Western 144, 145
    West, American 53, 171n7
WIFI 65, 73, 89, 151
Wikitude 157, 159, 161, 179n17
window 16, 21-22, 44, 48-49, 57-58,
    82-85, 90, 92, 107, 114-117, 124, 127,
    137, 158

car window, windshield 21-22, 26,
    28, 31, 34, 48-50, 137, 161
metaphor, screen as 16, 21-22, 49,
    57, 85, 90, 92, 114-116, 127, 137,
    158
Xbox 85
YouTube 178
Yellow Arrow 156